S0-ATL-568

L.A. LINE

L. A. LIVE

PROFILES OF A CITY

JUNE ROSE GADER

St. Martin's Press: New York

Copyright © 1980 by June Rose Gader
All rights reserved. For information, write:
St. Martin's Press, Inc., 175 Fifth Avenue, New York, N.Y. 10010.
Manufactured in the United States of America
Library of Congress Cataloging in Publication Data

Gader, June Rose.
  L. A. live.

  1. Los Angeles—Description. 2. Los Angeles—
Social life and customs. 3. Los Angeles—Popular
culture. I. Title.
F869.L84G32   979.4′94   80-14182
ISBN 0-312-46119-4

To Bertram, who kept saying, "Write faster."

ACKNOWLEDGMENTS

I am extremely grateful to everyone mentioned in this book—whether by their correct names or by necessary pseudonyms—for valuable time given up, and for hair let down, in revealing to me various aspects of Los Angeles life.

I owe special thanks to Deputy Mayor Grace Montañez Davis for suggesting contacts within the Chicano community; to Elizabeth Hayes for excellent contacts and for personal research; to Helen and Carl Mack for insights and introductions; to S. J. Diamond for producing valuable factual material; and to my husband, Bertram Gader, for handling so many onerous tasks.

Dominick Abel is largely responsible for the fact that the book was conceived, and entirely responsible for finding the right publisher—he is my agent, and he writes very funny letters, and I thank him for all of the above. Ashton Applewhite's sharp editing raised my ire and also, belatedly, my perception; I finally am grateful.

William B. Allen deserves separate and most special thanks for opening numerous doors to the people and places in several chapters.

CONTENTS

Introduction : XI

1 **: Seekers in Lotus Land :** 1

2 **: Kathy, the Queen of Disneyland :** 23

3 **: How to Escape the Valley :
The L.A. Triple C's :** 37

4 **: The Genuine All-American
Southern California Boy :** 57

5 **: The Dallas Memorial
Homecoming and Social Club :** 67

6 **: South Bay: The Beach Cities
Have Their Own Magazine Now :** 85

7 **: Gay L.A.: Where the Music Never Stops :** 100

8 **: "Lookin' Good" in Beverly Hills :** 124

9 **: "I Am an American!" :** 141

10 **: Town Hall Meetings in the Big City :** 155

11 **: In Old Pasadena :** 171

12 **: Stars and Stars Forever: Hollywood :** 188

13 **: East Los Angeles: Portraits and** *Placas* **:** 204

14 **: Christmas in Los Angeles:
A Very Personal View :** 223

INTRODUCTION

Two years ago *The Los Angeles Times* conducted a survey, asking its readers, "What do you think about L.A.?" When the results were in, the newspaper drew this conclusion: "For all the millions who live here (6.85 million countywide), no two people live in the same Los Angeles."

This scarcely is surprising in a city whose boundaries could contain, to use City Planning Director Calvin Hamilton's reckoning, all of New York, Chicago, San Francisco, Minneapolis, Miami and Pittsburgh, and still have room left over for several other cities. Nor is it surprising in light of the fact that so many people have come to Los Angeles in pursuit of a dream. Dreams tend to be unique.

Los Angeles is unlike any other city in the world in its structure. It has a downtown, but downtown is not its center for either business or pleasure; there is no one center. There are 464 square miles of residential, business and pleasure areas intermingled; they rise from sea-level beach communities to mountainous areas above five thousand feet; they are connected by the world's most extensive freeway system. With one car for every 1.8 residents, the population of Los Angeles is uniquely mobile—individually and privately so. It is possible to live out the dream on a day-to-day basis without ever rubbing shoulders with a stranger.

Structurally, and by historical bent, other cities require a certain conformity of lifestyle. Structurally, and with a notable lack of old guardism—political, social or other—Los Angeles permits individuality to flourish. The city as a whole does not impose rhythms or create atmospheres. Life here is as exciting or as dull, as free or as confined, as the individual in his choice of neighborhood and friends cares to make it.

Thus this is not an easy city to analyze, to "get a handle on." It is immense and diverse, and it is impossible to take a few bus or taxi rides and get a feeling for the essence of Los Angeles—as one can in almost any other city in the world. I have a deep sense of being an Angelino: I was born here and, with the exception of one year spent on the East Coast and three years in Europe and Asia, I have lived here all my life; yet I don't feel that I have begun to plumb the true nature of the city. I only know that I prefer it—as a place to live *my* life—to any other place I have seen. Perhaps because it reveals itself so slowly.

Many outsiders have the natural tendency to compare Los Angeles to more familiarly structured cities—and find it wanting. A recently transplanted New Yorker said to me, "Oh, you're writing a book about Los Angeles? That should take about half an hour." Others, especially Europeans, seem to delight in the fact that Los Angeles does not match up to their preconceived notions of what a city should look like or act like. A well-traveled French friend who was visiting Los Angeles for the third time after a stay in San Francisco responded to the usual "Didn't you love San Francisco, isn't it a beautiful city?" questions with: "Yes, it's charming. But of course it's not nearly as much of a city as Los Angeles. It's all on the surface, you see it and you understand it immediately. Los Angeles is deep—you have to study it and get to know it. A real city has mysteries. San Francisco is just a copy of a dozen other cities. Los Angeles is itself."

Part of this self is what I hope I have uncovered here.

L.A. LINE

1

Seekers in Lotus Land

It is Psychic Fun Night at the Temple of Soul-Truth on Wilton Place, a street that connects the raggle-taggle eastern end of Hollywood with the now almost entirely Korean settlements along Olympic Boulevard, via a long, narrow "speedway" with a hair-raising series of hairpin turns. Wilton Place used to be a street of middle-to-upper-middle-class elegance, at a time when business was still centered downtown and business people began to build their good-sized houses in this "western suburb" of the city. Norton, Wilton and Grammercy had the large, comfortable homes; a few blocks west, Lucern, Arden and Rossmore had the mansions. A major indication of the importance of the neighborhood in the twenties is that the exclusive and very large Wilshire-Ebell Clubhouse was built on Wilshire Boulevard near these cross-streets in 1928. It still exists and often is used as a theatre. Needless to say, this no longer is considered a "western" area; we think of it as being almost downtown.

The mansions also still exist. But Wilton Place, which never had mansions, is showing her age badly. The houses do not seem as large as they once did, and some have been replaced by the innocuous apartment buildings that slowly and slyly change the face of a city. The Temple of Soul-Truth is at the corner of Wilton and Eighth Street, in a rambling two-story frame house of the pre–World War I type, the kind of house that once was truly in the country and had a huge garden and a place to keep horses. Today the narrow windows have been filled with stained glass with a cross in each; the large living room is a chapel, with a line of pews reaching down to a one-step-high

1

dais. In this chapel pyramids of red plastic roses sit on side tables beneath the small picture of *The Last Supper* and the larger picture of Christ; four chairs resembling thrones—they have very low seats and very high tapered backs and are covered with either red or gold crushed velvet—are placed on the dais and just below it; there is a baby grand piano in one corner. It is sweetly tacky. There are a thousand other "churches" in the city just like it.

The Temple of Soul-Truth, which believes in "meditation and psychic experiences and attempts to reach the other world through teachers who have passed over," has a Psychic Fun Night every Friday.

"Please release me, let me go. . . ." The old country-western classic is being beaten to death by someone crashing away at the piano. We have arrived late, have paid our $3 love donation at the door, have written our "three questions for the guest psychic" on pieces of paper, signing them only with our initials, as requested, and placed them in a basket. Will there be any places to sit, we wonder in the foyer. Not to worry. Nine other people have placed themselves carefully apart in various front pews. The piano segues into "Home on the Range," followed by "Streets of Laredo," "Danny Boy," "Beautiful Dreamer," all played with the same crashing monotony and mangled chords by someone wearing a tall-crowned cowboy hat and a denim-blue leather jacket. "My God, he's terrible," I whisper to my husband. "It's a she," he whispers back.

A few more people filter in, bringing the congregation finally to sixteen: male and female, young, middle-aged and elderly, almost exactly half Black and half Caucasian, with one Oriental. The meeting is about to begin.

The crashing of the piano stops abruptly and we all applaud, mostly from relief. The gray-haired figure stands to take a bow, and we are introduced to "Grinnel Tinney, the Nationally Famous Denver Nell!" "Hi there, y'all," she booms in a voice that could drown out a tuba. Denver Nell and her protégé, a boy about fifteen, take seats in the front row and hastily write out their three questions to be placed in the basket.

The attractive middle-aged woman now on the platform

wears a long evening dress. This is Elizabeth Long, Doctor of Divinity. According to the flyer we have been handed at the door, she is "assisting Bishop Hali Hart at the Temple of Soul-Truth . . . attempting to bridge the 'old with the new.'" She is "a minister ordained by City Temple Church . . . this ordination enables me to deliver sermons from the podium [sic] of all faiths—Catholic, Protestant, Hindu, Judaism, Mohammedanism, etc." The flyer tells us that she is an author (*Developing Your Gift of Healing*), a teacher, a lecturer, a Healer (the capital is a must) and a psychic. Dr. Long introduces tonight's Guest Psychic, another attractive middle-aged woman in long evening dress, Gloria Perri, whose card says she does Tarot interpretations, group and individual counseling and spiritual meditation. Now Psychic Fun Night gets its real start.

"Gloria, you take the first turn," Dr. Long says rather playfully, handing across the basket with the slips of paper on which each person's three questions have been placed. Gloria closes her eyes and dips her fingers into the basket. "R.C.?" she calls. "R.C., please raise your hand." The elderly man toward the front of the room stands halfway, raising a hand. Gloria looks at his list of questions but does not read them aloud. Neither does she close her eyes, pause for a few minutes of psychic communing, nor do anything else that might lead the watcher to believe that any such thing is occurring. "Number one, no, definitely not. Number two, perhaps. Number three, yes, but not just now. Wait a week or two." Briskly, as though washing her hands of the whole matter, she hands the basket back to Dr. Long.

Psychic Fun Night zips along, the questions are answered with lightning speed, and nearly every person who raises his or her hand to be identified with a set of initials looks relieved and satisfied after the terse answers are given. Only "E.L." creates a diversion, for "E.L." obviously has come not to listen but to talk. When his questions have been disposed of, he leaps to his feet. "I meditate twenty-four hours a day. Saint Paul says, 'Pray without ceasing,' and I do. I have confidence now, I feel strength within myself—"

"Thank you, E.L.," Dr. Long interrupts before he can work

up to full steam. "The more you meditate, the sooner the answer will come."

Only one question, one of my own, as it happens, breaks the rest of the steady stream of answers. I have asked, "Is it possible to find my father?" My father died before I was two. Gloria is a little perturbed by the question, though I sense that she thinks I am seeking a father who deserted me, not someone who has "passed over." "When did you last see him, J.G.?" she asks. "Many, many years ago," I answer. "I believe this will take some time," Gloria says. "I will contact you after the meeting and we'll discuss this further. I can recommend the right person for you to talk to." (After the meeting, she slips me her card as she rushes out, saying "Call me!" in a rather urgent manner.)

Mine were among the very last questions. The session has lasted perhaps forty minutes. We all begin to rise hopefully, but we are too slow, for Denver Nell and her protégé are now on the stage with accordions in their hands, and they are riffling through sheets of music. The protégé is introduced. "He's only had lessons for about four weeks," Nell booms. No doubt a prodigy, for he handles his instrument somewhat better than she handles hers; that is to say, he knows two songs straight through and plays them. (Gloria the Psychic, with the aplomb of any guest of honor, walked swiftly from the stage, down the aisle and out the door before the entertainment even began.) After fifteen or twenty minutes, people begin to sneak quietly away little by little. My husband and I are among the last, leaving only when it is obvious that Denver Nell is planning to play all night.

For the better part of this century Los Angeles has had the reputation of being a primary breeding ground for eccentric religions. Perhaps Aimee Semple McPherson and her Four Square Gospel Church put us on the national map, but there was a reason why she chose L.A. rather than someplace in Canada, where she was born, or any of the cities across the country or around the world where she had preached: the market was here.

The original Angelinos were Spanish grandees and Mexican peasants, mostly of Indian stock (the native Indians were not large in number, perhaps four thousand, and most were wiped out quite effectively when the Mission padres rounded them up and tried to train them to Mission duties—many died of apathy, and many of those who managed to escape died of starvation). Later, "Yankees," mostly easterners, arrived and married into the grandee families; Chinese came to work in the gold fields and on the railroads; and there was also a quite large Japanese farming population. These were the beginnings.

Though established in 1781, Los Angeles remained small in population until the late nineteenth century, when boom-town schemes by land speculators lured thousands of people, mostly from the Midwest, to this city. The origin of the boomer activity was a railroad squabble. The railroads owned a great deal of land in and around Los Angeles, and it naturally was to their advantage to attract customers; but in 1886 the Southern Pacific and the Santa Fe had a falling out that turned into a price war. Round trips from points west of the Missouri dropped to as low as $15, and for one remarkable day, to $1. Midwesterners leaped onto trains, sold or gave away their return tickets, and stayed—and the mood and manners and attitude of the city slowly began to change.

But it was in the teens and twenties of this century that much of what now is considered the Los Angeles persona began to emerge. The migrations of the late 1800s were the tail end of the pioneering migrations; cheap transportation, cheap land and a late-recognized "new frontier" appealed to certain types of people for settlement, and to certain other types, from shopkeepers and saloonkeepers to hotelkeepers and churchmen, to attend to their needs. The later migrations, from the East, Southeast and Southwest, of course, but still predominantly from the Midwest, occurred for a different reason.

For so many people of that era, "California" meant palm trees swaying against blue skies, days that were warm but not hot, nights that were cool but not cold, a place where the sun shone all year round, a place where you could "pick the oranges right from the trees with your own hands." Amazing how important that last item was. "California" did not mean San Francisco or the cool north, nor the hot central valley, whose climate was so much like that of the Midwest in summer, nor, for some reason, San Diego. It meant Los Angeles. They came here, so many of them from the Midwest, searching for the good life. And because they so often came to escape the depressions and recessions that have racked this country nearly every decade and sometimes more often, because they came from Bible Belt areas where, despite their strong beliefs, God never answered their prayers during hard times in hard climes, they came to Los Angeles also searching for "An Answer"—the sort of answer the conventional Protestant sects never gave them. They were ripe for evangelism. And evangelism was ripe for them.

My maternal family was among those who came out from the Midwest (Nebraska) seeking "An Answer," and they sought it in every conceivable place: Science of Mind and Dr. Joe Jeffers's Ministry and the Great I Am and, yes, Aimee's Four Square Gospel, and among the Seventh-Day Adventists (luckily, a brief affair, since we were allowed to eat only Vege-Burgers and could not dance or play cards) and with the Rosicrucians and, very briefly, with the Christian Scientists and, finally and until everyone but me died, with Dr. Clem Davies' Ministry. He was English, so our first "hymn" was "There'll Always Be an England," a delight if you enjoyed attempting a really high soprano.

There were many others. Most were both anti-Catholic and anti-Jewish. (Of the Catholics: "They call them seminaries and I call them cemeteries," Dr. Jeffers would say—he was an Elmer Gantry type of great force and charm who would take his sermon from whichever page of the Bible opened when he threw it full-force on the floor, and who later ran off from his wife and children with the church secretary and all the church funds. Of the Jews: "Everybody knows Roosevelt's real name is Rosenfeld, and the Jews are running this country!") Though my family was mad, truly mad, about all of this stuff—my mother filled numerous small orange notebooks with tiny, tiny writing based on ideas taken from these sermons—they were not mad enough to assume that a five- or six- or seven-year-old child could sit through five-hour-long evening meetings in huge halls such as the Shrine Auditorium or the Embassy Auditorium without going into hysterics if she didn't have something else to do. And so I was allowed to bring a book, and to buy one comic book and five cents' worth of penny candy every Sunday before we entered the "church" at five; and that, and the hymn singing, which I loved, kept me satisfied until nine or ten P.M. when the service ended.

Consequently, a lot passed over my head. But I did enjoy the Great I Am, where everybody wore evening dress and real jewels and furs, and people went up onto the stage of the Shrine Auditorium and confessed that they had been George Washington or Napoleon in earlier incarnations; and I was impressed by one meeting we attended in a large house—I can still picture the house exactly, but have no idea of its location—where a woman was "elevated" through "psychic concentration"; and I did enjoy the sermons that insisted that every event in the world had been foretold by the Oracles of Nostradamus or by things revealed by the Great Pyramid of Giza and by the chapter of Revelations in the Bible ("the great whore of Babylon, who sits on seven hills," naturally turned out to be Rome, thus the Catholic Church). And I did believe, sort of, that the Twelve Tribes of Israel had fanned out to become all the great nations of the world, that the Stone of Scone had some mystic connection with all of this, and that such famous people as Anthony Eden believed the same and had joined our worldwide organization, and that one day Eden himself would come to address us. He never did.

Such things used to be typical of, and unique to, Los Angeles. No more. What with Scientology and the Moonies and the Hari Krishnas and all the other cults running rampant across the country—the Church of Jayne Mansfield of the New Atomic Age has just been registered in Utah—it is no surprise to find that there are 1,987 churches (not including synagogues—a different heading) listed in the yellow pages of the Los Angeles telephone book, among them the A-Di-Da Buddhist Temple, the Christadelphian Ecclesia, the Church of

God–Anderson Indiana, the Dial-a-Prayer Angeles Mesa Presbyterian, the Church of Naturalism, the First Temple of Astrology, Omni and the Self-Realization Fellowship. But— and this is not surprising, considering our background—the longest listings are Baptist and Roman Catholic. It *is* a bit surprising that there are so many Protestant churches whose names indicate that they are congregations of Orientals from every imaginable country, of Europeans from every imaginable country, of Arabs or of Jews. This listing gives a vastly expanded idea of the various nationalities that have taken enough root in this city to form their own congregations.

Yet Los Angeles still has the reputation of being a cult center. And today, with so many people searching for "An Answer" that is not religious—merely "how to get the most out of life" or "how to find the real me"—the city still is considered a mecca. Here are a few of the pilgrims.

Lee and Josh are the center of attention at this Saturday evening dinner party in a pristine contemporary house in Beverly Glen. They are talking quietly and seriously and a little wistfully about the many years they spent at Synanon, one of the earliest self-help organizations in Los Angeles. They are a middle-aged Jewish couple, fairly dynamic in their personalities, obviously well educated and oriented to things intellectual. Something like twelve years ago they sold their Brentwood house, Josh quit his job, and they moved, with their three children, into one of the Synanon-owned-and-run buildings near the beach. One daughter still lives there.

"It was not an escape," Lee says vehemently. "We were not going off to a farm to raise food and do crafts, we were staying in the real world. Or at least, we thought we were."

"We felt that all we were leaving was establishment rottenness and hip liberalism," Josh concurs.

Mal, our host, adds, "It was the excitement of possibility. The possibility that there was a better way to lead your life than devoting all your time to earning more and spending more. That learning about yourself and other people was more valid than being one of the exploiters, or one of the exploited." Mal and his wife, Enid, never lived at Synanon, but they used to attend the games.

Synanon was established by a former drug addict to aid drug addicts and alcoholics, and had had, or at least was publicized as having had, notable success. Later, it broadened its scope to offer therapy to straights—to take a more cynical view, it decided to try to reach the establishment market. At this writing the organization is under investigation for numerous abuses, including trying to murder a prominent attorney by putting a rattlesnake in his mailbox.

"He seemed to go crazy, that's about what happened," Lee says regarding Synanon's founder. "There was nothing evil going on while we were there, we saw no abuses. We felt that the whole premise was idealistic, that it was a way of helping people help themselves. We still feel that way about it to a great extent. We do not feel we wasted those eight years."

"But you left," I remark. "And you don't seem entirely happy that your daughter is staying on."

"We outgrew it. And it seems about time for her to outgrow it too."

The Synanon Games. There was a time about twelve years ago when it was considered rather chic to attend the games, at least among a certain group of people. There were games for the people who lived there and games for outsiders too. I did not know Mal and Enid very well during the time they attended the games but was very close to some close friends of theirs, a couple who attended to try and save a failing marriage.

"Oh, it was wonderful last night," Anita would tell my husband and me in those long-ago days. "I really was able to open up for the first time and say right to Jack's face some of the things he does that I think are horrible." Jack would grin, which seemed to me odd. "I'd already told Anita off. The others egg you on you know. They say, 'Spit it all out, scream it out, yell it out!' It's a great release. You learn not to be afraid of your hostile feelings, you learn that hostility toward the people you love most is perfectly normal." Anita and Jack got divorced shortly after their avid participation in the games.

Tonight Josh says, "We moved into Synanon almost as soon

as they opened it to middle-class straights. They had started a school. We had our own separate apartment, with a separate bedroom for each member of the family."

"It was the first time in my whole life that I'd had my own bedroom," Lee says, and the nostalgia is obvious. But then real memories return. "They gamed you if you wanted to cook in your own apartment instead of eat with the others. They gamed you over everything that didn't fit in with their ideas of community spirit, or the way you should act. They gamed you over just about everything.

"If you want help," Lee says finally and a little obscurely, "don't go to a reformed addict. Go to a Gandhi."

Fifteen years ago. Friday nights at, of all places, the Beverly Hills Hotel. My friend Angela had had a call from our mutual friend Harry. "Listen," she told me, "Harry knows this really funny thing we can do together on Friday. There's this sort of pop psychiatrist who goes for acting out with his patients—and they do it in front of the public! Anybody can go! Do you want to go? Harry says you almost die laughing!" Psychiatry as public entertainment. I'm sorry to say I did not go.

Susan's search for "An Answer" has been on a different level, a much more serious level. After her son was born she tried, four times in six months, to kill herself. After two days at Camarillo State (mental) Hospital, one of the most frightening names in the area to anyone who has had mental problems—"It was just like everything you've ever heard about an insane asylum, I was put in a section with lifelong patients," she says—she spent four months in another mental hospital, to which she since has returned many times. "It was like a haven to me, like a return to the womb. I never progressed there, but I could live there." "Live" is an important word to Susan.

It was during her last stay in the hospital that she met a man who told her about Emotional Health Anonymous—the relatively new Los Angeles–based organization that, quite literally, has saved her life.

"It's like AA, it was developed along the same theories. The thing that makes it work for me is that I know the people involved have had *my* problem—not alcohol, but depression and panic and the urge to get away from it all forever.

"Like AA, they tell you to live one day at a time. Like AA, there's a support system—if you're feeling low, you can call someone to come over and help. They tell you what to do when panic hits. There is a spiritual side—you do daily meditation. And there is counseling—you help other people, give back to others some of what you've taken. At meetings, you get up and tell others what happened to you—not a long speech, just 'this is the way I used to be, and this is the way I am now.' It's very upbeat and positive, the meetings are pleasure, not pain. I can involve myself every night of the week, at the times when I need to do that. It's like a religion, in a way.

"I've learned three great things, three major things, from Emotional Health Anonymous," Susan says. "One is to admit that I'm a neurotic. Anyone whose emotions interfere with their functioning on a day-to-day level is a neurotic, and that's what I am. The second is that I don't have to try to figure it all out at once. I can take the problems that come along and deal with them one by one—I know I'm making progress on that day-to-day basis, and I don't have to worry about an overall solution. The third is I've actually learned to laugh at myself. That may be the most important thing that EHA gave me—the ability to laugh."

"California is the center of spiritualism today," Gordon tells me. Gordon is the last person I would have thought would be involved with the occult—he is a confirmed capitalist and a happy hedonist. But, "When I lived in London I got very involved with the Spiritualist Association of Great Britain. I went into it as a complete atheist, if you can use that term. I came out a believer." We are discussing this because he has just mentioned, much to my surprise, that he had taken his dog to one of the many animal psychics in the Los Angeles area. "The dog was acting very strange, he was cowering, he was hiding under tables. He never had done things like that before. The psychic discovered that he was very upset because my house had been broken into and robbed three times. The vibrations of these intrusions disturbed him deeply. As soon as I moved to another house, he became his old self again."

If anyone should know whether this city is indeed a center of spiritualism, it is Samson de Brier. He is considered to be one of an elite cadre—one of the genuine witches of Los Angeles.

It is not a title he has sought, and he would much prefer to be known for some of his other remarkable accomplishments, such as the fabulous salon he held nightly for over ten years for artists in all fields, or the journal he has kept for half a century detailing, among other things, his friendships with such people as André Gide, Anaïs Nin and Gertrude Stein. Yet one could say he looks the role he tries to play down. He says he is seventy-five, yet the translucent skin is virtually unwrinkled on both face and hands. Eyebrows are dark, thick, devilish looking, over deep brown eyes that dart and rove. The hair is a silky silver, swirled casually into a Roman style. The face is classic, the whole effect is that of a Roman emperor with a sense of humor—or of a good witch.

He refuses to be darkly mysterious. "I believe that so many people speak of psychic powers when all it is is highly developed intuition. There's nothing remarkable about it, we all once lived and survived by instinct as animals do. Some people, because of their circumstances, are able to develop their powers more than others, but we all have them.

"I began to develop this ability in my early twenties," Samson says, "but I didn't put it all together until I came to Los Angeles. I had done the New York scene, had lived in Paris, then like so many people I came out here to start a new life. And I found the vibrations very good for me. I became increasingly aware of mystical energies taking over in my personal life. Back East one is battered, always running, life is difficult, even the weather is difficult. I was torn between so many different emotions that I couldn't concentrate—to develop your gifts you have to have a serenity, you have to have possession of yourself. Out here, I was lulled by the climate, yet fascinated by the wonderful vitality. Gradually, I was able to put practical things in the background, where they belong, deorganize, let a pattern for living emerge. Then the other could take over. Then I could become aware of my intuitive powers and how to use them.

"Yes, Los Angeles is a center for the occult, because it's a center for people who are searching. After every crisis there comes a fascination for the occult—a lot of people got into it here. It's become a panacea for everybody's insecurity."

The word *witch* has not been mentioned. I remind him of an article published in *Esquire* magazine, just after the Tate–La Bianca murders, titled "Light in the Heart of Darkness" and featuring a photograph of Samson, identified as "A good witch who deplores the evil obsessions of his fellow Californians." "Are you a witch?" I ask.

"A witch is a person who has magical powers and can perform benefits and curses on people," he answers. Then, "You know, *Esquire* came to me because someone had told them I could help them locate people who were involved in the occult. I didn't talk about myself at all. When they started taking pictures I asked why, and they said they were coming back to California later to do a series about unusual people, and they wanted to include me because I was interesting and they might as well get the pictures ahead of time. Well, when I saw they really had just used me in that silly witchcraft story, I was quite irritated. So I wrote them a letter and I said, 'You know, a bad witch is just a good witch whose patience has been tried once too often. So a pox on you and all concerned.' Right after that the man who wrote the article had a nervous breakdown." Samson gives me an utterly devilish grin. "Of course, I had nothing to do with that. But they're really scared of me back there now."

With self-help organizations listed in the hundreds, naturally, est flourishes in Los Angeles. An interesting offshoot is The Advocate Experience, a sort of est franchise operation for gays.

Outside the Balboa Room of the Pacifica Hotel near the airport, the large upstairs lobby is swarming with men and women, the former in the majority. A lot of people seem to know one another, and almost everyone has someone else in tow. Men greet each other with bear hugs and fanny pats, but they greet the women, most of whom have come with men, more conservatively, with discreet hugs and kisses on the cheeks. The big topic is not the meeting about to begin, but the upcoming costume party aboard the *Queen Mary* the following weekend. Someone introduced as Jerry says, "A friend of mine is coming as the Frog Prince. He's hoping everyone will kiss him." "You mean Mark?" somebody else says. "It would take a lot more people than can get on the *Queen Mary* to turn *him* into Prince Charming." The lesbians here are as excited about the party as the gay men. Apparently this is to be one of the still fairly unusual mixed events. "What are you going to wear, what are you going to wear?" everyone asks. "You'll recognize *me*," someone says. "I'm coming as Adam. *Before* the fall."

Finally, we are asked to sign our names, pay our $2 donation, and go into the Balboa Room to be seated. The sign on the wall says, "The purpose of The Advocate Experience is to *transform* your experiences of being gay or homosexual into richer contexts wherein your individual lives can be lived in ways that are truly self-enhancing and contribute to all of society." A mouthful.

David Goodstein, publisher of the national gay publication *The Advocate* and a good friend of Werner Erhard, founder of est, is one of two leaders of The Advocate Experience. But it is the other leader who addresses us tonight. A young and good-looking man leaps to the platform and grabs the microphone. "Hi, I'm Rob Eichberg," he says, "the Jewish-American princess!" Everyone applauds and laughs, but a middle-aged lady in the fourth row stands to applaud. "That's my mom," Rob says, pointing. "Hi, Mom!" More applause.

There is quite a lot of homosexual joking during the evening, but it is obvious that the orientation is more est than gay. All the buzz words are here: "space" and "love space" and "bad space" and "sourcing" and "transformation," and phrases such as "I want to put this out" and "get in touch with yourself" and "learn to accept the responsibility for your own life." There even seems to be a certain amount of mysticism: "I always feel David is with me when I speak, even though he's three thousand miles away," Rob says. And, "When I was returning from New York yesterday I had a chance to take a later plane and I was so tempted, but something told me I *had* to be on that plane, and I was seated next to this woman and she said, 'I knew I was supposed to meet you.' She turned out to be a professional seer. We both learned so much from each other. It was a meeting that was meant to be."

In fact, this is precisely the sort of open house that est has, the sort of gathering to which people who have "been through" take their friends in the hope that they will become excited enough to "go through." The sales pitch ends thus: "I can't wait for the day when straights feel as able to go through The Advocate Experience as gays. It's just fun. The whole space is fun, and we're all in the same space." Loud applause and cheers. My friend and I leave. It would cost us $250 to get in the same space as Rob Eichberg.

Of course some of the answers people search for in Los Angeles are very basic: they want a mate.

Presumably, one way to find a mate of the correct caliber is to rent an apartment at the Marina City Club, where the highrises go on forever; where there is, at ground level, virtually no walking space, only driving and parking space; where the best apartments are the highest ones, and the ones with the ocean view, and the ones closest to the tennis courts and to the pool. In this world the Muzak piped in is not "Raindrops Are Falling on My Head," but symphonies by Beethoven. "It's a very classy place," John, the short, brash, but very successful young attorney tells me. "Everybody here reads a lot."

We are at a pasta party. Linda, the hostess, an extremely attractive lady who gives her age as twenty-five, has received a pasta-making machine for Christmas. The apartment is not one of the top ones with an ocean view; it is on the fourth floor, and the view is of the balconies of other apartments. But it doesn't matter. She lives at the Marina City Club. She gets Beethoven piped in and she reads a lot. She is rubbing shoulders with the likes of smart young attorneys like John; in fact, some people think she almost has him hooked. She is a secretary. She can afford the $750 per month rent (soon to be raised) only because her mother lends her money every month, against her future security. John—not necessarily this John, but any brash young attorney—is, to her, worth the effort. She wants the kind of guy who can afford one of the apartments that cost $1,000 or more, who owns his own boat, who drives a sports car; the kind of guy who can help a secretary move to the top of the building. If she misses out on this John, she will have to take in a roommate.

This is part of the way of life at Marina del Rey. Not all of it. George and Paige, old friends who sold their big house and moved into a right-on-the-beach condominium down here, laugh uproariously when the Marina City Club is mentioned. "Jesus, they're all sick up there," George says. "They don't understand that the incredible thing about beach life is that you walk around in sneakers and Levi's and nobody knows whether you're a bank president or a bum. Down here [the Marina City Club is several blocks up from the ocean] everybody knows who they are, because everybody already has made it. Up there, they're all just trying to make it, to be recognized as Somebody. All the little secretaries going in hock to meet *the* man, and all the guys showing off their boats and trying to impress the ladies."

George was very accurate. Here is Linda, slim and sleek and pretty, showing off for John. She has invited the boss who gave her the pasta machine, she has invited several friends from other milieus, the kind of people who apparently really do read books, she has invited the potential roommate (a mistake, I think, because Joanna is positively gorgeous), she even has invited her mother, a cozy lady with a nice sense of humor. Linda is being quite witty, she is coaxing everyone to take turns pushing the fat dough through the machine until it comes out in ten-foot-long strips of raw spaghetti. She has set the table beautifully, made an excellent salad, bought good wines. This party is also a sort of housewarming for her new couch, one of those immense things advertised as "adult playpens," since you have to crawl into it. The fabric of the couch is handsome, the few art objects show a refined taste, flowers are abundant. It is barely noticeable how hard she is trying.

Living at the Marina is one way of finding—or trying to find—a mate. Another is the many city-wide singles events. *The Los Angeles Times* has taken to running a twice-weekly calendar of these. However, in a January 1979 article headlined "Lonely Hearts' Mingling Not for Today's Singling," they point out that the day of the strictly socially oriented singles club is virtually over, that now singles expect to mingle with others who share their particular interests. They list a club that accepts only members who have earned an advanced university degree; a club started by a concert pianist for other musicians of concert caliber; a club for people interested in gourmet food; a club for single boaters; a club for single tennis players.

Yet, there still are plenty of singles around town who go to the Oar House in Santa Monica or to the Saloon in Beverly Hills, and who continue to patronize some of the private clubs that exist strictly for social purposes.

One is a very unusual establishment—a house so far up on one of the winding roads of one of the canyons that you would never be able to find it on your own. You are met in a parking lot on Sunset Boulevard by a van, and later returned, safe and sound, by van. Whatever happens from that point on is your problem, not the club's. I was longing to go there with Beth and Joanie—except that if you are married, your attitude is all wrong and it is spotted immediately.

The club was started by a man who was, remarkably, looking for a wife, a swinging wife. He owned a large handsome hillside home, so he decided to give singles parties there. One night, the woman of his dreams walked in. They married. Now they give singles parties together.

Not too successfully. Beth: "It sounded like such fun. But it turned out to be such a bore. None of the men would talk to you. It was as though they were waiting for Raquel Welch and wouldn't settle for anything else. And it wasn't as though they were young and handsome and fascinating. Most of them were middle-aged and boring." Joanie (who is a little more outgoing, a little more aggressive): "Well, one man talked to me quite a lot, but he kept looking at the door, as though he were waiting to see if something better would walk in. There were plenty of hors d'oeuvres and lots to drink, and enough people of both sexes, but it didn't take off. And you had the feeling that you were stuck, because you had to wait for that van to take you back to your car."

Beth: "The house was beautiful, one of those big, sprawling hillside houses. But I kept getting this feeling that if this thing didn't turn into a success and start to pay off, they were going to lose it—the house, I mean. There was an underlying uneasiness with the hosts, and it didn't help the atmosphere. I met this terrific woman, one of those voluptuous middle-aged types who always looks wonderful. And she said to me, 'Honey, you don't belong here. Come to my place in the Valley. I give a wonderful party, very private, much more friendly than this, every week. Here's my card. Now you call me for sure.'"

There are two places in Los Angeles where the tensions are minimal. One is Barney's Beanery. Not essentially a singles' hangout, it is just one of the oldest hangouts in the city, a sort of landmark. It is in an old stucco building, a café really, on Santa Monica Boulevard just east of La Cienega. It is lighthearted and raunchy, and after ten P.M. it is jammed with out-of-work actors and a lot of people who know one another and know they will meet one another there, as well as a few lonely types. Barney's has a long bar, and some outrageous signs, and it serves such soul food as hamburgers-with-everything and chili-sizes. Even if you don't know a soul in town, it is difficult to feel lonely when you are at Barney's.

The other place where tensions disappear—at least with the right attitude—is new to Los Angeles. In fact, it may no longer exist since the police are trying to find some legal reason to close it down. But at this writing Plato's Retreat West, the West Coast version of the club that took over the formerly gay Continental Baths in New York, is creating a lot of fun for a lot of people.

It is on a rather shabby street in Hollywood, next door to a place that advertises "Live! Nude! On The Stage! Every

Night!" Almost next door, also, to the Hollywood branch of the public library and to the Hollywood branch of the USO. Both institutions would love to get rid of it. It is a two-story building that does not have a pool, but offers a Jacuzzi and a sauna and a communal shower. My gay friends, who have told me that Los Angeles is a beat behind when it comes to sexual extravagances, have lauded the fact that finally there is a place that gives straights the same privileges as gays. As far as I know, Plato's Retreat West is a first on the Los Angeles heterosexual scene.

Anna, who has been swinging around Los Angeles for nearly fifteen years now, has told me a lot about the swinging life, and not just singles bars. She moved for a while with a group that was into orgies—"Well, it just got to be boring, always the same people, and most of them married or going together." She has investigated the homosexual scene, since she is bisexual; she has done private numbers with so many top executives from so many top companies that it would be difficult to count them; she has visited nearly every type of club, from the lowest down to the highest up. "I like to try everything, once," Anna says quite often, and since this includes everything from the most dangerous sports to traveling alone in unsafe districts of unsafe foreign cities, one scarcely can doubt her motives. She says she has never seen anything like Plato's Retreat West.

"It costs something like forty or fifty dollars for a couple to get in, which includes a six-week membership," she says. "But I got in alone for ten dollars, a one-time fee. A single man can't get in at all." I wonder aloud what the single women are supposed to do if there are no single men. "Make it with the couples, make it with each other, or just stand around and add to the atmosphere," she tells me.

Anna finds the atmosphere very pleasing. "You can wear clothes or not, and there's absolutely no pressure to have sex. There are a lot of private rooms if you want that, and a room with lots of mattresses if the public thing interests you. But you also can just watch closed-circuit TV, or play backgammon or pool, or dance to the disco music. There are people there of all ages, and I guess from all walks of life. I talked to everybody from teachers to longshoremen to lawyers. But everybody looks pretty good. There's nothing sleazy there, I guess they're very careful who they let in the door. I might go back." If it still exists.

If you were lonely or bored or just wanted to get out and around and experience something new, here are some of the ways you might have done it on a typical winter weekend. You could have attended a Holistic Fair in Santa Barbara, a three-day event with demonstrations and hourly lectures by various holders of various doctorates: twelve hours Friday and Saturday, nine hours on Sunday. That could take the bruises off a lonely weekend.

You might have attended classes in "Beginning Sailing," or "Our Body Is Our Expression" or "What You Should Know About Your Car" (taught by two women, both with mechanics' certificates), as well as "Sharing Our Expertise," a seminar sponsored by Women in Business, which included lunch at the famed Coconut Grove of the Ambassador Hotel.

You could have let your fantasies run wild at the Southern California Boat Show, or Tridents International Custom Car and Hot-Rod Show. For sports enthusiasts, there were the Los Angeles Times Indoor Games, the Raquetball Doubles Tournament, and an NHL Hockey Game; or the Sunhawks Dinner Dance, a $12-a-plate fund raiser to help pay for exchange programs with German soccer teams.

There was a Contemporary Music Festival in Riverside, the 42nd Los Angeles Bach Festival in downtown L.A., Lucia Albanese and Enrico di Giuseppe appearing in Pasadena, the Santa Monica Symphony Orchestra at the Santa Monica Civic Auditorium, the Westside Symphony Orchestra at the Wilshire-Ebell Theatre, Troika Balalaikas in Riverside, the Los Angeles Master Chorale at the Music Center.

You could have taken a whale-watching cruise from Dana Point, or a seal-watching cruise to San Miguel Island. Or attended performances of a Folk Dance Festival, the Ballet Pacifica, Flamenco Dancers or Balinese Dancers, or even gone to the Dance-in-Action Awards Luncheon on the *Queen Mary*. Several folk singers also were appearing around town.

You might have seen Marcel Marceau in Claremont, or Phyllis Diller at Studio One's Backlot, or chosen from twelve different plays, or attended a Cat Club Show, also in Claremont, a Junior League Rummage Sale in Long Beach or the Pasadena Antiques Show. If none of this appealed, there were the Senior Olympics Talent Contest in Dominguez Hills, a performance of Jewish Entertainers at KCSN (an FM station in Northridge) and the downtown start of the Firecracker Ten-Kilometer Run, which began in Chinatown to help celebrate Chinese New Year.

You could have covered the entire length and breadth of the city and its suburbs doing these things; or, if you wanted to save gas and money and still cover the length and breadth of the city, you could have bought an RTD Super Sunday Ticket for $1 and traveled anywhere in Los Angeles County for as long as Sunday lasted.

Or, you might have gone to the Open House at the Vital Health Center in Encino in the Valley. The Vital Health Center has a dual message to impart. On the one hand, it is involved in a holistic approach to health, and if you had attended the Open House you could have sampled classes and lectures on such things as "Bates Method Vision Training," "Parent Effectiveness Training," "Hatha Yoga," "Color and Your Health," "Contacting the Healer Within," "Herbs in Chiropractic," "the Vitamin Syndrome," "How to Cope with Stress," even "Face and Fashion Image for Women" and a very beginning class for joggers called "Downhill Runners and Fast Walkers."

The other message the Center is seeking to get across is quite different, for one of its main interests is Feminine Energies. To quote from a letter from Janet Goodrich, Ph.D., one of the founders of the Center:

> We understand feminine energy to be that aspect of existence which is primal, the source out of which all creativity arises. ⊛ This view automatically frees us of all patriarchal and religious concepts and brings us into mythology and the power of the imagination. That this aspect is carried more explicitly in the female form is just beginning to be understood. . . .

The feminine energy is being expressed by us in a cultural form which brings in the process of personal change for the individual . . . as well as providing an experimental vehicle or model for larger societal transformation. We consider ourselves a tribe, indeed, a city tribe, because the technology of city life needs transforming the most.

We are a group of 22 men and women . . . we have our own art, dance and creative activities. We all keep personal journals, explore dream consciousness and meet at tribal seminars. . . . We have cut a record of our spontaneous tribal music which had the sound engineer jumping up and down . . . the classes are geared toward women realizing their fullest creative powers in all phases of life. The Casteneda books are used as texts. . . .

If you are a woman who feels her time is about to come, you may enroll in "Feminine Energies I" or "Feminine Energies II," both courses under the auspices of Dr. Goodrich. If you are unlucky enough to be of the opposite sex, no matter. Dr. Gary Robb, a chiropractor, teaches "Feminine Energies for Men."

2

Kathy, the Queen of Disneyland

Disneyland is not, of course, in Los Angeles.

It is a desperately boring drive away, thirty-five minutes to an hour, depending on traffic, on our most boring freeway, the Santa Ana. It is on this freeway that you encounter, nearly always, even on days that are clear in the rest of the basin, the yellow-gray pall that need not be smog but may simply be haze that a weak sun is trying to penetrate. The pall hangs over Bob's Big Boys and Sambo's and McDonald's and Wendy's and Denny's and all the other fast-food-chain drive-ins and drive-throughs and coffee-shops-labeled-restaurants that line the long streets that parallel the freeway—"next off-ramp, don't miss it," "easy exit, easy return." The pall half obscures, luckily, the billboards that stretch all the way to Tijuana, the lot after lot of car dealers, the end-of-the-dream desolation of mobile home parks and forties tract houses separated from the freeway by graffiti-tracked walls. The pall smells, a slightly burnt or perhaps decayed smell of things such as rubber and cow farms and exhaust fumes and factory fumes. The pall creeps among the cars which, even with the fifty-five-miles-an-hour speed limit, try to escape it at sixty or sixty-five or seventy; but of course it cannot be escaped, it seeps in through air vents and the merest crack of a window—you seldom see a car with windows open on the Santa Ana. And it cannot be outdriven. It follows you past the small industries of the City of Commerce and Pico Rivera, past the little ranches crunched between the bumper-to-bumper tracts of Santa Fe Springs and Norwalk and

La Mirada, past Buena Park and Knott's Berry Farm and all the way to Harbor Boulevard in Anaheim, where the fake-snow-covered peaks of the fake Matterhorn tell you that Disneyland lies.

Disneyland is not in Los Angeles. But to millions of people from every country in the world, to Australians and Thais and Russians and French, to peasants and presidents alike, Disneyland is Los Angeles—or vice versa. To write about Los Angeles without writing about Disneyland would be to leave out something peripheral but essential, like omitting what the police call an "identifying mark" from a realistic portrait. It is part of Los Angeles in a way that is not profound but possibly is important to understand. My friend Bill Allen is fond of saying that Disneyland is the cathedral of Los Angeles. That puts too much emphasis on it, but makes a point: for much of the world, Disneyland is a sort of shrine.

I would like to tell you about a girl.

Her name is (or at least it used to be) Kathy Smith, which is a perfect name, pretty but neutral, for the perfect Disneyland example of the perfect Los Angeles teenager.

Of course the quintessential Los Angeles teenager is the one who hangs out at Balboa or Newport or Laguna or Malibu all summer; whose lean body is the exact color of a McDonald's French fry; whose honey hair is sun whitened and reaches precisely to where the briefest bikini bottom does not quite cover her own brief and jaunty bottom; who, barely postpubescent, already has learned the ritual walk and swing and the indolent loll that promise something sensual that she could not possibly give—or could she? But that is not, never has been, definitely could not be, the Disneyland/Los Angeles teenager. Kathy Smith was.

As a teenager, Kathy Smith was very pretty, but not too pretty. Her hair was of a medium brown and of a medium length; her eyes were greenish hazel; she was, perhaps, a little too tall to be called average, but she didn't seem tall, she didn't tower, so it was all right; her figure was good, but it was a figure, not a body, and there is a difference. She had perfect teeth and a perfect smile and there was a sparkle to her; the smile came often and it seemed to be natural. She was as clean-cut and polished and wholesome as if Walt Disney himself had designed her. At the last minute, just before he set all the complicated machinery to work, he added a high-voltage dose of personality, so that the girl you might have passed by without noticing became a little bit special—at least, special enough.

Kathy was born in Japan, the only fact about her that is out of the ordinary. Nothing even vaguely foreign stuck to her; her service family moved to Los Angeles before she was old enough to remember ever having lived elsewhere. She does remember that her mother, an energetic and determined woman who seems to have had a little of the stage mother in her, took her exploring every single weekend to places that would help Kathy develop a curiosity about life. The father does not play a large part in Kathy's reminiscences; we can assume that he did not tag along on the jaunts to the arboretum and the museums and the downtown public library. We can also assume that the family was not wealthy, for Kathy makes a point of the fact that these weekend trips were to places that were free.

But for Kathy the most important place her mother took her, the only place she recalls that had an admission fee, was Disneyland. "I remember one day my mother said, 'We're going to Disneyland today,' and we got all dressed up and we came here, and at that time I remember the parking lot still had some orange groves left, and I really can't tell you exactly what we did here that day, because I was six years old. And every year after that we came back to Disneyland. We came at Christmas time, and that was sort of our family Christmas present to each other. It was just the two of us, and we would come and spend the day and walk around, and I remember, even as a child, I liked to go on the attractions but there were a lot of things to do, you could just sit and listen to the band, or go to the Pacific Telephone exhibit where it's a free attraction, and this is the type of thing that we would do."

When Kathy was twelve the first Disneyland Ambassador was chosen, and her mother clipped the article from the newspaper. The idea stuck in Kathy's mind— not so much as a goal, because it seemed so farfetched, but as a dream; the way a more ambitious (or less realistic) girl might dream of becoming a movie star. Perhaps the mother believed in the dream more than the girl. To become an Ambassador you had to work at Disneyland for some years. When Kathy was sixteen, the mother moved them to Tustin, which is only ten miles from Anaheim. For many years afterward the mother, who worked at Max Factor in the heart of Hollywood, commuted the nearly seventy miles round trip daily on the Santa Ana Freeway. As soon as she was old enough, Kathy went to work for Disneyland, the first step toward fulfilling whoever's dream it was.

In Los Angeles some people make fun of Disneyland. Some think of it as overblown and garish, and use the name as a synonym for those terms, as in: "How was the party?" "Ugh, a regular Disneyland." Some regard it as bland, a prechewed and predigested form of entertainment suitable only for small children and people who prefer not to think. Some consider it not a Los Angeles phenomenon but an Orange County one— Orange County being the place where the John Birch Society has its headquarters; where people would still vote for Richard Nixon for President, given the opportunity; where superconservatism in politics is coupled with a fervor for exotic religious cults—if Aimee Semple McPherson arrived in the West in this decade, Angelus Temple would be built in Orange County. If we have not too much good to say of the San Fernando Valley, at least we accept it as part of Los Angeles. Orange County is an area we repudiate. And Disneyland surely is one of the largest single enterprises in Orange County; for many of us, it is a defining element.

In fact, Disneyland is a delight, a place that seldom fails to please children and adults alike, the ingenuous, the sophisticated and even the jaded. It is the best of what might be defined as an "amusement park," though Disneyland itself prefers the term "theme park." It is both slick and homey, childlike and sophisticated, and there is scarcely a tacky element in its seventy-plus acres. Disneyland is plainly and simply fun, and it is fun every time you go, even if the relatives from Nebraska arrive just days after the friends from Paris have departed, even if you have to make that long, gray, boring drive for the second time in less than two weeks. It is fun to zip over the park in the sleek monorail (probably the closest Los Angeles ever will come to decent public transportation). It is fun to slip through jungle waters past jaw-snapping crocodiles and water-squirting elephants that seem utterly lifelike. It is fun to fly through the air like Peter Pan, and to see spectres in the Haunted House, and to take nerve-wracking rides such as the Matterhorn or Space Mountain trips, countered by relaxing cruises such as the Paddle Wheeler on the "Mississippi." Of course souvenirs are sold here, and of course hot dogs and cotton candy are available. But you can also find superb antiques at the shop in New Orleans Square, and have a unique perfume blended for you, and buy crafts, artwork and clothing from countries around the world, and eat at a restaurant that has beveled and stained-glass windows and brass and copper fixtures.

Disneyland is beautiful, always ablaze with seasonal flowers, always shaded by handsome trees. Over fifty thousand flowers are planted here annually, and there are more than forty thousand specimen trees and shrubs, but these facts are boring compared to the reality: a spread of deep-purple pansies that are more velvetlike than velvet, for instance; or the deep shade, on a hot day, of a chestnut tree that stands so tall you can barely see its top. In the summer there are spectacular fireworks nightly, and there is constant entertainment: rock groups and pop groups and marching bands, from the local high school talent to such stars as Pearl Bailey and Benny Goodman, Stevie Wonder and Duke Ellington and Helen Reddy. There is Main Street, U.S.A., which is so like a turn-of-the-century Midwest small town that some Midwestern oldsters have complained that they didn't come to Los Angeles to see what they had finally escaped from. And there is Tomorrowland, which catapults you into the future. And if a larger-than-life, moving, talking Abraham Lincoln strikes you as a little goulish, perhaps by this time you will be able to forgive the one aspect of Disneyland that is not quite tasteful; you may even be able to accept the fact that, odd as it seems, some people revere this attraction.

Los Angeles, surely, has nothing to fear from being associated with Disneyland. It may lend us the best image we've ever had. And yet, there is something a little strange about the place.

On assignment for various magazines, I have been invited there several times to see behind the façade. And, honestly, what exists behind the façade seems to be a façade. If perfection exists in an imperfect world, it is here. Things run smoothly as clockwork behind the scenes as well as in front. Oh, there are offices and corridors and stairways and reception desks; and in the subterranean depths there are miles of machinery for keeping the rides moving and the grass green, and for sending away the tons of trash collected daily and bringing in the tons of food consumed daily. And it is not like Futureworld: the reporter does not sense that she is being shown only the pretty part. If they keep things from you here, it is for your own good.

For instance, I find a note to myself made during one of those assignments. It says, "Characters are not allowed to be interviewed because they are not people." What this means is that the huge Mickey Mouse and Minnie Mouse and Pluto and Goofey who roam the park, shaking hands and posing for pictures with visitors, are considered, by Disneyland, to be the *real* Mickey Mouse, Minnie Mouse, et cetera. They feel that it would shatter—not fantasy, mind you, but—*reality* if the public found out that there were human beings inside those costumes, and normal-sized ones at that; and not even the same human beings all the time. According to the Disneyland credo, there is only one Mickey Mouse, and he is alive and well forever, roaming the acres in Anaheim. What is a little frightening is that not just Disneyland seems to believe this, but the world seems to believe it too. Last year Disneyland received over four million telephone calls. The name most frequently requested was Mickey Mouse.

Another strange thing about Disneyland is that it is spotless. Always. Is it possible that last year's more than ten million visitors did not drop one piece of paper on the ground, did not stamp out one single cigarette butt? One explanation is that being surrounded by such remarkable cleanliness has a psychological effect. (According to *The Los Angeles Times*, B. F. Skinner, on visiting Disneyland in 1979, credited "the designers for reinforcing visitors' anti-littering behavior.") It certainly worked on me. Watching the Bicentennial America on Parade show a few years ago, I let a cigarette burn down to its filter, then held it until the show was over and I could throw it in a trash can. During the same parade, when a pigeon flew over my head I started to duck—and then actually said to myself, "No, it wouldn't dare."

Of course, pigeons and people do drop things in Disneyland. And of course the real explanation is that hundreds of Disneyland's behind-the-scenes actors cope with the problem on a major scale. Nightly, they retrieve thirty tons of trash. Nightly, they steam-clean the streets, the only infallible method for removing chewing gum. (The previous method of using fire hoses with ninety pounds of water pressure didn't work. Neither did banning the sale of gum at the park.) Nightly, one dedicated worker spends eight hours polishing the brass on the Fantasyland merry-go-round. Every single dawn finds a five-man crew repainting the targets at the two shooting galleries. Every single day finds the boat painter repainting one or another of what he calls "his" boats. Every single day finds the Pirates of the Caribbean getting their costumes checked for dirt, and changed at the merest hint of it. The life expectancy of every one of 100,000 light bulbs is plotted to the second; when 80 percent of its lifespan is reached, the bulb is changed. It is comforting to know that the maintenance supervisor of the frightening Matterhorn ride does not merely rely on its $2 million worth of safety equipment to keep it safe—he personally walks every foot of track and inspects every link of chain nightly. But it is a little disconcerting to learn that every single one of these people seems to do his or her—surely boring—job so joyously, so willingly, and with such pride.

Which brings us back to Kathy Smith.

"I guess I first started thinking about working at Disneyland when I was about fourteen. The papers were doing articles about how you could qualify, and it was unique, because, for instance, there's always been a grooming code for employees, men's hair has to be short, and no beards or mustaches, and makeup and dress have to be pretty much conservative. And I really got to thinking about it."

The moment she turned eighteen Kathy applied for a job.

"My first job was right over there at the Plaza Pavilion. I was a cashier and I worked there for the summer, and along about that time I really became aware of the Ambassador program. And I remember at the time the Ambassador was a young lady named Marva Dixon, and I mean she was just my idol. I couldn't imagine how anyone could be so . . . poised and perfect and all those things. So I don't think it was something I ever thought about doing in reality, it was just something I dreamed about."

Actually, her initial dreams were on a smaller scale. "After I was in food services for a very little while, I became a tour guide, and that was a dream come true, because when I was a little girl I would see them taking people around in their bright red outfits and I dreamed of doing that. So I did that for about two years, and I thought it was just terrific, and about that time I became what we call a Permanent Part-Time Employee. We have what we call Casual Seasonal Employees who work for the summer or at Christmas, but I was a Permanent because I worked every weekend. And I knew at the time you had to be a Permanent to try out for Ambassador, and I thought, well, I know I won't win, but I'll try it, it'll be fun. And then I was just so absolutely nervous, I called the lady who did the scheduling to say I couldn't do it, but she wasn't in, so I had to do it."

The committee of supervisors who weeded through eighty to one hundred girls to pick ten semifinalists and then four finalists obviously saw something in Kathy that she didn't see in herself. "I was so nervous, I couldn't believe I was in the final four. I didn't win, another young lady was selected, but I was encouraged to try again the following year. And that's when I was selected."

One wonders whether such Victorian turns of phrase—

"another young lady was selected"—helped move Kathy up the
ladder of success, or whether an Ambassador is especially
trained to speak that way.

I first interviewed Kathy during her reign, if it may be called
that, as Disneyland Ambassador 1975–76. It was a marvelous
time to be Ambassador, the best ever, because it was during the
Bicentennial celebrations, and she and her counterpart from
Disney World in Florida were the first Ambassadors to be sent
all over the world, as well as all over the United States. "We've
been to Rome, Paris, London, Stockholm, Tokyo, New York,
Alaska," she told me then. "That last lap, we flew direct from
Tokyo to New York, then to L.A. via Alaska, and we never did
catch up on what time it was, or even what day it was. I was
interviewed in Mexico City once at two o'clock in the morning!
Oh, it's been hectic. But it's been wonderful. Wonderful!"

At that time I asked Kathy what her plans for the future
were. Would she return to her prelaw studies at the University
of California at Irvine? (She had taken her junior year off to be
Ambassador.) Did she plan to remain in Los Angeles? "Oh, I
think it's important to finish school," she told me. "I need to
find out who I am, what my special talents are. But I think I'll
go into communications. I've made so many contacts, I've even
been offered jobs." You almost could see the stars in her eyes as
she imagined a career in radio or television or film, see ambition
finally lighting up this near-child whose previous dream had
been to be a Disneyland tour guide and wear a red uniform. As
for settling down in L.A., "After seeing London and Paris and
Rome, how can you decide where you want to live?"

Nevertheless, she was deeply caught up in the utopian
fantasy that Disneyland either imposes on its employees or finds
there already and cultivates. "One thing we've done a lot of, we
take the characters and we visit hospitals and orphanages and
old people's homes. There's a company philosophy, sort of, that
there *are* people who can't come to Disneyland, so we try to
bring a little bit of Disneyland to them. At Christmastime we
started in northern California and toured just about every
hospital with children, all the way back down to southern

California. It can be a little depressing, but you know, they really appreciate what you can give. That's the kind of thing the company feels pretty strongly about."

Another thing the company feels strongly about is keeping its employees not just happy, but clasped as closely to the maternal (or paternal, if you will) breast as possible. There is a pretty cafeteria with indoor and outdoor eating areas where employees may order the same food that is served in the public restaurants—such dishes as shrimp creole and fresh crab salad and rare roast beef—and pay just a fraction over cost. Any merchandise sold in the park—and everything from silk dresses to gourmet cooking items to antique dolls is sold there—may be purchased at, again, just over cost. The medical benefits are so good that an employee doesn't even have to pay to have his teeth cleaned. Employees who wear costumes are issued clean ones daily—the cleaning bills six years ago amounted to $70,000 a month, and the company paid them. Disneyland wants you to love your job, so there is a placement counseling service where you can discuss your future; your job wishes are programmed into a giant computer, and when the right opening occurs, you are notified.

Camaraderie is encouraged at the Rec Hall, where there are lounges and conference rooms and where free beverages are available; and through ski clubs and tennis clubs and bowling clubs and golf clubs, even canoe clubs (in which employees have races along the park's waterways before the park opens); and there are group trips, and a Fifty-Five Club, to which people who have worked at Disneyland since it opened belong. Once a year there is Employees Family Night at Disneyland, when supervisors man the rides and shops and booths in full costume, and all the other employees and their families enjoy the attractions at no cost. Kathy says, "When people see their supervisors doing their own jobs, it makes them feel really good!" In fact, "feel good" seems to be the standing order for Disneyland employees. The "one big happy family" attitude is not merely encouraged, it seems to be mandatory. Forty percent of Disneyland employees marry one another.

And so I was not much surprised when I decided to find out

what had happened to the perfect Disneyland teenager four years after her reign as Ambassador ended, posed my question to a Disneyland telephone operator—"Could you connect me with someone who might know where Kathy Smith, the 1975–76 Ambassador, is today?"—and received this answer: "Oh yes, Kathy Smith Hall. I'll connect you with Merchandising."

She met me in the employees' parking lot the following week, zipped me through the Administration Building, a short cut to the park, whipped out her Disneyland employee charge card at the restaurant to which she had steered me, and proudly insisted on paying for lunch: "It's my treat. I have an expense account, you know." She has not changed; one can say that pretty girls do not change much between the ages of going-on-twenty-one and going-on-twenty-five, but that is especially true if their lives have not changed much either. She is perhaps a bit more poised, but she was quite poised before, despite the nervousness she used to claim. She was never flighty, so one cannot say that marriage or maturity has settled her down. She is dressed now as she was then, as a perfect lady—below-the-knee wool skirt, silk blouse, lightweight wool blazer, neutral stockings, medium-heel pumps. The medium-brown, medium-length hair is perfectly groomed, the makeup is subtle—that dress code she read about when she was fourteen will, no doubt, stick with her all her life. The smile still flashes. The personality still shines out.

She is as enthusiastic about Disneyland as ever. "After that wonderful Ambassador's year I came right back here to work full time," she says, without a hint of disappointment over a potential not realized or a challenge not met. "I got my degree in communications at night, because I thought it was important to fulfill that goal. But you know, I thought of communications in terms of television and things like that, but that's not really right for me. You can't just be on TV, you've got to go out and get the news and things like that. So I moved into merchandising. They have a wonderful merchandising training program here and I'm in that."

She seems a little confused when I ask where that will lead

her—as though she is not used to thinking in those terms. "Well, I'm a buyer trainee right now, and hopefully when I finish training I'll be an assistant buyer. Right now, I'm working in a lot of different shops, so I can get the feeling for different kinds of merchandise. And I go to gift shows and things with the buyers so I can learn how to select merchandise."

Then what? "Well . . . then I *could* become a buyer, and then a manager, and then a director, all the way up to—" She stops, she's about to say "supervisor," but cannot quite get that thought out. "To tell you the truth, I'll be very happy if I'm just a buyer someday. I think I'll be very comfortable being a buyer . . . I don't know, being a manager is a pretty big job, with pretty big responsibilities. So right now, that's all I'm thinking of. You know, I'm a trainee. I'm just starting at the bottom."

Surprisingly, she did not marry another Disneyland employee. She met her husband, who used to be a reporter, at a Disneyland press conference. He now works for a hospital. They have been married two years, and they recently bought a house. They continue to see a lot of Kathy's mother, who has great pride in her daughter's achievements. "She's just so big on Disneyland. It really means a lot to her that I work here."

After lunch we walked through the park together, Kathy pointing out her favorite places and expostulating on the (requisite but obviously sincere) pride and enthusiasm of the people to whom she introduced me.

A central circle of flowers, pansies and marigolds at the height of bloom and as carefully designed as a wedding cake: "This is where I had my coronation. I think of that wonderful day every time I pass here." The doll shop, where she is joyously greeted by the salespeople, and where we watch a teenage girl buy a $200 reproduction of an antique doll: "This is one of the first shops I worked in when I started buyer training. The buyer is so wonderful, she knows every single doll. She's a doll collector herself, you know." An Oriental shop with expensive jade and porcelain, plus the usual souvenir items. "Look at these things, just look! [A tiny brass elephant, carved Indian wood boxes, a nutshell with minute ivory elephants inside.] Even if you only can spend fifty cents or a dollar, you still can buy a quality item here. The company realizes that the items people take home will be their lasting memory of Disneyland, so they're always quality items." The perfume shop, a quite lovely replica of a turn-of-the-century French shop, with crystal chandelier, molded ceiling, back-painted mirrors: "Walt Disney designed this especially for Lily, his wife. See the lilies on the mirror? He used to just walk through the park, you know, just like he was one of the visitors, to see how people were enjoying things." New Orleans Square, with its narrow cobblestone streets and houses with wrought-iron balconies: "These are *exact* replicas of real New Orleans houses. You know, they never say here, 'Well, if we left out this and this we could save money.' They always do it absolutely right." The gourmet cooking shop, with handsome imported French and Italian items: "Disneyland owns nearly all the merchandise shops, even the antique shop, so they don't have to jack up prices like crazy. They don't have to make their money from the shops. They can afford to have some really expensive items that won't necessarily sell. They want people to see quality when they come here."

Shop after pretty shop. Willing, helpful, smiling salesperson after salesperson. Happy buyers who greet Kathy by name: "Every buyer feels just like these are his or her own shops. Because there are no two shops alike. Except for the Disneyland character items [the Mickey Mouse hats and Donald Duck T-shirts] you won't find the same merchandise in any two places in the park."

And as we walk along, past all the things that make Disneyland bigger and better and prettier and finer than any other theme park in the world—past the rivers and lakes with the fleet of boats that give Disneyland the world's eighteenth largest navy; past the tree where the parents of Ron Dominguez, who now runs the park and whose family once owned the land, were married; past the Golden Horseshoe Review, which has broken show business records for number of continuous performances; past the stands that sell 4.5 million hamburgers per year; past the elm tree that was the only specimen plant that Emperor Hirohito, a botanist, asked Kathy to identify for him during his visit here while she was Ambassador—as we walk through the fantasylands that are the public areas, and through the equivalent fantasies of the back lots and underground passageways that are the employee areas, everywhere we go, everywhere we turn, people call out, "Kathy!", "Kathy Hall!", "Hi, Kathy!" "Hi, how are you?" Kathy says to one man. "Better, now that I've seen you," he answers.

The permanent sign on the Disneyland marquee that greets visitors as they enter from Harbor Boulevard says, in huge letters, "The Happiest Place on Earth."

According to *The Los Angeles Times* reporter who accompanied him in 1979, B. F. Skinner, passing the same sign, jokingly murmured, "Abandon hope, all ye who enter here."

3

How to Escape the Valley: The L.A. Triple C's

Elizabeth wanted to buy a house.

She hunted and hunted through the western sections of the city—Beverly Hills and Brentwood and Westwood and all the western canyons—but she could not seem to find the perfect house within her $130,000 to $140,000 budget. After weeks of searching, she called. "I've got it," she said, "and it's wonderful." She proceeded to describe the Dutch doors, the greenhouse window in the all-tile kitchen, the huge used-brick patio with wrought-iron fence around the heated pool, the pegged-wood floors, used-brick fireplace, the raised-level dining area with French doors to the garden. It sounded superb. And yet there was something in her voice.

"What's wrong with it?" I asked finally.

"Oh, June," she said, "I'm so embarrassed. It's in the *Valley!*"

And that, admittedly, is the way many Angelinos, the ones who live in Los Angeles proper, the ones who do not cross the Santa Monica Mountains to go home at night, feel about it. The Valley. It is a different way of life out there.

The San Fernando Valley, as it is formally called, is an immense chunk of Los Angeles that stretches from Burbank, just over the hills from Hollywood, all the way to Chatsworth, on the Ventura County line; and from the Santa Monica Mountains (where the many canyon communities are) on the south to the Santa Susana Mountains on the north. It includes some separately incorporated cities, such as Van Nuys, Burbank and San Fernando, and a large number of cities that belong to Los Angeles and yet lead the Valley life, such as North Hollywood and Panorama City and Mission Hills, such as Sherman Oaks and Encino, Tarzana, Reseda, Woodland Hills, Canoga Park, Northridge. It is crossed by two of the longest streets in the entire city: Sepulveda Boulevard, running north and south, and Ventura Boulevard, running east and west. In some places it is as far as one can get from the city and still live in the city. In other places it is the northern extension of the canyon communities, or the link between Los Angeles and our northeastern enclaves, Glendale and Pasadena. It includes Universal City, a major film studio, now with its own "theme park," and Magic Mountain and Busch Gardens, two other favorite tourist attractions.

It was incorporated into Los Angeles for only one reason: it was necessary to bring water across it to serve the city. In 1913 the Los Angeles Aqueduct—a major project that went through 142 tunnels, crossed a desert as large as the state of Massachusetts, and eventually became a pipeline as long as England is wide—was inaugurated, bringing water from the Owens River to the thirsty basin.

The Valley is all of those things that make people think they will hate Los Angeles. It is the area which, viewed from an airplane banking in over the mountains from the east, seems to be one giant turquoise blob, since nearly every house and certainly every apartment building has a swimming pool. It is the area which is hotter than the across-the-mountains side of the city when it is hot, and colder when it is cold; but mostly it is hot. It is the area where some people still think doubleknits and leisure suits are chic, where most men do not wear ties when they go out to a restaurant for dinner (in fact, they often wear knit sports shirts), and where people who are invited over for a swim, with dinner afterward, often sit down to the dinner table in their bathing suits—perhaps with T-shirts over them, perhaps not. It is the land of barbeques and of air conditioning, of orange and grapefruit orchards where to this day "you can pick the fruit right off the trees with your own hands," as early comers from the Midwest used to marvel. It is the locale of that architectural phenomenon known as "the California ranch-style house," and today that house usually includes a sauna or a hot tub. It is the area where everyone drives and drives and drives, where they drive even if they are just going around the corner to a neighbor's house, where every fourteen-year-old has passed Driver's Education and Driver's Training, and every sixteen-year-old owns his own car. It is the area where Gelson's, which is just an ordinary supermarket with perhaps slightly better than average produce and meats, and higher prices to match, is the name to drop when asked where you shop; and every single woman in the Valley insists that she shops there—though the Ralph's and the Von's and the Mayfair are always more crowded.

As my brother-in-law, who lives in the Valley, says, "There are eight million stories here. All of them dull."

It is where the McDonald's and the Bob's Big Boys and the Pup 'n Tacos and the Burger Kings flourish as nowhere else, because almost everyone has kids, two or three or four or more of them. The Valley is the part of L.A. for families with kids; there are schools all over the place, there are plenty of other kids for them to play with, and there are plenty of hamburger and taco stands for them to work at when they're old enough to want jobs. The Valley is big, and it is crowded. And after ten o'clock almost any week night you could hear a pin drop anywhere on Ventura Boulevard.

Ventura Boulevard is "the Boulevard," as the kids who cruise it call it. It follows almost a straight line for the length of the Valley—from the Cahuenga Pass (which crosses the shortest span of the mountains from Hollywood, where it meets Cahuenga Boulevard) to Hidden Hills, at the farthest west end of the Valley—and it almost parallels the Ventura Freeway, which eventually turns into one of the main highways north to San Francisco. It also sets the dividing line of the area, just as "the tracks" used to set it in towns and cities long ago.

"Where do you live?"

"South of the Boulevard" is the correct answer. Because south of the Boulevard is where property is divided into one-half or three-quarter-acre tracts, where it is zoned for horses and other animals, where orange groves used to flourish (and some still do), where big old trees still exist.

North of the Boulevard is where the old, empty flatlands and small ranches and farmlands used to be before World War II, where the immense tracts of low-cost housing were established just after the war, and where nontract houses used to be ticky-tacky and many still are. It is where the apartment house neighborhoods grew up, and where some settlements of Chicanos and Blacks were established, again, mostly after the war.

There are some handsome places north of the Boulevard; indeed, whole cities have grown up in this area in the last thirty years, and of course, these cities have their own dividing lines, their own "other side of the tracks." New Valleyites might not even know that this subtle dividing line down the middle of Ventura Boulevard exists. But if you live south of the Boulevard, you know it does.

Ventura Boulevard can be fun. There are more antique shops along its length than on any other single street in the city; and there certainly are more restaurants of every persuasion—French and Italian and the ubiquitous Continental and Japanese and Mexican and Swiss and German—than any place else. It is much more of a Restaurant Row than La Cienega, which has held that title for so long. There still are neighborhood movies (besides the three- or four-theatre complexes in various nearby malls), and everything else anyone could want: book stores and toy stores and boutiques and fine shops for china and glassware, for plants, for fabrics; loads of banks and savings and loans and insurance companies and doctors' and lawyers' offices; hardware stores and drugstores and coffee shops and delis, too. It probably comprises one of the longest "neighborhoods" in the country, if not the world. It would be a delightful street to walk along, to browse along; but of course you don't walk and you don't browse. This is the Valley. You move from parking space to parking space. Anyway, it is too hot to browse. You get your business over and you get home. To the air conditioning.

There is a quality about the Valley that, I admit, I love. A lazy-summer quality. Breathless still air, hot enough so that you know school is out. Let's go out and pick some peaches or plums, let's go down to the stand on the highway for fresh corn, let's go down to the reservoir to swim. The reservoir—or, rather, many reservoirs, remnants of that early Owens Valley project—still exists, as do the highway stands and the fruit groves. Despite the postwar upsurge in building and industry, there are still some small farms here, some horse ranches, places where people raise a few chickens. And in the Valley it is almost a sin not to try to grow one's own corn and squash and zucchini and tomatoes. The soil and the weather are perfect for vegetable gardens; almost everyone tries to have one.

And, somehow, there still is a sense of dusty roads—of grass growing out of control so that it looks like fields of weeds, of pepper trees scattering their minute leaves at every puff of breeze, of the real country that used to exist here before the tracts came, and the office buildings, and the industrial "parks." The country feeling can be sensed even while driving in heavy traffic (it is always heavy) along the Ventura Freeway and staring out at the extraordinarily run-of-the-mill modern buildings that now punctuate the skyline that seems to stretch forever. Perhaps it is the way the light shimmers, with ripples of heat running through it; perhaps it is the fact that there are still stands of dust-colored trees, eucalyptus and pepper and California scrub oak; perhaps it is merely that one knows that eventually this freeway reaches the southern California ranch-land, where cows and sheep graze knee deep in bleached grass. Whatever it is, the Valley has a subtle essence that lies far beneath its burgeoning bourgeois lifestyle. It is very attractive to me.

Like so many other areas of Los Angeles, the Valley can be a delightful place to live, but it is not necessarily the place to find entertainment or intellectual stimulation. Many people try to escape it as often as possible. This is how a few of them manage to do it.

The LACCC, or Los Angeles Culturally Curious Club—obviously a tongue-in-cheek name—has existed for nearly four years now. It has only nine members ("We want to be able to travel in two cars, and share one table at lunch"), and its primary purpose is to find out everything possible about Los Angeles and its surrounding areas. The group is eclectic in its interests—it will travel across the city to watch picture frames or chain saws being made with the same enthusiasm with which it visits museums or landmark buildings. "Today we agreed upon plans which will soon put us all in the *Guinness Book of Records* for having traveled every freeway, surface street and alley in Los Angeles County in a three-year period," one member noted in her report of their January 1979 planning session.

The nine women met when they car-pooled on field trips during a "Discover Los Angeles" course at Los Angeles Valley College. All had come from somewhere else to settle in the Valley. Of vastly different backgrounds and with a wide span of age differences, they had two things in common: a desire to know more about this city where they now lived; and a desire to maintain the odd friendship that had sprung up among them. They decided to continue discovering Los Angeles on their own time, and they set up a club with rules and regulations— meetings once a week, written trip reports required—to do it. The club notebooks, now fat, start with the autobiographies of each member.

Go is the soft-spoken, languorous-appearing southern belle, the acknowledged leader of the group. "Originally from South Carolina, I married a Baltimore lawyer and had three daughters, and I taught art. Later, I married my best friend, and I feel very lucky for the life I now enjoy here." Tall, blond Lynn, "from a nice but boring small town in Indiana," is married with two children, and is getting an advanced degree in education. "After a vacation here, I vowed to return to California one day. And I fulfilled that vow!" Her opposite is Atsuko, so tiny that she buys clothes for herself and her children in the same department. "At college in Tokyo, I majored in American Area Studies. So I am lucky to have the experience to understand this country by myself, not by books only." Great-grandmother Elaine is from Decatur, Illinois, and has a record for never missing a club trip. "I have been in direct sales all my life," she writes, after a long, eloquent description of her girlhood. "I raised my daughters alone, but always with fun and happiness."

Brown-eyed Barbara has one child and is a part-time operating room nurse. Her five-sentence autobiography neglects even to mention where she's from, and ends with her usual directness: "Let's get on with the fun!" Margie, who "grew up on the periphery of John Steinbeck country," is a witty and outgoing part-time librarian who writes some of the most amusing reports. The most erudite and thoroughly researched are from quiet Olivia, who has four grandchildren though she is in her forties. "I was born in Coffeyville, Kansas, during the Depression. . . . We traveled with my dad to find work, living in our old car or a tent." Rita is the youngest, a blond, slightly shy graphic designer. "After Bob and I married, we toured Europe with a multimedia environmental protest rock musical. Our son was born in Chicago, and we came to California because of a good job offer." There have been various ninth members of the LACCC since Sylvia, the original, "just disappeared," but her memory remains, since the group always meets in a spot known as "Sylvia's lot."

Some of the L.A. Triple C's early trips could serve as the standard tourist guide to Los Angeles. The J. Paul Getty Museum in Malibu displays Greek and Roman art, plus visiting exhibits, in a replica of a Roman patrician's house in Herculaneum. The Los Angeles County Museum of Art on Wilshire Boulevard has a permanent collection that seems designed to offer a quick course in art history, but there are fine visiting exhibits and a park featuring Calder's works. The Page Museum just next door is devoted to finds from the prehistoric La Brea Tar Pits, on which it is located. Descanso Gardens in La Cañada has acres of roses, camelias, azaleas, specimen trees from all over the world, plus a Japanese teahouse and garden. The Huntington Library and Gardens in nearby San Marino offers a double treat: the magnificent mansion and art collection (Lawrence's *Pinkie* and Gainsborough's *Blueboy* are here) of railroad magnate Henry E.

Huntington; gardens representing every type in the world, including the West's finest cactus garden. Also nearby, the Los Angeles County and State Arboretum in Arcadia is on the estate of Comstock Lode millionaire "Lucky" Baldwin, and features an ancient adobe, Queen Anne cottage, Indian Village, immense bird sanctuary and superb gardens. The Norton Simon Museum on Colorado Boulevard in Pasadena has a fine art collection and beautiful sculpture garden. The Museum of Science and Industry and the Museum of Natural History, both in Exposition Park near the University of Southern California, offer intriguing permanent and changing exhibitions. The L.A. Triple C's have not visited the most basic tourist sites together; like all Angelinos, they have shown Disneyland, Marineland, Universal City, Knott's Berry Farm, Lion Country Safari, the Hollywood Wax Museum, the ethnic areas of Little Tokyo, Olvera Street and Chinatown, and the seaside attractions of Marina del Rey to plenty of visiting relatives. What the club has done is seek out unusual places, many of which cannot be found in any guidebook.

Though it may come as a surprise, there are landmark buildings in Los Angeles. With the exception of the Avila Adobe on Olvera Street, which dates back to 1810, most are not as old as the landmarks on the East Coast; but they trace the history of this city, and that is one of the LACCC's most avid interests.

"Today was our tour of Frank Lloyd Wright houses," Go reports. "There are only five of them in Los Angeles. We began at the privately owned Storer House on Hollywood Boulevard, where it turns into a residential street west of Laurel Canyon. It is on the north side of the street and you cannot miss it; it is definitively Wright. You cannot go in, but we parked and gawked. It certainly is worth a visit, a beauty.

"Next, we went to Barnsdall Park at the corner of Hollywood Boulevard and Vermont. There always are interesting art exhibits here, but we came to see the Wright house, which is open to the public. It is remarkable the way every piece of wood, every piece of stone and glass, seems to reflect his unique view of architecture, yet it all blends into a beautiful whole, which seems a natural part of this parklike site. A bonus, here, is that you can stand on the sloping front lawn and look across to the hills and see the incredible Mayan style house he also built on a hilltop near here. It looks like a primitive palace."

The Triple C's have explored downtown Los Angeles also, which hardly anyone who doesn't work there bothers to do anymore. There are many things of interest, including some landmark buildings.

Go writes of a day-long tour: "We began at the Bradbury Building, erected at Third and Broadway in 1893, and still a place which architectural students tour. It's something to look up to. You enter into a central court—and then, above you, you see tier upon tier of ornate wrought iron, polished wood stairways, landings and balconies, topped after five floors by an immense skylight, which bathes the interior with sun. Originally it was offices, and some still exist, but now it also holds the Parlor Restaurant, an antique photo salon, a general store and other tourist attractions. The famous cage elevator takes about five minutes to travel the five floors, so we watched it instead of trying it. Unfortunately, we did try the restaurant, which definitely is not a repeatable." (Go's terms, "a repeatable" and "not a repeatable," have been adopted by the entire club.)

"After lunch, we strolled across Pershing Square [which used to be a hangout for winos and soapbox orators, and now is a pleasant park over an immense parking area] to the Biltmore Hotel, which was recently restored. The restoration retained most of the twenties details, including the huge lobby and double staircase. There are interesting artistic touches, and a classy restaurant, Bernard's. Already having lunched [!], we settled for tea in the coffee shop. Then back to the Grand Central Market, which goes the length of the entire block, from Hill to Broadway, and is the largest market in the city, much like a European one, with vendors hawking fruits and vegetables and meats from their stalls. There are lots of lunch and snack counters, a supermarket downstairs, and many Chicano and Oriental specialties sold, including some really exotic meat items. A highlight was vegetarian Elaine almost being run down by a cartful of animal carcasses. Actually, we saw enough innards today to turn us all into vegetarians."

Rita writes of the Alexandria Hotel nearby at 501 South Spring Street: "It is a sixty-three-year-old landmark, and was a famous 'in' place for such legendary Hollywood figures as Douglas Fairbanks, Mary Pickford, Charlie Chaplin, Tom Mix, Rudolph Valentino. The hotel failed during the Depression, and became headquarters and training quarters for various boxers after the war. The recent restoration makes it absolutely elegant again. In the Palm Court Restaurant the beautiful Tiffany stained-glass skylight gleams again—it took three months to clean it of the black paint which made it black-out safe during the war. Tiffany glass is now brilliant throughout the hotel, suites are decorated in Victorian or Mediterranean themes, and there are lovely restaurants and lunchrooms, just as in its heyday. On our special tour, which requires reservations a week in advance, we also saw two hours of happy and interesting film clips from old-fashioned favorite movies."

Go describes another downtown tour of the Pacific Stock Exchange, Clifton's Silver Spoon Restaurant and the Los Angeles Public Library. Stock exchanges are not unusual, but the other two places are interesting. "At Clifton's we reserved the vault, a real vault, which is for parties of six or more. This is a very old cafeteria, with a section of antiques, a 'soupeasy' from Depression days, even a meditation garden. Very special." Clifford Clinton used to own two cafeterias downtown, where free or very cheap meals were offered to out-of-work people and uplifting tracts were placed on every table. The one dear to my memories of childhood had a waterfall and a fountain that spurted free limeade for children.

Go continues: "The Los Angeles downtown library is a beautiful Art Deco building from 1926, with murals, painted ceilings and French windows. We were lucky to have a guided tour to help us understand the basis for the current controversy. [Should a new library be built, or should this handsome building be saved?] Inadequate wiring permits only forty-watt bulbs. Lack of ventilation and air conditioning makes it uncomfortably warm. Fire danger is great, since the eight-level 'stacks' where 85 percent of the books are stored are connected by vents which would suck up fire like a chimney. Yet there are many interesting rooms for specialized study, records dating back to 1840, and such very modern systems as SCAN, which gives reference sources for a myriad of questions, and LINK, a community program which puts people in touch with various available sources. This library is a great heritage. I hope it can be saved."

Olivia reports on "a tour of three historical downtown buildings. The first was the Art Deco styled Coca-Cola Bottling Plant, with a façade in the shape of a ship designed in 1936 to enclose four original buildings. Few people see this Central Avenue historical site, which includes a display of bottles used over the years, as well as many years of advertising, which gave many of us a feeling of nostalgia. Next we went to the Garfield Building at 403 West Eighth Street, which features wrought-iron grillwork in the shape of birds, colored tile inserts in the front walkway and a beautiful penthouse. The original (1928–30) lower outside walls of forest green and maroon Italian marble were cleaned and installed in the lobby by the man, Mr. Grinker, who saved it from destruction. The lobby also features a goldleaf sculptured ceiling, German silver elevator doors and trims and numerous statues. The building has been restored so well that it has been declared a historical landmark.

"Finally, we went to Union Station nearby on Alameda Street. It is Spanish in its outer design, and has beautiful patios and plants, and is Art Deco inside the 1939-built building. The decorated wooden ceiling, brightly colored marble floors, Mexican ceramic tile accents, brass fixtures and massive rows of Deco-style wooden seats make the interior most impressive. The coffee shop, across the patio, is now open for special parties only; it has a lovely copper and tin engraved back bar. We enjoyed our day of historical tours, which ended at one of the oldest downtown restaurants, Little Joe's Italian Restaurant, with old murals, sawdust, and an Italian grocery on the premises. It was built in 1927."

A close-to-downtown tour is reported by Go: "Bullock's Wilshire, on Wilshire near Virgil, is one of the finest Art Deco–style buildings in the country. Built in 1929, it now is a cultural landmark. There is a motor court, where chauffeurs still drop off their employers under a rainproof roof—the ceiling of this porte-cochere features a fantastic mural of the history of transportation. There is a very tall copper tower, and inside the building so many beautiful details of marble, polished wood and brass and bronze, that you could spend as much time looking at the building as at the merchandise. We ate in the Oriental-Deco tearoom, which still offers a fashion show daily. The whole thing is like living in the past.

"Afterward, we walked the few blocks west to the Ambassador Hotel, another place filled with Deco delights, from chandeliers to carpets, railings, even phone booths. There are stained-glass windows, carved elevator doors, a lovely marble fountain. We looked into the Coconut Grove, and imagined that we were part of the famous crowds who walked down the aisles in the twenties or thirties."

Another nearby landmark, St. Sophia's Greek Orthodox Cathedral, at 1324 South Normandie Avenue, was reported on by Margie: "The interior of the incredibly beautiful cathedral is in stark contrast to its simple exterior. Inside, we were made speechless by the amount of art in the stained-glass windows and oil paintings, the profusion of gold filigree, the exquisite crystal chandeliers, portraits of donors' children, and the overwhelming presence of an immense painting of Jesus, looking down on *us* as we gazed seventy feet upwards into the rotunda. It is one of the most impressive buildings we have seen."

When Los Angeles began to expand out of the original downtown area, it moved south as well as west, moved along Figueroa and Hoover all the way to Washington and Adams. Many of the mansions in this area were built about the same time that the cornerstone was laid for the nearby University of Southern California—that is to say, around 1880. Olivia reports on a fine walking tour of this section: "Our first stop was St. Mary's College in an area of old mansions, chief of which is the former Doheny mansion, which was donated to this college. Mr. Doheny was a poor Irish workman who later became an oil millionaire. The mansion boasts sphinxes and lions at the entrances, red marble, a tower with a walkway around it, which once must have given a fabulous view. We continued on to St. Vincent de Paul Church, built in 1925, also by Mr. Doheny. It features a Spanish baroque tower, and inside is a tile-inlaid dome rising ninety feet over the altar. The pulpit was created from a single block of red marble, there are lovely stained-glass windows and there is gold and silver gilding on many of the shrines.

"After visiting this landmark, we strolled through USC, which now encompasses 138 acres, and has a student body greater than the entire population of Los Angeles when it was built—over ten thousand. The Doheny Library is a treasure, and Widney Hall, built in 1880, looks like an old southern mansion. We had walked so far that Go and Margie volunteered to go back for the cars while the rest of us saw the exceptional rose gardens at Exposition Park. There is so much to be seen in this area—the old mansions which now are fraternity houses, the two museums at Exposition Park, the Shrine Auditorium, where ballet and opera companies still perform, and the Coliseum, where all the big football games used to be played. It is a section most Valleyites don't know very well, and it is worth returning to often."

The Triple C's have eagerly explored all points of interest in the older northeastern section of the city, Pasadena/San Marino and Glendale. The Pasadena Freeway passes Heritage Square, an ambitious project that has not yet come to fruition. "We arrived about two P.M. and kept asking, 'Is this the place that we waited three months to see?' A man guided us through the Hale House, where, after hundreds of hours of volunteer work and much money spent, only two rooms of this Victorian mansion have been restored. The idea of the project was to save Victorian houses that were to be torn down, to move them here and create a whole street, including church and school. Not much has happened yet, though it is beginning to look good from the freeway." (This unsigned report is from 1976. Quite a bit more has been restored now, though there still is work to be done. The aim is to keep some of the cultural heritage that was about to be lost when the old Bunker Hill area of Victorian houses was razed to create a modern downtown.)

Moving on in this same area, Rita writes: "The Lumis House at 200 East Avenue 43 is a genuine early California landmark. Mr. Dudley C. Gordon, who has been studying Lumis since his college days, got us within his walls and wouldn't let us go. We never got a proper tour, but did get a lengthy history of Lumis's life." Lumis was the first city editor of *The Los Angeles Times;* he built this castle, now a Historical Cultural Monument, of granite boulders and concrete, with his own hands, between 1897 and 1910. There is a round tower, a bell tower, wooden doors and windows which look like arrow slits.

Further into Pasadena, Atsuko describes the club's visit to the old Huntington Hotel. "The hotel was built in 1907. Now the owner is Keikyu Corporation (Japanese). There are many dining rooms, meeting rooms and bars. The Ship Room has lots of model ships made of wood. The chandeliers of the Viennese Room, a magnificent ballroom, came in the 1930s and are copies of Mad King Ludwig's from his castle in Bavaria. The beautiful Horseshoe Garden can be used for wedding ceremony [sic]. There is a covered picture bridge of native redwood which has wisterias and forty-two murals by Frank Moore. This hotel shows that early Los Angeles had much elegance, which has lasted over seventy years."

In Glendale, the group visited the Brand Library, which Margie describes as "a miniature Taj Mahal. The Brands dabbled in Hollywood society, airplanes and east Indian architecture. An astute businessman, Brand added a bedroom which extended across the city line into Burbank, because in those days you were taxed according to where you slept, and Burbank's taxes were lower than Glendale's. There are valuable art and music books here, a gallery with works of local artists, and many photographs which show what life was like in the early days of this century."

The Triple C's have visited many unique museums, some in this area. The Pasadena Historical Museum is a handsome old mansion on Walnut Street, and an unsigned report mentions "a fine collection of furniture, paintings and needlework, the largest Finnish sauna museum in the United States; luncheon is served turn-of-the-century style, with gorgeous antique table service, wine glasses and sterling silver. The lunch was superb, and only $6.50, including the tour of the house." (Reports of the L.A. Triple C's quite often devote more time to restaurants visited and lunches enjoyed than to the main object of the day's trip.)

Go reports on the Pacificulture Museum, also in Pasadena, a building designed in the style of the Chinese Imperial Palace. "Fine Oriental antiques and costumes are on display here, there is a meditation garden, and even a quick visit offers the serenity one might expect from a trip to the Orient. There are so many diverse works of Oriental art shown, and the techniques employed are well-described. You can take classes here also, in such arts as brush painting and flower arranging. It's an incredible place."

Other museums the group has visited include the Cabrillo Marine Museum in San Pedro: "We went on a grunion hunt! You also can take a boat trip to see whales, and there are maritime artifacts and several acquaria" (Olivia); the California Pictorial History Museum on mid-Wilshire: "The center houses fifty thousand prints, negatives, books, albums and artifacts that illustrate the often rambunctious and flamboyant history of the Los Angeles area" (Barbara); the San Bernardino County Museum in Redlands: "A handsome contemporary structure with a striking dome. It has fine displays of the geology, history, agriculture and industry of this large county, plus Indian relics and ornithological and mammal displays. We learned that Mormons and their black slaves were early settlers. They freed the slaves and all lived in harmony" (Go); the Southwest Museum in Highland Park: "The history of the American Indian is here in its entirety" (Go); and the House of Iran in Beverly Hills: "We didn't realize how many different arts the Iranian culture offered. We were shown techniques for rug-making, glass-blowing, wood-inlaying and silver-embossing. Fine artwork and crafts were displayed, and the patterns and quality of the carpets were incredible—you felt as though you could dive into those rich colors" (Elaine).

There is one report that is too funny not to be quoted, and too damning for the museum to be named. It is a small one in Beverly Hills, interesting but not a must-see. The report is unsigned: "The curator moved immediately into his routine, apparently a self-imposed challenge to recite the correct name for every artifact in the immense room, along with the name of its designer and the dates of anything remotely relevant to the object. He did not hesitate for recall, response or resuscitation. He darted around the room, ricocheting off Chinese jades onto ornate paperweights and model ships, from bronze birds and antique rifles into silver toast racks and pottery Toby mugs, rattling off his litany at an ever-increasing tempo, like a pianist who realizes too late that he might not get through "The Minute Waltz" in sixty seconds. He obviously gave himself points for every name-and-date squeezed into a second, and subtracted points for such deviations as inhaling, and for such emotional outbursts as smiling."

The Triple C women have an avid interest in anything that relates to the history of the Los Angeles area (it even extends to collecting lists of how certain places got their names—Chilao, for instance, originally Chileo, was named for a Mexican herder who killed a grizzly with only a hunting knife and thereafter was called "Hot Stuff," or Chileo, by his friends), and they have traveled far afield to pursue this interest. They have visited Fort Tejon, nearly eighty miles north on the No. 5 Freeway, and Rita notes: "Tejon is Spanish for badger—the Spanish explorers found a dead badger at the entrance to this pass when they discovered it in 1806. The area was originally settled by Indians, then Dragoons patrolled here, and ten years before the Civil War the fort was built, and twenty-five camels were used for exploring the area. The fort was abandoned in 1864, and it was not until 1940 that the government bought some of the land for a national monument, and now some buildings are restored. On the third Sunday of each month from June through September, the Union and Confederate organizations have parades and stage mock battles here."

Geology buff Lynn led the group all the way to Calabasas and up into the Santa Monica Mountains for a fossil hunt: "Armed with chisels and hammers, we extracted fossils of the Miocene Age, at least fifteen million years old, from this section known as the Topanga Formation."

She continues: "After lunch, a tour of the Leonis Adobe in the Valley brought us into more recent history. Built 130 years ago, it was given to a daughter of Mission-raised Chumash Indians when she married Miguel Leonis; after he died, Espiritu had a long court fight to regain her claim. Fortunately, her descendants have shared the house, mementoes and photographs with the public." And far to the south, in Wilmington, the group visited the Banning residence, and Elaine, usually so brief, writes four full pages of enthusiastic description: "There are spacious, parklike grounds and a lovely old 'southern' mansion with a magnificent circular staircase. General (honorary title) Phineas Banning was born in Wilmington, Delaware, which accounts for the name of this area. He built the first railroad from San Pedro, then made connections with the Southern Pacific, and walls of the house are filled with old railroad photos. He had fleets of freighters and of stagecoaches, helped bring water to Los Angeles, and his sons bought Catalina Island and later sold it to Wrigley. The house is filled with Aubusson carpets, Chinese lacquered chests and other wonderful antiques, and there is a ballroom where the Virginia Reel was danced, and a champagne cellar with leaded glass. It was bought by the city in 1927, but restoration began only in 1970. It is a beautiful place to learn about part of our history."

Of special interest to the group have been tours of historic sites in the San Fernando Valley. Olivia seems to be the Valley reporter, for she researched and reported on most of these. "The San Fernando Mission was barely restored when it was somewhat damaged by the 1971 earthquake. You do get a feeling for what life was like for the Indians and the Padres here in the eighteenth century. Another memorable visit was to the Orcutt Ranch near the Mission. W. W. Orcutt, a geologist and engineer, was the first person to discover the scientific importance of the La Brea Tar Pits. This lovely Spanish-style home was built in 1917–20, and there is a guest room named for Toscanini, who visited here, and another named for Mario Lanza, who did not (but Mrs. Orcutt admired him greatly). The ranch is now Historical Monument No. 31, and is used also as a horticultural facility by the city. Ernesto Cornejo, who became the Orcutts' gardener in 1919, still cares for the property and the gardens."

Olivia again: "The Andres Pico Adobe in Mission Hills was owned by the adopted son of the brother of Pio Pico, the last Mexican governor of California. Built originally by Mission Indians about 1834, it is furnished in the style of 1870–90, when Pico lived here, and there are fascinating pictures of well-known early Valley inhabitants, including Van Nuys, Lankershim and Tapia. Later, we visited the Lopez Adobe, the builder of which was the brother of one of the first Valley residents, Catalina Lopez, who started the first post office, first English school and first general store."

Olivia writes of the Valley College Museum: "This deals primarily with the San Fernando Valley. There are photographs of early Valley days, and a collection of early books, mementoes from some of the ranchos, Indian artifacts, and items salvaged from Spanish ships sunk off the coast." She also writes of one of the truly unusual sites the women unearthed: "Daniel and James van Meter live on Magnolia in Van Nuys. We went to see the tower Daniel is noted for, which he built over the grave he found of a pioneer boy. But there is so much more—two acres of land filled with old wagons and farm equipment and buggies, an old cut-log building from the original rancho, a rare breed of duck, and birds once owned only by the Emperor of Japan. Both brothers are inventors, as was their father, a cousin of the Wright brothers, and James has almost completed a flying saucer, which works on aerodynamic principles. They told us of another brother who collects old beer cans, and still another who collects antique clocks and cash registers. What a fabulous family!"

On their most obscure travels the Los Angeles Culturally Curious Club members have visited: the Ethan Allen Showroom, where the tour showed how furniture from earlier days is reproduced; a General Motors Plant, where they learned how automobiles were assembled; the Sheriff's Communication Emergency Station, where flashing computers and a "tall, dark, handsome sheriff" showed them how disasters were handled; Judson Studios, where a fourth generation of Angelinos is making stained glass and mosaics in the tradition of a hundred years ago; Wattles Gardens, a historic family home in Hollywood with its own very specialized gardens, which now has made plots available for local people to till, and where young delinquents are sent by judges who feel that gardening will help rehabilitate them; the Mormon Temple in Century City, where Elaine, the reporter, felt they were heavily proselytized; the Self-Realization Shrine in the Pacific Palisades, where they saw the museum and walked around the lake of this ten-acre estate established by Paramahansa Yoganda in 1950; a Justice Walk, where they visited various courtrooms and were apprised of the workings of the small claims court; Leopard's Studio, with an extensive collection of Indian and Eskimo artifacts; my own house, where my husband activated most of his battery-operated toy collection for them, and where they brought lunch for us all and stayed to play and sing around the player piano; "Girls' Day" or "Dolls' Day" at Atsuko's house, a traditional Japanese holiday similar to our Valentine's Day, in that it is not a national holiday but is always celebrated among families; plus various antique hunts in Pasadena and as far away as Ventura, where they examined also the early-thirties courthouse; and numerous beach trips and luncheons and swim parties and Christmas parties and birthday parties, where they just had fun and everyone brought food specialties and they talked and laughed a lot.

Every year someone suggests that the club meet only every two weeks, and every year the new rule is voted in. After a couple of weeks, someone remarks, "Well, there's so much I want to see, I'm going somewhere every week, and whoever wants to can come along." And since nobody wants to be left out, soon the weekly meetings are voted back in. Go says, "Lots of people spend their lives saying 'tomorrow,' and never do anything. I'm scared. We might have to move away from here someday. I love Los Angeles and I want to see it all. And I'm going to!" She will, and so will the others. Every Wednesday the L.A. Triple C's take to the freeways and the back streets of Los Angeles once again.

4

The Genuine All-American Southern California Boy

The thing we always say about Los Angeles, the statement we most often use to rationalize living in a sprawling sort of noncity, with no center to speak of, with many of a city's disadvantages and perhaps not enough of a city's advantages, the single thing of which we seem to be the most proud, is this:

"If you live in Los Angeles you can be in the mountains or in the desert or at the beach in two hours or less."

"Why, you can ski at Waterman in the morning and look at desert flowers in the afternoon and have a moonlight swim at Malibu, all on the same day," we say.

Of course it is true. You *can* do this. But nobody does. Except Larry Owen.

Larry Owen is the only person I've ever known who really does do all the things one can do if one lives in Los Angeles, all the things which all of the rest of us talk about, and more or less brag about, and scarcely ever—or more likely, never—do.

Larry Owen was born in Wisconsin, and not so much later moved to Culp Bay, Oregon, where his mother worked in the post office and his father worked in a mill, and he came down to Los Angeles quite a long time ago to study art. He is very tall and rangy, he has big hands, the kind of hands you would more likely expect to see tearing an engine apart than painting a watercolor, and he seems very boyish, though by now he must be forty or perhaps older. It is not a puppy-dog quality which he has, it is not the kind of boyishness that seems vulnerable or makes you want to hug him. It is more a free-spiritedness, the sense you get of his wanting to get on something that moves out, a horse or a motorcycle, or into something fast, a fast car or a fast boat, and simply take off rather than stand around talking about things. Also, he appears to be a loner, someone who likes to do the things that one person can do alone. In an earlier time you might imagine him cutting trails through the wilderness.

But of course Larry Owen does not blaze trails. What he does do is work in an advertising agency—where there are plenty of rules set out, and yet a certain kind of freedom, too—and he does it very well. The reason he does it is interesting in view of the kind of person he is.

"I like toys," he says. "And to get toys you have to have money."

Working in an advertising agency, especially if you are a writer or an art director, especially if you move up from one of those jobs to become a creative director or a producer, is quite a good way to make money. There are a lot of politics to be played, and it often is necessary to be extremely tactful, especially around clients; but if you do these things well, and are good at your specialty, you will be paid extremely well. Well enough to be able to afford a lot of toys.

By toys, Larry Owen means exactly the things you would expect, the fast cars and fast boats, the fast bikes and the best ski equipment. He also means some unexpected things, such as antique furniture, and old bottles and tins, and Coke memorabilia. And the last thing you would ever expect from someone who seems to be such a free spirit—investments, such as apartment houses.

Of course many of the toys Larry collects have a direct relationship to the city in which he has chosen to live for so many years (twenty years or so now), because in Los Angeles he can use all of these things readily and regularly, as he could not in most other cities. The toys and the city present a kind of chicken-and-egg question: Does he live here so that he can have the toys, or does he have the toys merely because he lives in this city? As with most such questions, the answer really doesn't matter. What matters is the way he uses both.

Larry Owen lives at the beach, and has for as long as I've known him, which is now about fifteen years. It was not so much that he was a swinger, which is what "beach type" often implies. Rather, it was that the beach cities were (and are) quite free places, places where you could bat about on a motorcycle in the early morning hours, where you could rent a cheap garage to tear down the engine of a Porsche, where you could find a landlord or landlady who didn't mind that you kept a surfboard in the living room and a bicycle in the hallway and stored your skis in the basement. I don't remember if it was the bathtub Porsche that he owned when I first met him, when we were both starting out in the advertising business, or one of the many other cars that he tore down and souped up and later blew up, as the jargon has it. I do remember that he knew more about cars of all kinds than anybody else. When my husband yearned for an MG TC, Larry said, "Well, they're fun, but you know pieces fall off while you're driving along"—and, indeed, when we got the TC pieces did fall off. When I wanted a fast, hot car, Larry said, "Get a Corvette, they're hot but they last"—and my 1968 Corvette is still capable of tearing up the pavement (when I can get enough gasoline to fill its tank). I always thought of Larry as primarily a car freak—though I knew he also ran a bike, and surfed, and skied—because he spent so much of his office free time dashing off splendid drawings of cars and parts of cars and even parts of engines, like a medical student doing anatomical drawings. But in those days as a fledgling art director, before he learned to live with the rules, he never stayed at one agency long enough to accumulate the kind of money it takes to accumulate a lot of toys.

He was a very good art director, but generally a writer and an art director work as a team and Larry never was a good team player. At the agency where he works today, the agency where he has stayed longer than he ever stayed anywhere else, he does not have to play team games very often. He says, "I'm a senior art director who functions as my own creative director. I get new business, I go after the kinds of accounts I want to work on, and then I'm creative director on those accounts." So the boy who always looked and acted like a loner now is allowed to function as one in his professional life. Which accounts for his now being able to play in the true Los Angeles style.

Here is a typical day.

He gets up at six-thirty, an hour when the mists or the fogs still hang over the beach cities at most times of the year; an hour when sounds are muffled by the fogs, so that you are not too much disturbed by the coughing engines of the cars of the hundreds of early-shift workers at the aerospace plants that have proliferated along and around the Pacific Coast Highway; an hour when you cannot gauge whether the day will be sunny or chilly—and all too often at the beach, especially during July and August, the day will remain gray and chilly, while the inland parts of the city are bathed in sunshine. This explains in part why the Los Angeles coastline has never been outlined by resort hotels—the mist burns off too late during the summer months, and the surf can be rough, and the winds can be chill.

He gets up at six-thirty and, without a shower or even a cup of coffee, mounts his cheap three-speed bicycle and rides to the King Harbor Yacht Club, where he puts on a wet suit, takes his oceangoing kayak (he also keeps a river kayak at the club) out into the surf and paddles for an hour. He showers at the club after his workout, then bicycles back home to dress for work, stopping for breakfast at a coffee shop along the way. "You have to develop a habit," he says. "It's important. Otherwise you never do anything."

The drive from Hermosa Beach, where he lives, to the office near Hollywood and Vine is nearly twenty miles, and he makes it in "a souped-up Honda. I just can't let a car alone, you know." But he is considering a change. "I'm really a Porsche freak. The bathtub got me around at eighty miles per hour and thirty-two miles per gallon. It was my kind of car, I always felt good in it, it was the only car in the world. I've been looking for another one, but a good classic is hard to find, the weather here just eats them up. You have to get one from Europe."

Then he says, "A Ferrari," and there is a certain look in his eyes, but it is not the look of a dreamer, of a wishful thinker, it is the look of someone who knows how to get what he wants, if he wants it badly enough. "Something like that, something exotic, would be fun. But then I'd have to commute on a motorcycle, and I'm not sure I want to commit myself to that additional danger anymore. And then, a Ferrari, that means my next down payment on my next building. Still . . . you look at the Ferraris, you know." And you do know. Know that the consummate collector of toys is considering one of the ultimate toys. Know that what he really would like would be both, the Porsche and the Ferrari, and that it is quite possible that someday he will have them both—if some other toy that he needs even more doesn't come along first.

And so the long drive to the office is not as much fun as it might be, even though the Honda is souped up, even though he knows all the back routes that can be used as speedways, and gets a certain thrill out of outwitting the fuzz, a technique he has perfected over the years.

After work the schedule is different every night; the only thing routine about it is that he never goes directly home.

One night a week is a watercolor class for professionals in downtown Los Angeles. "I decided to obligate myself to doing it at night by paying for a really expensive class. You remember, I used to paint every weekend, but I never have a weekend free anymore." I remember—weekends at desert ghost towns or upcoast fishing villages or inland farms, commemorated by strong, yet delicate, very painterly delineations of old buildings. He always seemed to prefer the old, the lost, the derelict, the dying—he never minded driving five or six hundred miles, round trip, over a weekend to find them. Some of the best vacations my husband and I have taken have been to little old villages discovered by Larry on some of those weekends. "I still take photographs everywhere I go of old buildings, bridges, roofs, barns. But I'd just keep on postponing painting them if I weren't taking this class."

"Another week night, or perhaps two, he stops at the Westside Jewish Community Center to play racquetball. "I like portable sports. You know, when I go on a business trip I can take my racquet and sneakers along. I've got a client in Denver who has a company apartment in a building with a gym. And when I go up to Oregon to see my folks, I can take the river kayak. I like to have a whole stable of portable toys. But I won't play tennis—I won't stand around and wait for a court."

Other nights he'll stop off at the duplex he owns in Manhattan Beach, the next beach city up the coast from Hermosa where he lives. "I pay someone to do most of the landlord jobs, but I like to go look at it. The last owner was a pilot who lived there himself, and he put in a lot of personal touches, pegged wood floors, things like that. It's a good place, it pays to buy a good building. Kathy wanted to buy a house, but you know, that's no investment. So when she was off launching a rocket in Florida, I bought this place. Now that she's decorated it herself she's more possessive about it than I am."

Kathy! Yes, his wife.

It was ten years or so ago, when he had the tacky little beach apartment, no phone, you had to call his landlady to reach him, and she had to yell down the back stairs. He didn't have time for girls, really, he was too busy on the Porsche, and on the motorcycle he had then, too busy on the winter weekend ski trips and the summer weekend painting trips, and the in-between trips when he crewed on boats and dreamed of owning and racing his own P-Cat someday.

So there were girls, the usual beach girls, who came and hung around for a while and then didn't come back anymore, because, jeeze, it was pretty boring just watching someone take pieces off of engines all the time, or wax skis or something like that. It wasn't as though he hung out with a gang, it wasn't as though there were a lot of other guys around and beer being passed, and the evening turning into a party later. It was just this one guy, handsome, yes, but a loner, working by himself at the things he liked best.

And there was just one girl, red-headed Kathy with the good figure and the calm eyes, and the temperament that seldom seemed to ruffle; just this one girl who hung in there. If there wasn't anything she could do to help with the tearing down or the souping up, if there wasn't a tool she could hand him or an engine part she could clean, she would cook dinner. And eventually he would come back from the garage, and get the grease off his hands, and eat. She turned up at the oddest times, would be sitting there waiting for him sometimes at one or two in the morning when he had worked late. She did her own thing, as they say; she had a responsible aerospace job, she played tennis and swam, she went around finding old pieces of painted-over oak furniture for a few dollars and stripped them and refinished them. She wasn't a pest or a hanger-on, she just was there. He got used to her, in the slow way a loner has to get used to people. After a while she was going along on the ski weekends and the painting weekends. After a while they got married.

She doesn't interfere with the loner's life. She continues to do her own thing, as he does his.

"We're not into each other's sports," he says. "She plays tennis, she has a private instructor and her own circle of friends. She rides her ten-speed Peugeot while I creep around on this three-speed cheapy. She's into long-distance running. She won't crew for me on the P-Cat, not even for an important race—she says it's my toy. And she'll only go along on a trip to a race if there are good courts there, and if there are going to be other wives who play tennis.

"Twice a month she takes a day off and goes into Beverly Hills and spends the whole day going to Williams-Sonoma [a store noted for culinary equipment] or the Design Center. It keeps her from having babies and stuff like that.

"The only things we do together are eat dinner and ski."

And do they ski. "We're the first ones out, as early as the end of October, and the last ones in, as late as the first of July." The ski weekends used to be strenuous and hazardous, long hard drives to Mammoth or Waterman, but no longer. "We never drive anymore. We have a friend with his own plane who's an excellent pilot. We fly every other weekend to Mammoth or anywhere we want now—Sun Valley if we feel like it—and this way the whole weekend is skiing, not driving. Kathy's the better skier, she's had more time at it. I learned, believe it or not, on haystacks. She learned in the snow when she was a kid." The pilot friend also flies Larry to Oregon for weekends with his parents, or down to Baja to fish. Larry made all these same weekend jaunts—even to Oregon and Mexico— with the élan of the true Angelino in the days when he actually had to drive them. Nothing has changed. It's just a whole lot easier getting to these places now that he flies.

"Some winters I ski more and some winters I sail more," Larry says. "It's during the summer that I can save money, because I only sail. But in the winters there's skiing and sailing and motorcycle racing." Only in Los Angeles.

He always has been "into" boats, as he has been "into" so many things. Six or seven years ago he bought the eighteen-foot-nine-inch catamaran, and he races it with the same determination with which he does everything, though "I don't win firsts, I win thirds." He races in San Diego—"I tow the boat down with Kathy's Chevy on Friday night, and tow it back up Sunday night." He enters one race each year at Ensenada in Mexico, and one the McCulloch Corporation sponsors at Lake Havasu in Arizona. "I stay out there as long as possible, maybe not come home until Tuesday. It's in April or May, and after the winter of skiing and ocean sailing it's nice to get to Havasu where it's hot and you just have this big, calm lake."

He takes the cat on a few long-distance races, coastal races up to Santa Barbara, or "round the islands," but these are hard races. "It's just two guys, and you're on all the time. One year I put the boat away and crewed on some big boat races. It's a good mix, you're out there for a long time, you're with other people, but you can still be alone and have time to think. It's very regimented, three hours sleep, four hours on duty, three off, four on. There's a kind of freedom about that kind of regimentation. I still get a lot of invitations to crew, I might do it again."

And of course the loner tries to figure out more ways of being alone.

"The trouble with a cat is that it needs a crew, one man can't run it alone. I wanted a toy that I could go down with after work and play with by myself. I thought, what the world needs is a little cat designed for a single adult. So, like an idiot, I spent two years designing one. That was several years ago, and I still haven't found a backer or a way of marketing it. I put it on the Honda and take it to the yacht club and play with it, but to tell you the truth, kayaking and wind-surfing are easier ways to do what you want to do alone. Wind-surfing is a wonderful sport. It's my kind of thing. The one-man portable toy."

One wonders why the loner joined a yacht club. Was it because Kathy wanted it?

"Oh, I'm not a joiner, but you have to belong to a club in order to race. It's fine, because it gives me a place to keep the kayaks and the big cat, and I use the facilities somewhat. Kathy will go to the dances, she gets around the boat people a little that way."

What about the desert? Of course—that's where the motor-cycling comes in.

"You know it's a funny thing," Larry says, "skiers sail, motor-cyclists don't. Or so they say."

"Well," I ask, "do skiers bike?"

"Well, they say motocross skiers often do motocross biking. They both take a lot of energy. More energy than football, they say."

"Where does that put you?"

"Just a maverick, I guess." He grins.

He used to work on the Yamaha Motorcycle account and on Norton-Triumph. "I still get invited to the Petersen Ranch a lot, to ride bikes, and my brother-in-law has a trailer and we'll go out to Red Rock [Canyon]. Kathy will go out to the desert with us. I forgot about that, that's another sport we sometimes do together. She likes to ride, and she'll go to Ascot or to the National Motorcycle Races.

"I enjoy motorcycles. They require balance, and I like that. It's not my major sport, but I enjoy it. I enjoy working on motorcycle accounts. I wouldn't want to work on a boat account or a ski account though, you know. You don't want the pleasure things you're closest to to become part of your work life. It spoils the pleasure for you."

And the rest? Is there room for anything more in this life that spans the city daily, just in the normal course of events, and takes in all the rest of southern California, and goes as far as Oregon and Idaho and Arizona and Mexico on weekends?

"Well, once a year I go up to the High Sierras and pan for gold. You have to get out there every once in a while, you have to do that. And I still get to Nevada occasionally, you know, hunting for old bottles and tins around abandoned places, but I don't do it so much anymore. And I still hunt for Coke stuff—I got a great poster recently in Sutter's Creek [in the gold rush country inland from San Francisco], it's fifty-four inches high. But I don't have any more room for the big stuff. I can only collect the little stuff now."

"You know the trouble with Los Angeles?" he asks suddenly and grins, looking very boyish, looking like the same tan beach type I used to know all those years ago.

"The trouble with Los Angeles is you never can become a millionaire here. There are too many things to do here to keep you from getting rich.

"You know what I'm thinking about doing? I'm thinking about going to Chicago. Get a high-paying job. There's nothing to do there, so you'd just work and save all your money. Stay maybe four or five years. Then come back here. Why Lord, you could buy every toy you ever wanted then!

"You know, I think I'll do that. You know, that would be the really sensible thing to do."

But he didn't. He is still in Los Angeles, and what he has done is buy another apartment house, a big one, and a few more toys, but not the Ferrari, at least not yet. And somehow I don't think he ever will go to Chicago. He is too much the genuine southern California boy.

5

The Dallas Memorial Homecoming and Social Club

They have come a long way, all of them, to get here tonight. Not just the ones who came by Cadillac from 110th Street or Arlington or Jefferson to the Top o' the Crock in downtown Los Angeles. Not just the ones who have jetted in: the Reverend A. S. Jackson, guest of honor, down from San Francisco; or F. H. Madison, the musical director, up from La Jolla; or special guests such as Atlanta Mayor Maynard Jackson's sister, all the way from Georgia, or Sing Baby who still lives in Texas. I mean every one of them, each one of these, the handsome, middle-aged, middle-income, middle-class Blacks who are here for a special dinner meeting of the Dallas Memorial Homecoming and Social Club. They have come much further than miles can tell.

They have come, via numerous circuitous routes, from a dark way of life in Dallas to a considerably brighter life in Los Angeles. It is that which they are celebrating here, as much as anything else.

You may think of Dallas as a glittering place. Neiman-Marcus and the Regency Hyatt House. The Cotton Bowl. Love Field. But there was nothing glittering about the Dallas that these Blacks have left behind. In spite of the heat, in spite of the days that dawned so early and dusked so late, their Dallas was dark. There were the dark apartments and dark little houses near enough to White Rock Lake so that someone, mother, or father if there was one, or a sister, an aunt, could

67

slip down every morning and catch enough catfish so that everyone could be fed decently that night. There were the dark buses that took them to choir practice or the football games and parades where they performed; dark because the bus shades had to be drawn so that other sections of the city would not be offended by seeing their black faces. There were the dark quarrels, between parents, between brothers trying, literally, to carve a niche for themselves. There were the dark jails where so many of those quarrels ended; where so many of them still end today.

And for some reason someone from dark Dallas came to brighter Los Angeles. The others followed. It is no different, of course, from the Swedes settling in Minnesota, or the Germans in Pennsylvania, or the Jews and Italians coming to New York. Someone told someone, "Go here and find a friend of your own kind."

And so, five or ten or twenty years later, here they all are at the Top o' the Crock. The streets outside are empty and silent, as downtown Los Angeles streets always are at night; except, just now, for the soft hiss of the tires of long, lean and lovely shining cars turning into the parking garage at the Crocker Bank Building at Sixth and Olive streets. There are certain flutters—the gentle whipping sound that long dresses make when they move through the wind tunnels that all parking garages seem to be. There is a certain chirping—soft southern voices greeting each other in the subdued manner of people going to a party that is not yet in full swing.

Forty floors up in the circular lounge of the restaurant, the lounge that to us seems to offer a fantastic panoramic view of this city with no skyline, the ladies dominate. They are an exultation of gorgeously plumaged tropical birds into which a funeral of blackbirds seems to have dropped, merely to feed. Or perhaps to admire. The blackbirds are amused, sleek, indulgent. They drink Scotch and soda, they speak in undertones, they occasionally dig each other with an elbow or slap each other on the shoulders; but mostly it is a quiet camaraderie. The ladies, the exotics, strut and preen their plumage, rustle their feathers—their dresses are edged or topped with ostrich or marabou. They take short flights across the room, they twitter and chatter endlessly and make their varied calls. They are orange, silver, fuschia, emerald, sapphire, white, multi-colored. They are bejeweled. They are beautiful. They know it.

Leah, my Leah, is fat; she is the first to admit it. She is just over five feet tall and she weighs well over two hundred pounds. But tonight she is svelte and sinuous in a long flow of sea-foam green silk with feathers at the deep-cut neckline. She wears long earrings that glitter like diamonds. Her wig is a high swirl of dark brown waves. She is over fifty, but she looks thirty-five, her skin is as silky and unwrinkled as her dress. Black is as much a misnomer as gay. She is the color brown I yearn to be after a summer at the beach.

Leah is the chairman of this banquet and she greets us at the entrance to the lounge. "You're here!" she cries. "Ralph's out looking for you. He said you weren't coming, but I said, no, they'll be here. I knew you'd be here." She takes our friendship absolutely on faith, as we take hers. Leah has worked for me for twelve years now. We are the only "Caucasians," as she is careful to call us, in this party of three hundred Blacks.

Ralph arrives, one of the tuxedoed blackbirds. Tall and handsome, he has a frothy white frill on the front of his shirt which is delicately edged in the same sea-foam green as Leah's dress. "I told him he had to match me," Leah says. "Now you take them upstairs and get them some camel's milk," she instructs him. "I've got things to do."

Camel's milk is, of course, the euphemism that Leah and all her friends in the Eastern Star and the Daughters of Isis and the Herions of Jacob and the Shrine use for liquor. Typically, they would call the cocktail hour "attitude adjustments hour," but this is not a Masonic gathering and so we can refer to this as the cocktail hour. Despite the camel's milk.

We are not precisely ill at ease as we mingle in the lounge with these people. We are more or less of the same age group and the same income group and we all, now, are Angelinos. If we are short of conversation, if we find ourselves saying, over and over, "What a wonderful view!" and, "I've never been up here before, have you?", it is not so much because everyone else is Black and we are not; it is because they are all old friends. They all went to Booker T. or Lincoln High, they all were in the Ambassadors or the Aristocrats, they all come from the same "back home." And "back home," of course, is Dallas.

Fifty or sixty percent of the people here tonight drive Cadillacs. Of the six or eight women I know here tonight, all of them have worked for me when Leah was ill or on vacation, or they have come to help her out with extra jobs. Of the rest, many of them work in the post office, as do many of the men; they have not been shunted aside there as they might have been in other businesses—Ralph now is a top supervisor—and the benefits are good. But stereotypes only go so far. Most of the men here are the financial supports of their families. Most of them are twenty- or thirty-year men who get four weeks vacation and have a solid pension to look forward to. And most of the women who still clean or act as maids occasionally do so because they're bored with being at home, and because they do it well and efficiently, and because they have a real attachment to their employers. Leah started working as a cleaning woman when she first came to Los Angeles because she had little children and it was a good way to earn money without being stuck in a nine-to-five job. She still visits, on a social basis, many of the women she worked for and whose children she helped raise in those days. I am the only person she works for now; she does it because she likes to get out of the house, and because she likes me. There are certain rules, of her making. When she works for me at my house, she calls me Mrs. Gader. When we are in a social situation, as at this dinner, or when we go to one another's house for lunch, then I am June. When she introduces me formally, it is as "my boss, June Gader." When she walks in every Friday we say, "Hello! How *are* you?" and chat for a given fifteen or twenty minutes. But if one of us is going away on vacation or has just come back, then we hug and kiss, as friends do.

On the one hand, Leah is a middle-class matron: she goes to church on Sundays, she owns her own house, she belongs to numerous clubs that have banquets and parties, she is energetically involved in fund raisings and other altruistic activities, she has parties and house guests and goes on long vacations. On the other hand, she lives in an area where burglaries and dope-inspired crimes are not uncommon, her older son has been in and out of jail, all four of her children are by different husbands, and she is, by profession, a cleaning woman. I have asked Leah why she and Ralph don't move somewhere safer, say up here in the Hollywood Hills where I live. "I wouldn't live up there if you paid me," she said. "Too many burglaries. I get scared every time you ask Ralph and me to stay at the house when you go away for the weekend. Why, I'd never answer my door if I lived up there!" I feel very safe up here. She obviously feels safer down there.

An old-fashioned education shows: she writes a beautiful hand, she says *vase* with a broad "a" and pronounces *aunt* with the "u" in it; she uses the conditional tense correctly. She is careful to refer to Whites as Caucasians and to Negroes as Blacks, but this is relatively new, a concession to the Movement; she still praises a woman's or a man's good looks by mentioning how "white" or "pale" they are. She also describes a rather giddy girl as one who "high-heels around," and condemned her pregnant sixteen-year-old daughter by telling her, "All this time you told me you was walking right, when you been walking left." Though her knowledge of grammar is excellent, she will slip on the proper occasion into idiom and "Black talk." During the Nixon administration, she described a club meeting as an event where "they have these carcasses and that's where all the Watergatin' goes on." Club election times are where you "jolly with the losers and go home with the winners."

What is remarkable is that she is so Black and so White at the same time. It may have something to do with the Los Angeles way of life.

We are still so new. The city that started as a mere cluster of buildings around a typical Mexican plaza in 1781 had less than ten thousand residents a century later. When we did begin to grow, we spread outward and outward and never upward: across the wide basin, which is like a plain, leading from the yellow brush-covered hills down to the sea; up, into and over the hills; out across a valley that seems to stretch forever. The people of this city have been like the pioneers who first settled into the West; when an area has worn out or become too crowded, they have just pushed on. The hills seem to sprout new developments almost daily. Populous and popular areas such as Marina del Rey didn't even exist a few years ago. Of course we rediscover older areas of the city and rebuild them too. But it seems as though this city is always on the move. Consequently, we have not had the time to get quite as entrenched into stereotyped areas as other cities have.

Yes, Watts exists. But we do not have tenements in Los Angeles, and we do not have what anyone from anywhere else in the world would recognize as slums.

Watts is an area of small individual houses: frame houses built in the twenties, stucco houses built in the thirties. The streets here are not precisely aligned; a ravine cuts through on a diagonal in a general east-west direction; tracks from the old Red Car line, which used to link the widespread areas of Los Angeles so efficiently, cut a general north-south swath. The Disneyland-like towers of Simon Rodea's fantasy rise as a landmark in the stark skyline of telephone poles and electric poles and wires—find Watts Towers and you have found Watts.

Not all the individual houses in Watts are newly painted or free from weeds, but many of them are. Of course, all of them have TV antennas, and a lot of them have recent-model cars parked in the driveways or on the street, and most of them have fences to protect gardens or closely mown lawns. There are a lot of dogs in Watts. It is not the safest section of town. And there is a slight feeling of desolation here, as though perhaps this area has been forgotten by the rest of the city. But it does not look like a depressed area: there are no cans and bottles in front yards, or garbage in the streets; if laundry is spread out on lines, it is at the backs of the houses, never at the fronts. In fact, many of the families have washer-driers.

On the main north-south streets of Western or Vermont, deep down in the deep Black section of town, you will see some of the results of its fleeting period of fame, the Watts riots.

There are stores that look as though they know they exist on sufferance, not too well painted or well kept, as though the owners are ready to pick up and leave the second the Santa Ana winds blow in the wrong direction. Here, indeed, are sidewalks with bottles and cans, and papers clogging the sewers. Young men, lazy-limbed but sharp-eyed, lean against buildings that are pockmarked from the stones and bullets of the riots, or express their own Saturday Night Fevers next to bus stops. There still is unrest, unemployment, most importantly, uninvolvement, and there still is a certain tension. But the riots were more than ten years ago and there are other things going down today. Watts is just a place, not a cauldron waiting to boil over. And the side streets, those certainly not ugly streets of small houses, are where people live, not where revolutionaries hatch plots against the honkies.

I have taken visitors to see the Watts Towers in the evening, when all the other sightseers are long gone; I have stopped to ask directions on those all-Black main streets; I never have felt threatened.

Watts has been a symbol to the entire country of what Blacks can do when they become enraged. But it is a very small part of the Los Angeles Black community.

It would be inaccurate to say that Blacks are integrated into Los Angeles, in spite of the fact that one may find Black neighbors everywhere from Sherman Oaks to Santa Monica. A broad line down the center of this city, from La Brea or even La Cienega on the west to Figueroa or farther on the east would mark our Black belt—though Koreans and Japanese and Vietnamese and some Chicanos have encroached on the area. Here, mostly, are well-kept, low-rise apartment buildings and small houses, and well-cared-for yards and cars. The only things that tell you you are in a Black area are the restaurants advertising soul food and "genuine Southern BBQ," and the outdoor boards showing Blacks instead of Whites drinking beer.

When I was a girl, we lived near Arlington and Adams Boulevard, in one of the grand old houses in this section of the city that once was almost country, where the important businessmen of the twenties built their mansions. In the late forties the big houses were being turned into rest homes and libraries and other institutions—the John Tracy Clinic for the Deaf is here, as is UCLA's William Andrews Clark Memorial Library. A group of apartment buildings was built, a handsome contemporary complex that covered six or eight blocks. And everyone who moved in was Black. "Look out," everyone said, my parents included, "in five years this will be a slum."

Over thirty years later those apartments still look contemporary, oddly enough; even more odd, given the gloomy predictions, the buildings are well-painted, the lawns and gardens beautiful, the whole area a charming suburban site.

It is from areas such as these that Leah and Ralph and all their friends at the banquet have come. And it is, indeed, a long way from Dallas. In these areas most—not all, but most—live comfortably. Many own their own houses; if they rent, the prices are no more exorbitant than any other rental prices in Los Angeles; and they do not get taken at the supermarket any more than the rest of us do. In fact, they live as everyone else in Los Angeles does: a little over their budgets, but not too much; a little easier than their counterparts elsewhere, because here one does not have to buy winter coats or antifreeze or snow tires; a lot better than middle-class Blacks in most other parts of the country, because, somehow, most things are less complicated in Los Angeles. When the Dallas Memorial Homecoming and Social Club wants to have a banquet, no restaurant with adequate space will turn it down.

Tonight at the Top o' the Crock there is a special attitude of excitement, of anticipation, and so the cocktail hour ends rather quickly, and we repair with our camel's milk to the big round tables in the adjacent banquet room. The anticipation is due to the presence of the guest of honor, the Reverend A. S. Jackson. Everyone here is pleased that his nephew, Maynard Jackson, became the first Black mayor of a major southern city, but it is the kind of pride they would take in the achievement of any of their friends' relatives. The fact that Mayor Jackson had to cancel his appearance here at the last minute is no great disappointment. It is the Reverend Jackson who is their hero. For good reason.

If they have become solid middle-class citizens, if they have good jobs and a good way of life, they hold the Reverend Jackson partially responsible. He was their music teacher at Booker T. Washington High School in Dallas, he organized the Ambassadors, which was the singing group, and the Aristocrats, which was the band. But he did much more than that. He taught them to be resourceful. He taught them how to make the compromises necessary to live in a White world, and showed them ways to give vent to their energies instead of to their anger.

The evening begins with the singing of the Negro National Anthem. Announced as such. The children and grandchildren are not here, no one under forty is here, and so no one has to call himself Black tonight. They are Negroes, it is the term they are familiar with and more or less comfortable with. They know from personal experience how tough it has been to be a Negro. Black is still a euphemism in their book. The Negro National Anthem is not a militant song. It is a song of hope and of coming through adversity to a better life. The melody is very lovely, and as voices trained to harmony rise to catch the high notes of the chorus, it is very moving.

In her welcoming speech Mrs. Vivian Reid, the mistress of ceremonies, makes the crucial remark. "Well, I guess everyone here went to Booker T. It was the only school we had." Everyone laughs and applauds—as always seems to happen, the bad old days have become the Good Old Days. The fact that there was only one high school in all of Dallas that Blacks could attend is what drew them together. In fact, by the time Leah was a senior, another school, Lincoln, had opened across town, and she attended it for her final year; and Professor Jackson divided his time between both schools. But nothing had changed. These still were all-Black schools. All-Negro schools, to be precise.

The Reverend Jackson must be in his seventies. He doesn't look it. But he started teaching at Booker T. in 1928, a long time ago. What he does look is White. As Leah says, "When we had to pull the shades of the bus down to pass through Grand View, Professor Jackson could leave his shade up." It is an accepted joke among all his friends and pupils, and it is mentioned a number of times. Somehow, they have gotten over the hurt.

The early part of Reverend Jackson's speech is pure nostalgia. As befits someone who was a professor of music and is now a minister, his voice is beautifully modulated; there is just the faintest trace of a southern accent, and no Negro inflection at all—except when he chooses to use it.

"When I came to Booker T. there was no band, no music class, no chorus. I went to the school board and I said, 'I need money for instruments, because we're going to have a drum and bugle corps.' Of course they said no, they said no to anything that cost money for a Negro school. So I organized my kids. They called them Professor Jackson's Street Beggars, because I set them out on every corner, asking for money. And we got it. Then I went down to the pawn shop—you all remember the pawn shop?" There is a soft flurry of applause. "Now I knew Mr. Johnson pretty well, because my daddy had a watch that he used to pawn just about every week, and then he'd send me back later to get it out. So I said to Mr. Johnson, 'You must have some used musical instruments here that we can buy cheap for the school.' Of course he did, and that's how we got our drum and bugle corps." More applause.

"Now you all remember what happened with the uniforms? We had to march all the way across town to perform at the game between Booker T. and Lincoln, and I felt we just had to have some snappy uniforms. So we went to Kresge's [applause] and we bought crimson sweaters, and white skirts for the girls and white pants for the boys, and we bought little white hats with black celluloid bills. [Extra applause, everybody remembers those uniforms.] Well, the day came and we started marching, and it started raining. And the crimson sweaters started running down on those white skirts and pants, and the black bills came unglued from the white hats, and at first we couldn't figure out why everybody was laughing at us. Then we looked at ourselves, and were we a mess! But we played! [Much applause and laughter.]

"But you all remember, I never taught you any cheap music. I wanted you to know about good music, I taught you Haydn and Handel, I taught you barcaroles and chorals. There was no cheap music at Booker T." A rising chorus starts here. It is almost like the sound of bees, as three hundred people show their approval with a sort of under-the-breath um-hum. There is something very nice, very reassuring, about this quiet chorus of approval.

"Well, I see a lot of my friends here from those good old days," the Reverend Jackson says. "I see Sing Baby, she was one of the first members of the Ambassadors. Sing Baby, stand up!" And a tiny woman in her late fifties, with bright orange-red hair, stands and is applauded. "And I see . . ." He names several others, mostly women, and they stand and are applauded. "And now," he says, "I'd really like to hear the Lincoln High Anthem. All of you who know it, go stand by Reverend Madison at the piano, and let's hear some singing!"

We all turn to our programs, the mimeographed kind that lists charter members and officers and committees and hosts and hostesses and speakers, so that one way or another nearly everyone's name is in print. On the front it says, "To Strive, To Serve, To Find And Not To Yield." On the back it says, "MAKE NEW FRIENDS BUT KEEP THE OLD, ONE IS SILVER AND THE OTHER IS GOLD." The back also has the words for some of the songs, listed under Alma Maters. "Dear old Booker T., we love you. You are always good and true. You have always led us through, and I shall always be true blue." But the Lincoln High song is not printed here, because Leah made up the program and she couldn't remember the words. Consequently, she doesn't join the group of seven or eight elegantly dressed and beautifully wigged women who gather around the piano.

The Reverend F. H. Madison—also something of a hero, since he has a degree in music and worked many years as a musical director in New York—starts the song too high. Sing Baby tries valiantly to get the high notes, but her voice quavers badly. Then, somehow, in the chorus all the voices suddenly catch the notes and blend into a beautiful harmony, and the women spontaneously begin making certain rhythmic gestures—it is a little like watching the Supremes in action. And suddenly you almost can see them as they were thirty years or so ago, young, learning to express themselves through music, finding camaraderie and some measure of hope; all of those things that have carried them through the bad times to bring them together tonight. They all started out Black and poor and southern; and now they wear mink stoles and their husbands drive Cadillacs, and they can afford to pay $12 a head for a steak dinner. They can afford to remember their roots, as they know them. Because they have made it in L.A.

The mood is very upbeat now, but the Reverend Jackson has something quite serious to say.

"I had a lot of notes," he begins, "I had a lot of things I was going to say about the past, but let's forget all that. I would like to talk, for just a moment, about the future.

"I would like to talk about your children. Our children. About what we owe to them, and what we have to teach them."

There is a pause. Everyone is listening carefully now, the table-side chatter and the clatter of knives and forks has ceased.

"Now the important thing," he continues, "is to let them know that separate but equal is not any good! (The *um-hums!* of approval begin again.) The important thing is that they put themselves into the *mainstream* of society. And the way you do that in America is to make money! (*Um-hum!*)

"They go to college and they major in African Studies, and what the hell good is *that* going to do them? (*Um-hum!*) Now there's nothing wrong with knowing the history of our people. They think it's something new, these children, but we studied Negro History back at Booker T. in 1928, and we all know it's nothing new! (*Um-hum, um-hum!*) Now I'm proud of being Black, and we all are (*um-hum!*), but being proud isn't going to help us get ahead. Making money is going to help us get ahead! (*um-hum, um-hum!*)

"Your kids study Swahili, and what good is that going to do them when they talk to the boss? The boss doesn't speak Swahili, he speaks English. They'd do better to learn good

English, and you'd do better to tell them so!" (The *um-hums* rise and rise, and the man at the table behind me says, "Africa!") I've been there. I hated Africa!")

The Reverend Jackson continues: "The time for 'We Shall Overcome' is past! *(um-hum!)* And the time for 'Black is beautiful' is past! *(um-hum!)* That was fine for its purpose, but its purpose is past, it's over now. And the Black handshake ["Doesn't mean a damn thing," my neighbor behind me murmurs] and the African hairdo ["Afros!" a handsomely wigged woman mutters in derision], all of that is past. Done. Over! (The *um-hums* get louder.)

"You tell your children to study computer programming. You tell them to study electronics. Forget Swahili. Forget African Studies. The way they're going to get somewhere is to have a skill which can make them money. Because this is a capitalist country, and if we're going to get anywhere we have to succeed *as capitalists!* Separate but equal is a joke—there is no such thing. The only way we can be equal in this country is to make as much money as the next guy!" This from a pastor!

"If you want to help your people, you tell your children this: Work hard. Study hard. Learn good English. And learn a skill. That's how you can help your people. By making them equal with all the other people—in every way that counts. When they're just as good as everybody else, they'll be treated like everybody else. And not before!"

The *um-hums* have risen and risen to a buzzing chorus. Suddenly everyone starts to rise and applaud. The music of the Negro National Anthem comes up again. There is a great emotional surge—a combination of happy memories of a sad past and of enthusiasm for the future the Reverend Jackson has set before them. We are caught up in it. We are included.

And yet, not separate, just equal. But why are they playing the Negro National Anthem?

The formal program is over, and as we prepare to leave, Leah rushes over to us and surrounds us with her friends. She is pleased and, yes, proud, to have us here; in her introduction speech she mentioned us by name: "When I have tickets to sell, my boss doesn't even ask what they're for, she just says, 'I'll take two.' So please welcome June and Bert Gader!" Now she wants to introduce us to everyone. There is a great deal of warmth expressed, and no indication that anyone feels strange about our presence. Part of this is that very real and natural quality known as southern hospitality. Part of it is our age group; despite the fact that these middle-aged Blacks suffered far more discrimination—especially in their earlier days in the South—than their children and grandchildren ever will know, they were raised with a certain attitude toward Whites, and hostility was not part of it. Perhaps it was a myth, but they felt they were part of those families for whom they worked. Consequently, they seem to have more of a sense of being "equal" than later generations may ever have.

And yet all of us here know that the Reverend Jackson's speech is irrelevant. No matter how much we all agreed, no matter how great the applause, the children to whom he referred have already gone their own ways, and they are not the ways of "equal but not separate." None of them took African Studies or learned Swahili, and none of them wear Afros—but neither did they study computer programming or electronics. Leah's Jim was a brilliant student, but he contracted TB and couldn't go to college; all his jobs have been as a retail salesman, and none has lasted long. Her older daughter has married two or three times, and has three children, and she has worked at some good jobs; but then she moves on to some over-the-rainbow ideal of a better man, a better place, a better deal. The younger daughter studied dental hygiene at great expense to Leah, then got a job as a salesgirl, married young, wants a baby. All the children of Leah's friends have done the same—not one of them has gone to college. Nothing has changed.

Some of these children even have joined the Masonic groups to which Leah and *all* her friends—not just the Dallas ones—belong. If there is a single connecting thread among the middle-class Blacks of this city it is their Masonic memberships. And that is indeed a plural; there are so many different organizations that an outsider cannot begin to keep count of them. It seems that Leah mentions a different "court" every time I see her, and I cannot keep track of which one she is referring to when she says that she is "going up" to a new position as Matron or Worthy Matron or Most Worthy Matron, of Ancient Matron or Most Ancient Matron or Grand Ancient Matron, or several other even more exalted titles. There are weekly meetings and monthly meetings; there are bistate meetings and state meetings; there are regional meetings and national meetings. How Leah finds the time to come to me once a week I cannot imagine.

"Equal but not separate" is a sentiment that seems to be in direct contradiction to these Masonic memberships. Since these organizations are so secret, I cannot categorically state that no Blacks belong to White groups or vice versa; but I do know that the groups to which Leah and Ralph belong are all-Black. Perhaps at the national conventions there is a mingling; if so, Leah has never referred to it.

There well may be as many White Angelinos who belong to Masonic groups as there are Black Angelinos, but I never see the ring or pin on anyone other than Blacks. And though my own father was a Mason and I occasionally wear his locket, no White person has mentioned the Masons or Shriners to me in thirty years. The great Shrine Auditorium on Jefferson Boulevard is an indication that Masons once were very powerful in Los Angeles. But as far back as I can remember, this huge pseudo-mosque with its onion dome and elaborate decorations has been used by visiting ballet and opera companies. If it has any use today as a Masonic temple it is not among Leah and her friends—they use small local halls for their regular meetings, and convention centers and hotels for their larger ones.

Whether or not Whites still follow the Masonic code in Los Angeles, Blacks of a certain income group and class will continue to take pleasure and pride in these organizations for generations to come. Leah recently sponsored a drill team for one of her chapters; she raised over $3,000 to pay for their uniforms and transportation to Kansas City, where they performed for the national convention. The girls on the team were eight to fourteen years old.

Naturally the youngsters are not true members of these Masonic groups. To become a full member one must pass through a "Creation," which has all the ritualism of a fraternity hazing. Presumably all secret orders go through such rites, but they seem anachronistic to outsiders—throwbacks to simpler ways of life in other times and places. Of course it is the combination of many such throwbacks that makes Los Angeles what it is today. Since it was the Second World War that brought the most recent population boom to this city, many of us came from somewhere else in the United States. If there is a major difference between Los Angeles and cities in the East, it is that while they are melting pots of European cultures, we are a melting pot of people from other parts of America—primarily from the Midwest and the South. If Los Angeles sometimes seems to be nothing more than an amalgam of crazy religions, crazy buildings and crazy politics—everything more extreme here than anyplace else—it is because each of us has brought with us a measure of things we thought we left back home, wherever home may have been.

Just so, these Blacks have brought with them from the South this desire to belong to organizations that are nothing if not separatist, and that create their own elite. It is interesting that so many of the younger generation—though none of Leah's children are involved—have continued in the same pattern. They will be the Black Masons and Black Shriners and Black Daughters of Isis of the future.

We went to Leah's youngest daughter's wedding. It was in one of those intriguing old areas of Los Angeles where Victorian houses with cupolas and turrets exist on shady side streets just a stone's throw from a main street of Korean markets and Vietnamese restaurants. Usher's Interdenominational Church is in one of the old houses. The wedding is to take place in what used to be the living room.

The groom was late, with the usual not-so-good excuse of his car breaking down; in fact, he was having second thoughts, and Georgetta knew it and was ready to walk out and call the whole thing off. Leah and Ralph were trying to hold it all together. Leah's oldest daughter, Amber, was helping by making sure that everyone had plenty to drink. It was a hot day, and there was a lazy southern summer feeling: men drinking bourbon or rum or Scotch, women fanning themselves with hats or handkerchiefs, the smell of barbecue wafting from the kitchen. Amber likes us, she spent a lot of time talking to us and plying us with drinks, introducing us to her friends. But she is the oldest of the second generation; her oldest children, two daughters with the same gigantic and slightly slanted velvet eyes that her first husband has, almost the same age as their aunt whose wedding this was, looked at us coldly. They are of the hostile generation. Bright. Both got scholarships to college, but neither used them. They watched their mother with disdain as she talked to us. They do not take crap from honkies.

Dan finally arrives, a handsome boy of twenty, backed up by four equally handsome brothers. The organ begins to sound, and a pretty girl in the bridesmaids' dress of red-and-white polka-dotted organdy sings "I Love You Truly, Truly Dear," with only a slight show of stage fright. Georgetta comes down the stairway on Ralph's arm, holding up her long train. The bridesmaids and the brothers gather, and Amber's youngest, six-year-old Rich, wearing a baby-sized tuxedo that matches his eyes, presents the ring on a velvet cushion. Leah sobs uncontrollably, and my husband, who is sitting right behind her—the best seats in the house had been staked out for us—helps to comfort her. The "I do's" are pronounced. The wedding is completed, a success, and now we all can drink and dance and have fun.

A large cement patio behind the house is set up with tables and umbrellas for the reception. There is only one other "Caucasian" here, a woman whose children Leah helped raise, but we are not drawn toward each other—I'm not quite sure why. Because it would not have been in good taste for the three Whites to move together? Or because we know and enjoy many of Leah's friends and see no need to rush to meet a stranger? Whichever, we are surrounded by Paula and her husband, by Ginny and Tommy Thompson, by a marvelous elderly man who had the brains to quit his job as a watchman and go to work for an airline just a few years short of retirement age; now he travels the world at reduced fares, and enjoins us to go to work for an airline quickly, before it is too late. "I'm having the best retirement anyone ever had," he tells us. "I've been to Paris, to Tokyo, just got back from two weeks in Hawaii. What a life!"

Georgetta, though she is only twenty-one, is not cold toward us as her nieces are. On the other hand, she is a little shy, as are Dan and the rest of their friends. Yet they agree, without any hesitation, when "Mamadear" says a "family" picture must be taken: the bride and groom, his brothers, Leah and Ralph, Bert and I. Less than two years later, this marriage has been through a trial separation and a trial reconciliation; it probably will end as four of her mother's five marriages have ended. But long after Georgetta has moved on to other things, our pictures will be in that family album.

The wedding party ended in the same way that tonight's banquet has ended—with a lot of hugging and kissing and promising to get together. I like Leah's term "jollying"; we do a lot of jollying when we are with her and her friends, and there does not seem to be anything phony about it. A genuine camaraderie exists here, and it does not seem to matter to either side that some of us are Black and some of us are White.

Down in the wind-tunnel garage, after the banquet, we exchange good-byes even with people we didn't meet, soft words wafted away in these cavernous spaces. I hug my long black feather boa to ward off the cold, as the Black ladies hug their minks. We rev up our BMW, but its throaty sound is lost among the even throatier purrs of so many Cadillacs and Lincolns and Chrysler Imperials. We head home, they turning south, we turning north to the Hollywood Hills, where Leah is afraid to live. We are a little jazzed, and I am sure that they are too, by the Reverend Jackson's speech; the sentiment is so fine. But they have found their way, and they know it; and they know the kids will have to find their own ways. Luckily, Los Angeles is as good a place as any—and a better place than most—to find one's own way. They did what they could, by bringing the children here. Now it is up to them.

6

South Bay: The Beach Cities Have Their Own Magazine Now

Paul, the advertising executive, called as he does approximately once a year for approximately the same favor. "Listen," he said, and then there was quite a long pause, so I knew what he wanted. "Listen, there's this girl, she's a friend of the family, and she wants to be a writer or something, and I wondered if you'd have lunch with her?"

So I met Sheridan Crawford, and talked to her for two hours. And a few months later *South Bay* magazine came into being.

We arranged to meet at the Studio Grill, which, from the outside, looks as tacky as its Melrose Avenue location, and inside reveals the intimate charm that has made it so popular with people in advertising and television. I was early and Sheridan was late. I had two glasses of nice house wine and had Luncheon Lecture to a Young Writer all ready when she finally came breezing in. "I'm sorry," she said, "the office was a madhouse and I just couldn't get out. Listen," she said, "what I really want to do is quit this job and settle down in the South Bay area and start a magazine. I'm young, I have a little money saved, I have a few contacts and I don't have any responsibilities, so don't you think this would be the perfect time to try?"

By the time lunch was over, I had convinced her that since she was young and had money saved and had a few contacts and no responsibilities this would be the perfect time to quit her job and start a magazine. Four months later, in December, a very slick little number filled with advertisements and called *The South Bay Gift Guide* arrived in my mailbox. In January Sheridan phoned. "How did you like our *Gift Guide*? That was the seed project for the magazine, which we're calling *South Bay*. How would you like to write a regular column for us?"

Sheridan is a pretty girl and at the time we met, in August of 1977, she truly was a girl, only twenty-three or so. She is soft-spoken and there is a ladylike quality about her that reveals her Pasadena/Palos Verdes upbringing. She also is intense and hard-working and dedicated. Ten months after the first bi-monthly issue of *South Bay* magazine appeared, the issues had doubled in size, the circulation was nearly thirty thousand, they were at break-even and approaching profit-making, and they were preparing to turn into a monthly. "There's a market down here at the beach that no one ever really tried to tap before," Sheridan says, "and we're tapping it and people really are beginning to react."

The South Bay consists of the cities that edge the southern section of Santa Monica Bay. Its northern tip is Marina del Rey, the posh, sailboat-encircled area of high-rises and condos and quaint bay-front shops, of crowded restaurants and bars; its southern tip is Palos Verdes, which is so old-line and old-money it doesn't even know it's a beach city. The hard-core center is comprised of four cities: north to south, El Segundo, Manhattan Beach, Hermosa Beach and Redondo Beach. For the purposes of the magazine, the area is extended inland to Torrence and Hawthorne, and farther south around the tip of the bay to San Pedro, which is at the harbor.

One thing makes the beach areas of Los Angeles very different from those almost anywhere else in the world: there are no large resort hotels here. No one seems to know why that type of development never occurred, either in the glittering era of land speculation and development before the Depression, or during the postwar period of wild expansion. The beaches do tend to be foggy during the summer months, but they would have made exceptional winter resorts. Now it seems too late: the California Coastal Initiative of several years ago created so many restrictions for building along the entire coast that, in some areas, it is difficult to get the necessary permits to build a personal dwelling. But that does not account for the omissions of the past. There are resort hotels down the coast at La Jolla and San Diego, and up the coast at Santa Barbara; Los Angeles just never developed that way.

In fact, until the real estate mania began between ten and fifteen years ago, most of the beach cities were just sleepy reminders of other eras. Each has always had its individual personality, but many of the cities had fallen into a comfortable, run-down tackiness. Until quite recently, it was not chic to live at the beach.

That is, it was not chic to live in Santa Monica or Venice or Ocean Park, nor in most of the South Bay cities. The acceptable areas were Malibu to the north, especially the Colony, noted for its movie stars; Palos Verdes Estates (the oldest, old-money section of the large Palos Verdes Peninsula) or Rolling Hills Estates (newer money) in the South Bay; and Balboa Island, Newport Beach, Emerald Bay and Laguna, farther south. San Pedro was, and is, a melange of Portuguese and Yugoslavs and Chinese and Samoans and Greeks and Mexicans and Armenians, workers drawn by the harbor—one of the few non-Wasp sections of our coast. El Segundo was and is predominantly a blue-collar city, where the people who work in the factories and aerospace plants that dot the area live. Marina del Rey attained instant chic because it originated just when living at the beach was beginning to be an "in" thing to do.

Manhattan and Hermosa and Redondo had, and for the most part still have, narrow streets with tiny beach cottages nestled cheek to cheek. In the past these cities were categorized as places where elderly original homeowners eked out their lives or where absentee landlords made easy money on run-down properties; and, later, where hippies and drug-takers were to be found. Still later, when a few apartments were built to cater to the pilots and stewardesses who wanted to live near the airport—and drew also all the young men and women who wanted to live near the pilots and stewardesses—this area became known as the most swinging "swinging singles" section of the entire city.

Outwardly, these cities appear to have remained much the same. But there have been major changes, not the least of which is that these usually tiny lots with their usually tiny houses cost a fortune today.

Two years ago some close friends decided that, since the children were grown and help was so expensive, they should sell their Benedict Canyon house and buy a condominium at the beach. They were told that they could expect to get $350,000 to $400,000 for their view property, which includes a contemporary house designed by a noted architect, acres of fine gardens and citrus trees, a pool, an artist's studio and a Beverly Hills postal address. After months of hunting, they found only one beach condo that appealed to them—a two-bedroom place, not in chic Malibu but in Manhattan Beach—and it was $375,000. They remain in Benedict Canyon. But a number of people in similar circumstances did make the move, despite the high prices.

There has been a notable change of demographics in the South Bay area. Some of it is due to successful people in their forties and fifties choosing to exchange their big houses in the city for a more simple lifestyle. Some of it is due to owners of beach properties tossing out their low-paying tenants, putting in picture windows and patios, and renting for much higher prices or moving in themselves. In Redondo Beach—and oddly, only in Redondo—there has been heavy building of slick condominiums that sell for extremely high prices. Since the remarkable success of Marina del Rey, which was wrenched from a sandy no-man's-land between Venice and El Segundo, marinas and yacht clubs have begun blooming like wildflowers down the whole length of the bay. Singles still are swinging around here, but they are earning more and spending more than the "beachies" of old; and some of them are single parents, which makes a difference; and some of them bought run-down apartment buildings and fixed them up and traded them up, and have turned into entrepreneurs. In short, these still are lively cities, but it is a very different kind of liveliness than ever before, and it now is appealing to people who are willing to spend quite a lot of money to enjoy it.

A fact that makes Sheridan Crawford something of a seer.

Of course, *South Bay* was not all her idea; as usually happens, a few people with similar goals came together at exactly the right point in time, and the right publication was born. But as editor she has shaped its direction; and her previous experience had given her important knowledge of which chances to take and which pitfalls to avoid.

The daughter of a journalist, she studied "a little bit of everything at Stanford, but I ended up in creative writing and communications. Trying to express myself creatively just made me feel more alive than when I was studying European history. I didn't really know how I was going to use it when I graduated, but I worked for *The Stanford Daily* and I had published in literary magazines and I had written a lot of fiction, and I realized that that was what made me feel best."

After graduation Sheridan took a job in the university's communications department for a while, then uprooted herself to go to Washington, D.C., "to test my survival skills. After a year I realized that Los Angeles was my place. So I moved back, came back to the South Bay, because I felt an almost magnetic pull to that area."

She first took a free-lance job at *The Easy Reader*, a give-away guide to events in the beach cities. Then she went to *Coast Magazine*, which originally had been called *Coast FM and Fine Arts* and featured radio listings and articles on music. When it dropped the end of its title and tried to be a wide-ranging city magazine, it failed.

"I was assistant to the publisher. You might say I was taking its pulse all the time the magazine was dying. You learn a lot when a magazine dies, it's a fast lesson in the ways of the world. I had a chance to analyze why it happened. Having been in on the death of one magazine made it much easier to be in on the birth of another; I just had to reverse the process." She had moved on to a company that published consumer aviation magazines—again on the administrative side—that day when we first lunched together, and she was itching to get back to writing, longing to create a publication of her own.

Her original idea basically involved public relations. "I started out thinking about King Harbour, which is one of the marinas in Redondo Beach, and I thought they ought to be attracting more tourist trade. People come to Los Angeles and look at visitors' guides, and all they read about are places like Disneyland. And I thought, here's all this real southern California experience to be had, boating and surfing and good restaurants and bars, and no one knows about it. Then I realized that this was true, not just of King Harbour, but of the entire South Bay. I thought I could invent a publication that could be mailed out on a controlled basis that would be good for the merchants and good for the tourists.

"Then, lo and behold, the Monday after I resigned from the aviation magazine, I had a call from Dick Sandres, who's now our advertising director, saying, 'Come work with me for a few months, we're going to do a South Bay gift guide for Christmas.' And there it was. God, I could feel it in my bones!"

Sandres, whom Sheridan had known from her *Easy Reader* days, had an idea for a city-type magazine, and had approached a local entrepreneur, Lee Eggert, about putting up the money. Eggert agreed to finance a gift guide to see if the advertising dollars were there. "Dick knew I'd been fooling around with similar ideas, so when Lee said okay, he called me right away. Then he got William Fridrich, who now is our art director, involved. We all knew we wanted a magazine, Lee included, but we didn't spread the word around that we were using the gift guide as a test. We sought out all the classy retailers in the entire area, because eventually we were going to offer them a publication that would appeal to a very select market. There was no other vehicle available to them that had class or clout. To find out exactly where the market was we did a controlled circulation, and sent out forty thousand free copies of the gift guide.

"The gift guide turned out to be fantastic. Very lucrative for us, and very successful for most of the advertisers. We proved that we were going in the right direction. So the day after

Thanksgiving we had a meeting at Lee's house, and we all were sort of dry-mouthed, but we all agreed, 'Let's do it. Let's take the leap of faith.'"

The magazine began rather cautiously: beautiful in design, but a little pallid in contents. The first issue, March/April 1978, headlined these features on the cover: "Beaches" by Leonard Wibberley; "A Poem" by Ray Bradbury; "Marineland." Inside were articles on a commercial vessel that nets anchovies; the beauty of tidepools; five South Bay women; cruising the warm waters of the world; how to become a volunteer for community projects. There were also five regular columns: "Billboard" (an entertainment guide); "Cuisine" (a restaurant guide); "Simply Cooking" (recipes); "Weekends" (my travel column); and "Sampler" (highlighting interesting products or services). The cover—a concept that has been retained—was glossy black with thin-line white lettering for the masthead, and a large photograph of a beach scene set into the black background. The effect was one of romantic opulence combined with contemporary chic, and it stood out handsomely on magazine stands. A lot of people did pick it up, did buy it; a lot of rave notices came in saying, "At last! A magazine for *us!*" A trickle of letters grumbled, "Not controversial enough;" but Sheridan Crawford, editor, was quite certain what she was about.

"Our purpose was to serve a community, serve the affluent market within that community, and serve a retailer who so far was not reaching that community through available media. Yes, I was cautious. At first, all we tried to do was reflect the known interests of that community, which basically came down to the good life. I figured that as time passed, *they* would tell *me* what they wanted. I was willing to move into a more aggressive stance, little by little, but I didn't want to do anything initially to scare anyone off." She remembered the lesson of *Coast*— don't go too far too fast.

The second issue had two articles that were not about the beach or sports. One was a series of profiles of people who had given up commuting to live close to their work. The other was about the issue that was the talk of the entire city at that time,

Howard Jarvis's tax-cutting Proposition 13. It was a seriously considered topic, and it was given the center-of-the-issue spread; but it was difficult to find among all the ads for leisure clothes and all the articles with full-page photos about jogging, racquetball and tennis.

The following issue retreated totally. The cover was head-lined "Summer!", the cover photo was a close-up of the most interesting aspects of a girl in a string bikini (occasioning several letters of rebuke, mostly involving using women as sex objects). The table of contents listed a photo essay on summer, an article about a surf festival, "Books to Take with You to the Beach," "Hot Tubbing and Wine Drinking," "Fire Up the Summer Barbecue!" and articles about outdoor spas and Jacuzzis, dancing from disco to ballroom, the youngest sports achievers, and (on the serious side) lifeguards.

But by the September/October issue Sheridan had reached stride. A four-page spread entitled "It's Not New and I Didn't Name It That!" was a serious interview with economist Arthur Laffer and an explanation of Laffer's Curve. "Media Makes the Man—or Does It?" examined an upcoming congressional race between a former television commentator, Robert Dornan, and the son of a movie star, Carey Peck, with several pages devoted to their stances on various issues. "The Birthing Market" discussed the current trend toward having babies at home; while "Why So Many Caesareans?" was a long article covering not just caesarean births but the role of midwives and the possibility of career women taking their new babies to the office with them. There were twelves pages devoted to new fashions, and the full-page photographs were so imaginative that one had the momentary impression of looking at *Vogue* or *Harper's Bazaar*. "Wine and Politics" was a funny article about the favorite vintages of various Presidents. "Emergency!" told whom to call if you have one, and how to deal with one if you can't get help. With this one issue, *South Bay* turned from an attractive but frivolous "ten-minute read" to a serious magazine worthy of settling down with for an evening.

"We're trying to explore our community more in depth now," Sheridan says, "but we're still cautious, we're taking a feature-oriented approach, not a politically oriented one. I think it's interesting to note, and I'm not embarrassed to say it, that many of the subjects we've covered—the roller-skating mania, women astronauts and several others—have turned up later in *Life* magazine. I'm not saying they copied us; I'm saying we're moving to the right beat. Southern California and the things that happen here are often just a hair ahead of the rest of the country; what we reflect today turns out to be a sort of microcosm of American life tomorrow. I feel our magazine is keeping the pace up in a substantive manner. We've shown we can survive. We've shown that the market is there—we've had advertisers make forty to a hundred thousand dollars from a single color ad in a single issue. Now we can progressively take more and more chances in the direction in which we grow."

If the media basically ignored the beach areas until *South Bay* magazine came along, it is no surprise; Angelinos in general tend to ignore this section unless they live there. For one thing, it is so far away—forty-five minutes to an hour from Hollywood or Beverly Hills or even midtown. For another, old impressions die hard: San Pedro has nothing but a harbor; Manhattan, Redondo and Hermosa are tacky; Palos Verdes is stuffy and El Segundo has factories. In fact, these are among the most interesting cities in the Los Angeles area: rich in architecture that spans a century; colorful in their juxtaposition of the new and the old, the smart and the seedy; interesting in the varieties of people who live there and the lifestyles they pursue.

San Pedro, for instance, far from being just an adjunct to the harbor, spreads to encompass almost every conceivable kind of living condition; and does it not just at the turn of a corner or a bend of the road, but two or three times in the length of one straight block.

There are, of course, the docks, the oceangoing vessels, the cargo-loading cranes; and Ports-o'-Call, a Tahitian-style village of restaurants and shops, is no surprise. But the old downtown area, with buildings from the thirties nuzzling buildings from the teens, with signs proclaiming ethnic restaurants of every stripe, with pool halls and pawnshops keeping rakish company next door to stodgy banks and insurance companies, is an intriguing chapter from Los Angeles's past, as are the residential areas just a few blocks away.

Here there are big old houses with big yards and gardens, and, half a block away, tiny houses with no yards or gardens. There are two or three blocks of steeply rising lawns; the houses perched on top are story-book style with pitched shingled roofs and variously colored stucco walls. Just beyond is Fort MacArthur, with parklike stretches of grass and cottages with red-tiled roofs. Next door is Point Fermin Park, with century-old trees and perhaps the world's smallest amphitheatre. Across from a long palisades (a miniature version of the palm-lined park at Santa Monica that keeps falling down into the ocean) are houses and stores representing every decade and style from 1880 to the present. There are even brick houses here, a surprise, since brick seldom is used in Los Angeles except in mansions trying to re-create a foreign style.

"This area is changing fast," Sheridan says. "A lot of young couples are buying here because it's still inexpensive, there still are fixer-uppers here. They don't work in the area, it's not that. It's just that it's a way of moving into the housing market, which is prohibitively expensive everywhere else now. And they can live the beach life, and there are all these good, cheap ethnic restaurants nearby."

There is also a Korean pagoda-style monument, on a hill. And there is Walker's Cafe, such a genuine example of the typical beach café of the thirties with its signs that say "burgers" and "cold drinks," with its white stucco façade and its pictures of mermaids on the door that it was featured in *Chinatown*, the movie that tried so hard to evoke the spirit of that period. "There's a jukebox inside," Sheridan says, "and the walls are covered with old photographs. It's the kind of place where strangers talk to you."

North of San Pedro, the ocean is edged with palm trees, the very tall, lean palms that for so long have seemed to the visitor to be the hallmark of Los Angeles. "I never see them," Sheridan says, "they're just so *there*." On the coastal side of the highway are ghostly dunes covered with brush, not unlike the English moorlands, though in the spring the shocking fuschia of ice plant spreads across the dunes like an alien floral force. Occasionally, there are little colonies of houses or condominiums, lost between ocean and brush-covered hills, looking like pioneer settlements from another time and place. "Isolation is part of the beach idea," Sheridan comments. "People who live here like that. They're accused by their families and friends of deliberately choosing isolation, moving down where no one really wants to visit them, because the drive is so long."

The yellowish rolling hills to the east identify the monied, horsey area appropriately named Rolling Hills. Suddenly the highway is all lumps and bumps and strange curves and potholes, though obviously it has just been resurfaced, and the roadside signs warn "Constant Land Movement." This is Portuguese Bend, once the most elite of beach cities and still carrying that banner high, despite the fact that many of the houses on the ocean side of the highway have slid into the sea, and many on the other side have been damaged. An unusual kind of soil, which turns oily and thus unstable when wet, did not deter estate builders even after the problem was discovered. And while the community behind the gates labeled "Portuguese Bend" in hand-painted tiles is notably Wasp, the other side of the highway holds many Japanese-owned farms, and a roadside stand, owned by an attractive fortyish Japanese woman named Annie, is said to have the freshest vegetables and flowers in this section of the city.

The Wayfarer's Chapel is here also, a landmark in an area otherwise noted only for Marineland. Designed by Lloyd Wright in 1947 and always controversial, it has a cobalt blue roof as bright as that of the Matisse Chapel near the Côte d'Azure, a bowerlike interior filled with greenery and much wood, and so much glass that even on a cloudy day the light comes pouring through, as though the heavens were making a benediction. Cracks in the Visitors' Center, behind the romantic garden toward the rear, indicate that this, too, may one day sink into the sea.

Just beyond, a place actually named Inspiration Point has a Spanish-style Coast Guard station with a lighthouse surrounded by palm trees; the lighthouse is said to have a ghost. A few curves up the coast, at Long Point, Resort Point and Flatrock, the whales gather for a rest during their migrations. People who live in the South Bay and have ocean views often give "whale watch" cocktail parties during the migration seasons.

Malaga Cove Plaza sits at the entry to the expensive section of Palos Verdes known as the Estates. The plaza, an early version of the shopping mall, features Italianate brick buildings with arched loggias running past book stores and drugstores and real estate offices and markets. Old pepper and eucalyptus trees line the edges of this little village; line the streets all called "Via" something that run behind it up into the hills; shelter the *de rigueur* Spanish-style houses with their red tile roofs, their from-here-to-eternity views of the entire city stretching behind the crescent of Santa Monica Bay. At night, when the bay is encircled by lights and the coastal highway is strobed by headlights, the effect is outrageously gorgeous.

Down below on the "flatlands" and just to the north is Redondo Beach. It begins with Riviera Village, a shopping center of small boutiques; continues on, beyond the King Harbor marina with its quaint shops and restaurants, to the area of tall new condominiums. "There's something happening here," Sheridan says, "and we don't know what it is. Money seems to be changing hands, small businesses are being driven out, and there seems to be a move toward Miami-cizing the area. A lot of people are quite angry about it—but why didn't it ever happen before?" Just beyond is Redondo Pier, where Howard Rumsey's jazz club, Concerts By The Sea, has become as famous as his former club, The Lighthouse, in Hermosa Beach. "You used to be able to walk around the pier with an open can of beer," Sheridan continues, "but the area has been under a lot of criticism lately, there have been a couple of stabbings out there, and the City Council is trying to curb the activity at night. They keep trying to make this a family-oriented place, and they're finding that it's an impossibility. So of course they blame the jazz club, and the beer!"

It is in Redondo that Sheridan has pointed out "my favorite

street in the entire South Bay." Five or six blocks of Broadway are like all of San Pedro scrunched together: immense Victorian houses sit watching their huge lawns being nibbled away by the concrete driveways of fire stations and medical centers; tiny frame or stucco beach cottages are dwarfed by large churches of diverse style and denomination; liquor stores and grocery stores and dry cleaners with façades from the low-life end of the Art Deco period stand in the shadows of elegant contemporary apartment buildings. "You can read Redondo's history, decade by decade, just by driving down this one street," Sheridan says.

Cross the borderline into Hermosa Beach, where Redondo's Harbor Drive turns into Hermosa Boulevard, and the ambiance is instantly different. Most of these cities are individually incorporated, so they have their own zoning laws, their very different rules and regulations. "Look!" Sheridan virtually yells as we drive through on the way to her apartment. "No yards, no grass, you can build shoulder-to-shoulder here. Why do I live here?" But, Hermosa, with its remnants of the past, is one of the most interesting parts of the South Bay. It was a prosperous city long before the turn of the century, and some of its original "cottages," many of them immense shingle houses, still stand. In those early days, materials were brought by boat to the beach, or to Pier Avenue by train, and then dragged across the sands by mule teams. A certain large frame house with gables, terraced gardens and full porches is known to have cost only $500 to build; the frame-and-glass house at 84 Seventeenth Street was built by a noted contractor, Carl Broneer, and his sister, entirely by hand; the Pueblo Apartments, still standing on Hermosa Avenue, is a 1924 stucco replica of a Pueblo Indian adobe village. It is the winding, hilly side streets that are fascinating here. The main north-south streets are ambivalent about past and future, quaint shops mingling with run-down buildings and fast-food chains. Many artists and craftspeople have made Hermosa their home, and Sheridan finally admits that she lives here because "I like the mixture of people, and it's very relaxed. There seems to be a less frantic attitude at the discos and bars. It's not as upwardly mobile as Redondo, and it's not as family-oriented and conservative as Manhattan. And I'm only two blocks from the beach. Why am I complaining?"

At the border of Manhattan Beach, Hermosa Boulevard turns, naturally, into Manhattan Avenue; and again the ambience changes. This used to be the most swinging of the swinging singles areas, but it is much more conservative now that a lot of money circulates here. It has a main shopping street that vacillates between the quaint and the hip, and Sheridan calls it "a funky Rodeo Drive," indicating that it is also expensive. The extremely narrow streets—narrower than any other beach city's—which slope down from the main street to the ocean, are sensibly alternated; every other street is for driving, and the garages and carports for pretty little houses and apartments are located on these; alternate streets are for walking only, and are faced by front lawns and gardens. Manhattan Beach has the look of a true resort town, without the big hotels—almost everything is picturesque, every building is painted a pretty color, every front yard is filled with pretty shrubbery and flowers. It looks almost too cute to be true.

El Segundo, just to the north, has a factory-town atmosphere that is difficult to disguise—the factories are everywhere in evidence. Still, a few years ago a group of forward-thinking people got together and restored some turn-of-the-century buildings into an Old Town. They hoped to draw antique dealers and craftspeople here; to siphon off some of the singles from other more raucous areas; to encourage building and override the sedate, lower-middle-class, 1940s ambiance of the rest of the city. It may be that they were too forward thinking; or that El Segundo was too engrained in its ways to change. Old Town remains a pleasant two-and-one-half-block-long nod to the past. But nothing else happened, no new building commenced, no new blood came in. "It's the biggest anomaly in the whole area," Sheridan says. "It's part of our market, it's *there,* but it doesn't fit into our market at all. It's still living in 1945, and I don't think it will ever change."

Farther north, Marina del Rey is definitely the market that *South Bay* magazine wishes to reach and cultivate. It is a built-to-order city, almost entirely condominiums and apartments—

mostly high-rise and mostly expensive—interspersed with dozens of those chain restaurants that look virtually identical and serve virtually the same food, and with numerous bars that swing late into the nights. Many of the more exclusive condos have private spas and restaurants and discos; many of the people who live in them own their own boats, and some of them are in the yacht class. It is an area that appeals to people with money, and to others who would like to know people with money. It is exactly the other side of the coin from El Segundo, and like that city it stands out as unique in the South Bay.

The term *South Bay* originated with the media. *The Los Angeles Times* has a Thursday and Saturday supplement called "South Bay" that is distributed only to subscribers here. There is also a small visitors' guide called *The South Bay View*. Most of the rest of Los Angeles would not know what you were talking about if you mentioned the term; and up to a couple of years ago, even the people who lived in El Segundo and Manhattan and Hermosa and Redondo and Palos Verdes and Rolling Hills and San Pedro might have had difficulty identifying themselves with it.

Not anymore. Sheridan Crawford and her group have shown the people in these cities who they were and what they are, and are moving on to show them what they can be. They no longer are just "the beach cities"—they are the South Bay, and they have their own magazine to prove it.

7

Gay L.A.: Where the Music Never Stops

All the names in this chapter, except place names and those of Scott Forbes and Ray Sanchez, are fictitious.

My very dear, very old friend Derrick is coming to the house where I live in the Swish Alps, which is the Hollywood Hills, to take me where a lot of the action happens, on Faggot Flats, which is West Hollywood. Derrick lives in the Alps himself, so it is not too much of an imposition for him to pick me up. In fact, he is delighted to pick me up, delighted to take me on this series of tours that, he hopes and believes, will help explain to me something of the way of life that is so important to him now. Now that he has admitted to himself that he is homosexual. Now that he has admitted it to a number of other people, though never to his mother. His father, however, knows.

My husband is not joining us tonight, nor on any of the forays we will be making in the future. He, too, is an old friend of Derrick's, and Derrick would love to have his company. But tonight we are going to the places where the music never stops, the hot places, and while the appearance of a fag hag will not change the ambiance or the mood of these places, or at least not very much, the appearance of a straight couple might.

I am using these terms, *Swish Alps* and *Faggot Flats* and *fag hag,* because they are the terms that my friends, the old ones like Derrick and Luke, and the new ones like Judd and David and Sal and Erin, use among themselves, or at least use to explain something of their lifestyles to me. I do not think there is anything to ridicule about homosexuality and my feelings about that are even stronger since I've been to the bars and the restaurants and the discos that welcome primarily gays.

We are going first tonight to Gipsy, which Derrick says has "the best gay food in Los Angeles." It is on La Cienega Boulevard between Santa Monica and Third Street, that section of the city that has, for as long as I can remember, been called Restaurant Row. In fact, there are five or six times as many restaurants along Ventura Boulevard in the Valley; and today only Lawry's, the noted prime rib house, and the Captain's Table and the Tail o' the Cock remain from the original Row, and none has the drawing power it once had. Cugat's and Alan Hale's Lobster Barrel have been fairly long-time tenants, and l'Orangerie's rather recent arrival has added some gloss to a street that was fading. There are many antique shops, interior design shops and art galleries along this section of La Cienega, and some of these are owned by gays; while the Garden District long has been a gay hot spot for lunch. But the prevailing mood of the street is straight, and it is interesting that "the best gay food" in the city should be available on what is perceived as a street of family restaurants and expense-account restaurants.

Straight couples do wander into Gipsy, for there is nothing about it to set it apart from any other restaurant on the Row. The only clue, if you understood it, is the disco music blaring out. There is not a gay restaurant or bar that doesn't throb to the disco beat.

If the straight couple got as far as Gipsy's bar, they might notice the small dance floor to the left, and they might notice that men are dancing together there, some of them in tight embrace. On the other hand, both the bar and the dance floor are dark, though the dance floor does offer a "sky" flickering with tiny "stars"—as usual, this on-off effect of lights makes the darkness seem darker, and it would be easy enough to mistake the long-haired man dancing with the short-haired man for a heterosexual couple. Assuming that our mythical straight couple gave only a quick glance toward the dance floor, there would be nothing about Gipsy to put them off, and certainly no one to put them out. There are women as well as men sitting at the bar—"Dykes," Derrick whispers, though they look straight enough—and the hostess who asks if we have reservations is slim, tall, great looking and wearing a very décolleté long dress. "Is she gay?" I whisper. "Oh, no," Derrick answers with absolute certainty, the kind of certainty Gide said was a sixth sense among homosexuals. "Then why is she here?" "It's a great place for a woman to work. She won't get pinched, she won't get propositioned, and she'll get big tips because everybody wants to be here and they'll bribe her for a good table." He passes her $10 for the booth he wants when she starts to seat us at a tiny table in the center of the room.

"Of course having a straight woman is an advantage to the management," he continues confidently. "They don't have to worry about her disappearing during the rush hour with one of the customers!" Later, Sal says a lot of gay restaurants have straight female hostesses because they're "mother figures," while Judd informs me that they're all "fruit flies. You know, they're afraid of sex or straight men or something, so they'd rather work around gays."

The hostess seats us instantly after Derrick's bribe. "It's the best service we'll get all evening," he warns. "They have to have pretty young boys for waiters, and of course they're never experienced, so we'll wait forever for our order." In fact, the very pretty young man who serves us is both pleasant and willing. It is somewhat better service than one often receives at the more expensive restaurants in town.

The dining room is brightly lit, and while it is too large and too open to be cozy, it is not unattractive: there are used-brick walls, plants in pots, high-backed, comfortable booths along the sides, white linen at the tables, fresh flowers. The dance floor is separated from the dining room by a divider, which, unfortunately, does nothing to separate the diners from the sound of the music. "Intrusive!" Derrick shouts over the disco blare. To say the least. It is a little difficult to whisper shared observations here.

Still, with something less than subtlety, he happily points out the different "types." The room is filled predominantly with male couples. Often one man wears the tight cap-sleeve T-shirt that admirably shows off arm and chest muscles, while the other man dresses more conservatively. "If it looks good, flaunt it; if it moves, fondle it," Derrick says. In other instances the current "gay uniform"—tight chinos or Levi's, plain T-shirt, plaid Pendleton shirt worn as jacket—is featured by both partners. At one booth there are five people, a woman included, and the men look to me like mechanics or other laborers in their blue work shirts or leather jackets. It is the only table where anything that might faintly be considered an overt sexual act is occurring—two of the men are sitting rather closer together than men usually sit. At one table are two men dressed in suits with vests, shirts with ties—one is Black, the other Caucasian. A young man and woman, obviously straight, have the booth next to us. Just beyond them, a middle-aged woman holds court between two extremely handsome young gay men. Derrick instantly defines her as a fag hag, instantly defines another similar group, a thirtyish woman with two thirtyish men, as just friends. A few of the other men in the room are dressed as Derrick is, collegiate style, with V-necked cashmere pullover over an open-neck sport shirt. Sal, known by Derrick and his friends as "the hottest of the hot," assures me that this is an outmoded style of gay chic "Two years ago, that was the uniform." It seems much more appealing than the plaid-shirt-jacket look, or the tight T-shirt, and it is exactly the right style for Derrick, who, at forty, still has that pleasing collegiate charm. Luckily, he is not into uniforms.

Our drinks are large and remarkably inexpensive. The menu is reasonable: complete dinners from $6.95 to $9.95, with many à la carte specialties as low as $2.95 (such things as chili con carne and "Heavenly Fried Rice.") The salad is excellent, filled with crunchy things and dressed with something both tart and sweet; the lamb kebob is tender and juicy. Perhaps the "best gay food in Los Angeles" should be amended to read the "best reasonable food in Los Angeles." But of course there is more to it than that, and Derrick wants to be sure I get the message. He gestures around the room. "Everybody can be comfortable here. Whether you're straight or gay, no matter how you dress or what your number is, nobody's going to make fun of you.

That's not true in most straight restaurants. Do you feel at all uncomfortable being in a gay place?" I hadn't thought of it, which undoubtedly proved his point.

I leave Derrick to finish his cognac while I go to the ladies' room. "Pay attention to the graffiti," he tells me, unnecessarily. I always pay attention to graffiti.

Surprisingly, only one message seems to be gay: "THE HOT BLOND at Palms and Peanuts (medical student) would kill me if she knew this!" It is signed with a heart. The rest of the messages convey the typical straight woman's view of the homosexual male—that if only he would try a woman, especially that particular woman, he would find out what life and love are all about. There are many offers, pointedly made to males, not females, complete with phone numbers. One message berates homosexuals in foul language and then commands, "Read your Bible!" Another states wistfully, "Dancing with each other such fools if only a boy/man would know how good it is to bed a woman and how a girl could bed a man."

We move on to Studio One.

La Cienega Boulevard is a very long street that runs from Sunset Boulevard at the north, way down to the airport area and beyond at the south. Around Wilshire Boulevard, it is a few blocks west of the eastern edge of Beverly Hills. Around Santa Monica Boulevard, where we are now, it just touches the eastern boundary of Faggot Flats, also known as Boys' Town, Derrick now tells me. To get to Studio One from Gipsy, we must go west on Santa Monica a few blocks. We pass the Blue Parrot, "absolutely the hottest bar," where people are lined up in the streets outside of a corner store-front. We will return here later.

Studio One holds a unique position in this city. It is the *only* hot disco to straights and a major hot disco to gays. It is an "in" place to go, even if you do not go to discos. It has been called the Los Angeles counterpart of Studio 54 in New York, and yet it is quite different: it does not draw the celebrities that Studio 54 drew at its peak; it is not as difficult to get into—though if you are not the right person for the right night, you will find many perfectly legitimate regulations to keep you out; it is unquestionably predominantly homosexual male. It has kept its hot reputation since mid-1974, which is possibly a record for this city. It is quite something.

Scott Forbes was a successful optometrist when he conceived the idea for Studio One. He has been quoted as saying that he was tired of having to go to gay bars via back doors and back alleys, and felt that L.A. gays deserved a place that was both respectable and chic, and could be entered from the front. (This was not a pun. Many homosexual places in this city are still entered through back alleys, including the now-hot Numbers bar-restaurant, which is nestled between the eminently respectable Greenblatt's Delicatessen and Ah Fong's Restaurant on Sunset near Laurel Canyon—both old-line Hollywood establishments.) Within a few weeks Studio One became *the* place to go, and Scott Forbes became wealthy. Rather surprisingly, he chose to devote a fair portion of his wealth to benefiting the gay community: he is a senior member of the board of the Gay Community Services Center, which offers, among other services, peer counseling; he gave numerous parties to raise funds to keep the antigay amendment, Proposition 6, from passing; he gives seasonal parties to thank his patrons, parties so lavish that he consistently loses money on them; he is, at this writing, president of the Tavern Guild, an association of gay bar owners that has helped to keep gay bars from being hassled by the police and has pulled off such fund-raising coups as Gay Night at Disneyland (an event that ever-conservative Disneyland had no idea it was taking part in—who would suspect such an innocuous-sounding group as the Tavern Guild?). He is also said to be a liaison between the gay and straight business communities—his success has made him as legitimate as they come.

Studio One has one fast rule: No open-toed shoes are allowed. Even I know that rule. And yet every single night women in open-toed shoes are turned away from the doors. The rule keeps out a few others too, a few Blacks, a few Chicanos. When that rule doesn't work, others do—you must often show multiple I.D.'s, sometimes three, which not all minority groups (or women) can offer; or, simply, the club is said to be full.

The object is to keep Studio One primarily a club for Caucasian homosexual males. A nice mixture of other groups is allowed: beautiful female model types almost always get in; a few single straights of both sexes are allowed; a few straight couples are welcomed; a few middle-aged people, a few Blacks, a few Orientals, a few Chicanos. When Derrick and I arrive, we are behind quite a handsome party that is being turned away because one of the women is wearing open-toed shoes. We are admitted with the most cursory glance and no I.D.'s requested. We climb the stairway, mirrored and lit on both sides, and are blasted by disco music and by our images, endlessly reflected, on both sides.

The building was once a factory, and later a very expensive, though not very exclusive, private club called the Factory. The club died after a few years, as most clubs of all sorts (except the old-line ones, the Jonathan Club, the Los Angeles Athletic Club, the California Club) do in Los Angeles; I was amazed when so many of my friends bought expensive "lifetime memberships" in the Factory—the lifetime of a Los Angeles private club is so short. Later, the place became a sort of covered market, with health food restaurants and antique and craft shops filling its long, lonely spaces. That lasted a year or so. Then Scott Forbes took it over, kept the factorylike motif, added a few twirling mirrored balls to the ceiling, a few neon signs that flash or not, according to the music, some strobe lights that do the same, hired absolutely the best disc jockeys in town, and devoted so much of his own time and energy to the place that it didn't dare to fail. Studio One plays, and it plays superbly.

In the large upstairs bar-lobby Derrick goes to get drinks while I try to tune in on what he calls "the cruising mood" of this section of the club. Actually, it seems quite tame. There are some pinball machines, and one very handsome young man is having a very hot streak and a lot of people are watching him. The rest of the people seem merely to be trying to get close enough to the bar to get a drink, or to work up their courage to get out on the dance floor, which from here is obscured by a mass of onlookers. Cruising there may be, but there certainly does not seem to be any hustle. The reflections from the strobe lights create eerie patterns. The mood is a little like that of a Greyhound Bus station—everyone just kind of hanging around, kind of hoping that something will happen.

Derrick rejoins me and we slowly push our way to the dance floor. Finally we are there—*the* disco spot of L.A.

It is the first time I have seen *posing*.

The dance floor is jammed with gyrating couples, nothing new. But it is along-the-walls that is fascinating. Men line the walls, and they are of all different heights and weights and shapes and nationalities and kinds of "good looks," and they all wear different homosexual "uniforms."

The only thing they have in common is that they are posing (I did not know that this was a word in the homosexual vocabulary, it was just the word that first came to my mind).

Posing is simply standing in the same position for quite a period of time. It does not necessarily mean taking a stance— that is, arms outstretched, or profile silhouetted against the wall, or affecting a certain slouch or a certain gesture—though it can mean all of these. But for the most part, it simply means standing still. And as the strobe lights come and go across the faces of these men, it is like a freeze-frame in a movie: the strobes freeze the impression of each face in the viewer's eye; when the dark comes after the light, the impression remains.

Posing is not a social act. It is a lone and lonesome thing.

Judd, later, was derisive. "Posing," he said, "is precisely the kind of thing that puts people off homosexuals. It's so juvenile. And so silly. It's just like a bunch of teenagers showing off. Only the men who are doing it are thirty-five."

But the posing at Studio One doesn't seem to put anyone off; everyone seems to be having a very good time. The music is a miracle of timing, heart-attack-pace songs segueing into the slower beats that one can relax to and just jiggle to a little, lights matching music so that the slower tempi command less flash, more soothing darkness. This is necessary, because the dance floor never empties. It is like a Depression era marathon, the dancers just go on and on and on.

And the music never stops.

In an April 23, 1979, cover story, *Time* magazine stated: "The outstanding example of gay taste going straight is the popularity of disco lights, dancing and music, which swept the homosexual clubs of Fire Island and Manhattan long before they caught on among straights." "Gays are on the cutting edge," Derrick says. "We start things, and by the time straights discover them, we've moved on to something else." But gays have not moved on from the disco scene. "If it feels good, do it," is another of Derrick's favored remarks. Obviously, disco does.

Derrick and I work our way slowly past the posers to the upstairs bar, where young male couples are having the kinds of conversations one hears in singles bars the country over: "But really, don't you think that Marcuse has the *real* answer?" juxtaposed against: "My shrink says I should mingle more, so I'm trying, but what kind of people am I going to meet *here?*" We browse around, showing our stamped hands frequently; there are two entrances to Studio One, the front one for the disco and the back one for the Backlot, a nightclub that features top performers; and you pay separately for each. Still, we manage to slip in to see the nightclub, past the line of people waiting for an Eartha Kitt performance. This club is very intimate and must be a pleasure to perform in. Phyllis Diller has just ended a run. Joan Rivers has agreed to do an annual show. This is another example of Scott Forbes's showmanship; he does not make much money on the club, but feels it lends class to the whole enterprise.

Finally we are ready to leave, but we are at the far edge of the dance floor and it is even more jammed than before. "There's only one way to get out," Derrick says, "we'll have to dance across."

Suddenly, I am in a Ruby Keeler movie, only the beat is different. My purse is an encumbrance in this crowd, as is my jacket. It is extremely hot; indeed, many of the men are dancing shirtless. Derrick takes over the purse, I tie the jacket about my waist, and for about twenty minutes we do our antique-movie number across the up-to-the-minute floor of Studio One. It need not have taken this long, but a strange thing occurs out on the floor—it is as though you are not *in* the movie, but *are* the movie. The beat throbs in your body rather than in your ears; the strobes become part of your movement instead of an accent to movement. People turn to you from all sides: the beautiful model dances with me for a moment, as does the very butch homosexual male; Derrick is lost to others, but it doesn't matter, I have been found by everyone. It makes no difference that they are gay and I am not, or that they are younger or older or prettier or not so pretty; there is a oneness to it that I have never experienced in a straight disco. Watching from above, I thought everyone solemn and self-involved; down here, there is lots of eye contact, lots of smiles, camaraderie, anything goes. It is enchanting, mesmerizing—I am startled to find myself caught by the arm and taken from the dance floor. It is Derrick. I had forgotten about him.

But we cannot go yet because there is a show-within-the-show taking place at the edge of the dance floor that must not be missed. The two men look like construction workers. One is bare from the waist up. Both wear Mexican-style bandanas tied around their necks. Both look absolutely straight. They are doing the most erotic dance I have ever seen—yet, there are no overt sexual gestures. It is simply that there is so much sexual energy behind their dance, and the energy is zapping between the two of them so vibrantly that everyone around them is caught up in it. It is like that archetypal movie scene where an entire floorful of dancers stands back to let the stars strut their stuff. But Studio One is not a movie, no matter how much it appears to be one. The moment passes. The beat goes on. Derrick and I leave.

We walk back to the Blue Parrot, where there no longer is a line of people waiting to get in. I have always believed—a nice conceit—that I could tell a homosexual male from a heterosexual one at a glance; there is a certain look, a certain tone of voice. At the Blue Parrot there are, perhaps, two hundred male homosexuals. Two thirds of them look straight to me.

The single room has tropical plants and some nice Art Deco touches, and it is bumper-to-bumper people. The DJ's in the record booth on the balcony are very professional, but there are no strobes here, no twirling mirrored balls, and no dancing. There is no room for dancing. There is barely room to stand.

This is the first place where we have seen overt sexual gestures. A male couple standing next to us engages in an extremely long kiss and embrace, perhaps four or five minutes. A group of four males does a lot of touching, and much of it is pats on the fanny. Yet there is also so much posing going on that, to the uninitiated, it might seem that half the room was in a catatonic state. It is not possible to get close enough to the bar to get a drink, and while there are two waitresses, they cannot seem to push through the crowd either; it would be entirely possible to come here for an hour or so, to listen to the music and see and be seen, and not spend a dime. Does it pay to be as hot as the Blue Parrot is said to be?

It is another night and we are at Numbers to have dinner with Judd. Derrick has told me that "you *always* have to wait for your table at Numbers." Unless you're with Judd. Judd, who considers no spot in Los Angeles really hot, who "deplores the costume syndrome you find at every gay place now," who is against posing, who almost always uses the word *homosexual* instead of *gay,* who now eschews every gay-rights march—"I've gone to them and I see people I wouldn't invite into my home. I have no respect for them as human beings, all those limp-wristed queers doing their fag-drag numbers out in public"—is very well known at Numbers. And at Gipsy. And at 8709, the private baths that are said to be the only hot baths in town. Judd is already seated at the best booth in the best part of the room, the place just across from the long bar where you can see everything and be seen by everyone. There is a maitre d' here, not a hostess, and I fancy I see the merest flicker of respect in his eyes when we ask for Judd's table. The service is even faster and more ingratiating than that at Gipsy.

Like all—literally *all*—of Derrick's friends, Judd is extremely attractive. Not tall and collegiate like Derrick; not muscular and Italian-actor-style handsome like Sal; but a man with quite perfect features, very cool pale eyes and the look of—an old-fashioned term—a gentleman. He is very serious, very verbal and lucid, and Derrick and some of his friends refer to him as the Patriarch, although he is several years younger than everyone but David.

Judd has not wanted to talk to me about homosexuality. Derrick has worked for nearly two weeks to overcome this reluctance. "I want you to see all sides of the coin," Derrick has said to me, "and Judd is interesting and has lots of opinions." Of course what Derrick meant was that he wanted me to see all sides of *his* side of the coin—since not one of his friends knows any of the people they term "queens" or "drag queens" (the gays who have what they consider female tendencies, such as bitchiness, or who wear makeup or women's clothing); nor do they know the "Levi's-and-leather" macho types (or if they do, they don't admit it).

Now that we are together here, Judd seems still a little anxious. He is playing host: ordering drinks, getting menus, recommending dishes. Like Derrick and Luke, who was Derrick's roommate when I first knew him, he has been raised in a certain way, and being protective toward women is part of this. He is so busy lighting my cigarettes, getting my drinks and making polite small talk that I begin to despair of ever getting down to our subject. And so I am startled when he breaks off an extraneous conversation about pets to remind me that he had been at my house once, many years ago, "with Luke, when he and I were lovers." Equally casual, I remark that I didn't know that they had been lovers, and ask what broke them up. "He was too old for me," Judd answers. I burst out laughing because I always have thought of Luke, who has, truly, the face of a young Greek god and who is as tall and slim and collegiate as Derrick, as being *so young!* The ice is broken. The conversation flows.

The bar at Numbers is very crowded and becomes more so as the evening progresses. The disco music blares from a point that seems to be just above my right ear. The tables and booths are full, and since the distance between bar and booths is not large, there is a constant sense of being involved in the action. And yet, unlike Gipsy, this place is very cozy: it is like the bars you find in New York and San Francisco that cater to people from a single business, advertising or stock brokering or the theatre. The business, or pleasure, here is homosexuality.

The lighting is intimate. The long bar features glasses with numbers on them—the bar was named for the glasses, or the glasses were numbered because of the bar's name; no one knows which. Judd assures me that the numbers are not obscure homosexual codes, nor are certain glasses reserved for certain customers. It is merely a gimmick. There are men of all ages, from those who look too young to be in a bar ("chickens," I am informed) to quite elderly types ("chicken hawks"). I see three Blacks during the course of the evening. I am the only female.

Judd points out a man standing at the bar who wears a black leather open vest over a tight white T-shirt. He is moving up and down the bar, talking to various people. "That's Gene, a noted butch hustler around town. He gets fifty dollars a trick." He then points out a tall man further down the bar. "See the man with the makeup? He's called a nelly or a fluff. Nellies want to be passive and play the female role, butches want to play the male role of aggression." Indeed, there is a man with plucked eyebrows and faint tinges of makeup, a little white around the eyes, a little rosiness on the cheeks and lips. People are talking to the butch, but studiously ignoring the nelly.

"I don't believe that all forms of sexual expression are equal," Judd says sternly. "I believe that there are parameters and values—not necessarily those of society as a whole, but you must have your own values and your own integrity. I went to Griff's [a major leather-and-Levi's bar where Derrick has said he will take me only if I go in drag], and there were all these men dressed up in leather, with caps with buttons on them to clue you into what kind of sex they liked, and they were all talking about making curtains and taking piano lessons. It's grotesque. People who are ribbon clerks by day dressing up as motorcycle riders by night!"

"Role playing is seventies America," Derrick interjects. "Role playing is unhealthy," Judd answers. "Go to the Blue Parrot and see everybody in uniform. I have no respect for people in costumes. I call them the West Hollywood clones."

"Then why go there?" I've been told that he does.

"To pick up somebody. That's why you go to gay places. To meet people. To have the maitre d' know you and the waiter know you. To be 'in.' But I hate myself for being there every time I go."

"Judd would never admit that he went to the baths," Sal has said, "so don't ask him that, he'll clam up." "Do you go to the baths?" I ask nevertheless.

"Of course. But only to 8709. It's a private club and it gets the pretty people. The oldies and the fatties go to public places, and most of them are pure sleaze. When I was at Princeton, I went to the Everhard Baths in New York and it was so dirty and rank that it turned me off baths for years. New York was far ahead of Los Angeles on the baths scene. But when Los Angeles finally got into it, it did it better."

"Los Angeles's contribution to the baths was carpets," Derrick says.

"No," Judd replies, "California's contribution was cleanliness. Everything in New York was damp and dank and disgusting.

"The largest and cleanest place is 8709," he continues. "You walk up the stairs to a locked door with a buzzer and a window with a grill—it's just like a speakeasy. You present your membership card, and then you pay four or five dollars, depending on which facilities you want. Membership is cheap, maybe ten or twelve dollars per year, so you pay each time you go, and the fee varies according to the time of year and how old you are."

"How *old* you are?"

"Of course. Hot young kids get discounted memberships and entrance fees, because that's the kind of clientele that makes a place."

"You have to be twenty-one," Derrick interrupts.

Judd ignores him. "You can have a private room, which really is just a cubicle, but there are beds built into the walls and they have real sheets and they're clean. Or you can just rent a locker and undress in public. There are showers and orgy rooms and mirrored mazes—that's to heighten the sense of pursuit."

"Are there different levels, like the old Continental Baths in New York, with pools on some floors and rooms on others?"

"Pools?" Judd says, startled. "There are no pools at 8709. Did you think baths actually were *baths?*"

Sal already has told me something of 8709, but he didn't tell me there were no baths. He said that it is designed to appeal to a variety of fantasies: "There's a barracks room done in military colors and insignia, with rows of cots, a jail with bars and cells all painted in shades of gray, a room for exhibitionists with windows and mirrors and lots of lights. And there's a toy room, not quite S&M, but close. But the best thing," Sal said, "is that every bunk or cot or whatever has a fitted sheet—and they're all *designer sheets!* Vera, Bill Blass, the signatures are on every sheet!"

Sal is an actor, easily recognizable as such—not because the face is familiar, but because of the look, the manner, the deep voice that could melt metal. He is winning and charming in that nice-tough Italian way, and he exudes masculinity. He came from New York to Los Angeles to pursue his career.

"God," he says, "I went into shock when I first came out here. In New York the competition is on an intellectual level. Out here it's on a purely physical level—everybody is slim and tan and gorgeous, and if you're not, nobody looks at you. It's very rejecting. At first, I just went to the baths all the time, trying to adjust.

"Of course," he adds, "I hadn't really accepted my homosexuality when I came out here. I think, in the long run, the California cult of the body helped me to come to terms with my sexuality. I mean, it's not just gays who are concerned with the physical, everybody is. And the attitude here is such that just about any lifestyle is acceptable." Learning that Derrick has called him the hottest of the hot, Sal laughs heartily.

"Well maybe. Maybe I *was*. I was a new face and a new body when I came here from New York. I knew a couple of people who invited me to a couple of parties, and suddenly *everyone* was inviting me. I wanted to be accepted for my brains, not just what I looked like. But I took it while it was available. It was interesting.

"I don't know if that kind of entertaining is done as much now," he says. "The parties would start on Sunday at noon, with drinks and snacks and dope around the pool. Then about seven dinner would be served, and at eight-thirty there'd be a screening of a movie. It was all very lavish, crab and shrimp and lobster, five or more desserts—people competed to outdo each other. My very favorite was a very pretentious party in Beverly Hills, with parking attendants and a bar in the entrance patio and another at the pool. There were at least twelve people serving, there were tents with an incredible amount of lavish food and flowers, and real silver, china, linen. Finally you went to the dessert table, and there were silver tea and coffee pots and at least a dozen desserts, all from Michel Richard [the king of pastry in Los Angeles]. And on this table, with all this lavishness . . . there was a jar of Cremora with a spoon stuck in it! The Rolls in the driveway and a jar of Cremora on the dessert table. That's what I loved most—the combination of pretentiousness and lack of taste!

"That particular party was all gay males, but many were mixed, and I much preferred those. The sexual vibrations aren't as intense at a mixed party, so you can relax and have a good time. When it's all gay males it divides automatically into two groups, those who are sought after and those who are seeking. So you have your young, muscular pretties, posing usually—and then those who are pursuing, and making quite a spectacle of themselves usually. Actually, there's also a third group, the heavy drinkers and smokers. They hang around the kitchen sampling the food and pretending not to acknowledge what's going on."

Derrick has told me that dope is big among homosexuals, that everyone smokes pot or snaps open a capsule of butyl nitrate before going to a bar or disco, and that it's done openly at parties. "Oh, it depends on your era, like anything else," Sal says. "If you came out in the early sixties, it was a drinking environment. Late sixties to mid-seventies, it was all dope, really heavy using. Now the kids coming out have reverted to booze. It follows the same pattern as what's happened on college campuses—you know, it used to be all booze and fun, and then it became dope and political activism, and now it's booze and fun again. Homosexuals just reflect what's happening in their own times."

None of Derrick's group is especially politically active, except David, the young Jewish lawyer from Texas. He is good-looking, with an engaging grin and an easy laugh, and is very easy to be with. He did not come out until after he moved to Los Angeles, for the simple reason that he had no idea he was homosexual.

"I came out here with my fiancée," he says, laughing, "but we didn't move in together. As luck would have it, I knew two couples out here, both straight, but they lived in West Hollywood, so I moved into the same neighborhood to be near them. At first I didn't even realize that it was predominantly a homosexual neighborhood, and it took me a long time to recognize that I had those proclivities. But when I did, there was no trauma. My younger brother is gay; he came out while I was in college and it was a very painful and guilt-ridden thing and our parents were terribly upset. I think, since I sort of lived through that with him, that it took care of all those problems for me."

David works for a noted law firm. "The head of the firm is homosexual and is often involved in gay causes, so it wouldn't do my career any harm if they knew I was gay. But I've never mentioned it because it hasn't seemed important. I just work for the causes in my own way." He scoffs at Judd's analysis of the types of people who turn out for marches. "They're all serious people now, working hard for something they believe in. The best thing is that now gay women are getting involved in the same projects as men. It used to be so separated."

David's newest involvement is with the Gay Community

Services Center, where he has been accepted (only one out of about fifteen is) as a volunteer peer counselor. He is now going through training, which will last many weeks. Both men and women are in his training group, and he is excited about the challenge of giving counseling to women. He thinks of running for office, though there is a chance he may be offered a judgeship. A great amount of David's free time is spent helping gays, yet he seems much less involved in the gay lifestyle than Derrick's other friends. "I don't go to gay restaurants because I'm a vegetarian," he says, "and I don't smoke dope because I don't smoke. The only disco I go to is Oil Can Harry's in the Valley."

"Good God!" Derrick says.

Erin is the most obviously gay of all the gay men I know. He is just twenty-three, is tall as a basketball player, and bounces about like a puppy—in fact, the first thing you think of when you see him is an Afghan puppy—and he speaks in exaggerated faggy tones and loves to do takeoffs of "limp-wristed" types. Despite his Irish name, he comes from an Italian Catholic family in upstate New York. He has four brothers and one sister. All six children are homosexual.

I met him not through Derrick or any of his hot friends, but because he came to paint my house. He is the only person I know who belongs to the newest, the hottest, the most "in" private club (at this writing, as must always be said), The Probe. At this particular time he also is working at the club.

"Women cannot get into places like The Probe," Judd told me.

"You want to go to The Probe?" Erin asks me gleefully. "Hey, I can get you in. When do you want to go? This Saturday? Midnight is best, if you don't mind listening to conversations that don't make much sense. I mean, everybody is *so stoned!* But you'll love it, you'll absolutely *love* it. Hey, that's great! I can't wait!"

Saturday arrives and something has occurred that makes it impossible to keep our appointment. At about a quarter to midnight, I telephone The Probe.

The man answering the phone is brusque to the point of being rude. "Erin? Erin who?"

"Erin who watches the upstairs door."

"Listen, I haven't got time to hunt people down. Call Erin on his own time."

I never yell.

"Stop!" I yell, realizing that he is about to hang up. "Just wait a minute!" and find out that, indeed, he waits. "I'm supposed to meet Erin at the door at midnight. I can't make it. I don't want him standing there all night waiting for me."

"Oh my God," the voice says, "are you the Writer?"

"Yes."

"You mean you can't come?"

"Not tonight."

"When can you come? You will come, won't you?"

"Next Saturday at midnight. Definitely. Tell Erin."

"I'll find him right now. I'll tell him. Listen, I'm the owner, I'll meet you myself next Saturday. I'll be at the door."

The word *writer* is better than *open sesame* for opening many doors. Even the doors to private clubs.

Derrick has told me, sadly, that gays are fickle, that they will go to a place for a few weeks or months and then drop it, that some truly great places, such as Dude City, died because they didn't get support. Derrick is wrong, at least about Dude City.

Ray Sanchez, owner of The Probe, which is on Highland Avenue near Melrose at the exact site of what once was Dude City and later the Paradise Ballroom, was the owner of both of those places. He knows that it is Los Angeles that is fickle; that to be hot you've got to keep moving. "I opened the first disco in California in 1969," he told me, "a place called the Gas Station. The Probe is the first private club I've tried, and it's much more difficult because you have to build a core of regulars. People come and then stop coming, so you need that core to sustain the business."

Sanchez indeed is at the door to greet me when I arrive at midnight the following Saturday. There is a huge crowd, but he spots me. "You the Writer?" he yells across the crowd. I nod. "Let her through, let her through!" he commands. "Go right on up. Erin's at the top of the stairs waiting for you. Somebody'll get you a drink, have whatever you want, it's all on the house. Come back and talk to me when you're finished up there."

I walk down the hallway to a door that is another checkpoint. "You the Writer?" the guard asks. I'm beginning to believe it. "Go right on up," he says. "Erin's waiting for you."

Music blasts. The first clamor of disco music always shocks. Strobes flash. Et cetera. I am getting jaded. Erin comes bouncing down the stairs, hugs me, kisses me, as full of excitement as if he hadn't seen me for months. In fact, he saw me yesterday. He leads me to his station, a perch outside the DJ's booth with a fine view of the dance floor below. The DJ waves out at me. Someone brings another stool. A waiter rushes upstairs. "What would you like? Have anything, it's on the house." "This is my friend, this is my friend," Erin says happily to everyone who passes by. "Isn't it great?" he says to me. "Isn't it *just great?*"

The room below is small and it is packed, and though no one seems ever to leave the floor, the people who keep coming in in a steady stream seem to be absorbed into the gyrating crowd with no difficulty. The music never stops.

There had been a costume party earlier, and apparently someone made arrangements ahead of time, for everyone appearing in costume simply is waved in, no I.D.'s checked, no names asked for. And so there are "soldiers" on the floor and "sailors" and "cowboys." Three men, very tall and muscular, are wearing huge high-piled wigs, lots of makeup, spike-heeled shoes, rolled socks plus rolled-to-the-thigh black nylons, black bikini bras and panties and filmy black short negligees. They are dancing, stony-faced and stiltedly, at the edge of the floor. "Don't know how to move with their costumes on," someone behind me says disdainfully. I see a lovely woman with cream-colored silky long hair, wearing a cream silk shirt and silver pants. "That's a guy," Erin says.

Mostly, the crowd looks exactly like that at Studio One: a

few pretty women, a few Blacks and Chicanos and Orientals, mostly Caucasian men in tank tops or T-shirts or bare-chested. Two differences: the men here are slightly older than at Studio One, and there is relatively little posing. "Look at them, look at them!" Erin exhorts. Aren't they a great crowd? So different from other places. Really *beautiful* people!"

Waiters keep rushing back to see if I want more drinks. Friends of Erin come up to say hello to him, with the usual greeting, a bear hug and a fanny pat, and everyone is excessively friendly to me. Finally Erin says, "Come on, let's go down and dance. You never get the real feeling of a place until you're on the floor."

"You can dance me out," I tell him. "It's nearly two, and I want to talk to Ray Sanchez." And so, out we dance.

Sanchez stands, as he. stands every night, Wednesday through Sunday, at the booth at the front door. He has an immense list with names on it. He is, quite literally, being mobbed by people trying to come in. "No, your name isn't on the list," he tells an attractive young man. "Don't go on the street and try to solicit a member," he warns him. "If you come back tonight I won't let you in." More people are turned away than are allowed in. He recognizes every member and waves each past, but studiously checks I.D.'s of everyone else. "Hey, when are you going to join?" he asks an older man, but waves him through. Oddly, it is mostly pretty young men he turns away, often letting pretty young women through, even though their names are not on the list. "It works like this," he tells me, between phone calls, between greetings, between I.D. checks (I now understand why he was brusque on the phone), "if a member calls to tell me some of his friends are coming, I put their names on the list. But he has to call before ten P.M. That way, no one can get in by stopping a member on the street and asking him to slip him through."

He is so busy, we can only talk in snatches. "You have to have a member sponsor you to join," he manages to explain, "and there's a waiting list for membership, though we've only been open four months." Later, "Sunday night is the biggest,

Saturday night is big, Friday it's hit or miss and week nights are slow. Ninety-five percent of the people take drugs of some sort before they come here, only a few are drinkers." Still later, "God, this is hard. A private club really is hard." Nearly every person who passes by in this long two A.M. line says hello to me.

"You know," Sanchez says to me, as somebody douses a cigarette in his drink, "if I were a boozer or doper, I'd be smashed on both after an evening at the door. Luckily, I don't care for either. Boy, do you need patience."

I walk outside to find my husband leaning against the car, grinning (we had been to a dinner party, so he decided to drive me directly to The Probe). "Have you just been standing here for two hours?" I ask, feeling guilty.

"No, I went to that coffee shop on the corner and had a couple of cups of coffee. You know, every single person in there was homosexual, I think."

"Of course," I answer, smug in my expertise. "That's one of the top gay hangouts in town."

"It's been an interesting evening," he says. "All those people in costumes. And a guy came up to me and said, 'Are you a member?' So I said, 'No, are you?' And he said, 'Only my hairdresser knows for sure.' 'Well, then, where's your hairdresser?' I asked him, and he said, 'One never knows. Are you sure you're not a member? You look like one.' I thanked him. After all, this is supposed to be the hottest private club in town, isn't it?" Yes.

There are many different homosexual scenes in Los Angeles. There are the leather-and-Levi's places, such as the Stud and Griff's, the places Derrick has said he would take me only in drag—not because a woman would not be allowed in, but because her presence would change the mood. These are the places where key codes and handkerchief codes and button codes are used—for example, the fact that a man lets his handkerchief or his key chain hang out of his left rear pocket indicates that he is interested in one type of sex, while the right rear pocket indicates a different preference. The color of the handkerchief or the number of keys on the chain also have sexual meanings. There are places that cater to what Derrick and his friends call the drag queen crowd, places that hold contests for "emperors" and "empresses" and "dukes" and "duchesses" for various "courts"—a clubby approach found primarily in distant suburban areas such as Downey and Monrovia. There are places whose publicity hints at sado-masochism, though Derrick says nothing "really tough" goes on in Los Angeles, nothing to match New York's most extremist S&M bars, such as The Anvil and The Toilet. A publication called *Data Boy* gives all the information about gay bars and clubs for both Los Angeles and San Francisco. Available free in bars, it is filled with near-pornographic ads and raunchy columns such as "Trash from the Old City" and "Midnight Cowboy"; but it is a serious publication editorially, reprinting articles from other publications that are of interest to the gay community, and announcing upcoming events both gay and straight. All of Derrick's friends deplore its sleazy look, but most of them read it regularly.

"Robertson is a cruising street after the bars close," I have been told, "not for prostitutes, just for people who haven't scored in the bars." This north-south street is Decorator Row. "The beach areas are pretty hot, but since Pacific Ocean Park [an amusement park] was torn down it's not dangerous anymore." "The police really cleaned up Selma [Hollywood]— all the chickens used to hang out in front of that church, waiting for the hawks, but there's no action there now." "There's no police hassle now, none at all. All they do is disperse."

Derrick drives me through West Hollywood, pointing out the gay hangouts. Drake's Coffee Shop close to Ah Men, the longest-lived homosexual clothing store in the city. Drake's Too, farther east on Santa Monica. Then the spate of leather-and-Levi's bars: Rascals, the Spike, the Rusty Nail, the Eagle, the Jaguar. "The Spotlight Room in Hollywood is a hustler bar," he says, "but nobody I know would go into Hollywood, West Hollywood is much classier." He adds, "Every single area in town has its gay scene, but the scene reflects the type of people who live there. I could have taken you to the Valley—it's much closer over the freeway than West Hollywood. But I never, never go to the Valley. Jesus, I wouldn't dream of living there, so why go to a bar there? Valley gays are just like Valley straights." He shudders. "But there are a lot of scenes that are interesting. I could show you a dozen gay scenes, all different."

"Los Angeles attracts gays because it's a hedonistic place by nature," Judd says. "You've no idea of the guilt trips that go on among homosexuals. It's especially hard for the Texans and the East Coast Italians, because Daddy was always doing his macho number. So they had to escape, and a lot of them escaped out here. Here the homosexual can blend right in and not feel so guilty. The whole city is on a hedonistic high."

8

"Lookin' Good" in Beverly Hills

"Lookin' good!"

I can't remember ever using the expression, ever even hearing it that I particularly noticed. Yet now I find myself saying it. Admiring the bathroom that I have just painted terra cotta: "Lookin' good!" I say to myself. Remarking on the tan I finally achieved after a rainy spring: "Lookin' good!" Every time I say it I think of Jackie Rubinstein, the Girl from Beverly Hills.

Her name is not really Jackie, but it doesn't matter, because all Jewish girls of her era were named Jackie or Debbie or Sherrie. Her name is not Rubinstein, either, but that is close enough. She is not a girl and she is not from Beverly Hills; at least, she wasn't born there. But she has a childlike fragile quality and a voice that dies into whispers, and she will seem like a little girl even when she is old. And she was raised in Beverly Hills, Beverly Hills formed her, molded her values and even, in the way a place like that has of doing, her traditions; created the cocoon from which her fabulous marriage could emerge, and, equally, the type of abyss into which it could fall; created, to the nth of a degree, her image. Although she will tell you that she created the image herself.

The image, nothing surprising, is this: She is a mover and a shaker of the kind rarely found outside politics or high social echelons. Name a chic shop on Rodeo or Camden, Dorso's, say, or the Right Bank Clothing Company, it was due to her patronage that they became chic. Name a caterer, take Milton, he is the most famous: "Milton admires me. I taught him some things. I was one of the first to use him."

Think of a style, any one, short skirts or long, tough chic, the thrift shop look, the peasant look, she was there first: "I guess I was just very individual. I'd buy Galanos or Gernreich samples when nobody had ever heard of them. Gene Shacove, *Shampoo* was about him, you know, was my hairdresser in *college!*, nobody knew him then." Pick a fashion in collecting, pre-Columbian art, classic cars, soft sculpture, Art Deco, she was into it before anyone else. This last claim is verifiable—she and her handsome, wealthy, insecure, mixed-up ex-husband were noted young collectors on the California scene. "I knew nothing about it, I had no training, but I did have an eye. The curator of a famous museum told me, 'You have an incredible eye.'" Which is not to say that the rest is not true as well, or at least somewhat true. Her picture has been in fashion magazines and she has been photographed among the movers and shakers. I asked about her at the shops along Rodeo. "Jackie Rubinstein?" Pause. "Oh yes. Yes, she's been in here." The image does exist. It's just that such eager insistence on the image tends to strain credulity.

"Of course I don't care about those things," she will tell you. "I just did them; if people paid attention it was just an accident. They seemed to, you know, just follow my lead." The voice whispers off, down to the quality of the gentlest breeze.

"Lookin' good!" When she says this her voice picks up stamina, there is a buoyancy to it. She is showing me the picture of her ex-husband; young, he looks like a young Arthur Kennedy; he is clean-shaven and short-haired and wearing a tuxedo; he is standing with his arm around a minor film director, here also young, clean-shaven, short-haired and tuxedoed; both are grinning. It is only later, when the director has, presumably, dragged him down to depths barely hinted at—drugs, nut cults,—and the pictures show him bearded, long-haired, solemn, that he has lost her approbation; no doubt deservedly. But for now, "Lookin' good!"

There are very few sections of Los Angeles today that have a distinct image, that instantly identify the background and economic status of the people who live there. More than most cities, we have tended to tear down the old and build up the new in a regular pattern over the years, so that many of the original dividing lines have blurred. There are, of course, exceptions: San Marino has kept its social distinction, East Los Angeles and Watts their ethnic identities. One of the major exceptions is Beverly Hills.

Beverly Hills is not Los Angeles and never has been. It is a five-and-one-half-square-mile oasis with such odd boundary lines that at certain places you can cross the street and be in another city. It extends just beyond La Cienega to the east, just beyond Olympic to the south, just beyond the point where Wilshire and Santa Monica cross to the west. Northward, it zigzags all over the canyons—parts of Benedict and Coldwater canyons are in, Franklin Canyon, between the other two, is out. Very oddly, you can have a Beverly Hills postal address in some of these hill areas without actually living in the city or enjoying any of its other services. People will spend thousands more on a house to have that address.

It is a separate city with a separate government, taxes, and school system. It is in most ways polarized from its surrounding areas, and in many ways provincial. The police in Beverly Hills are particularly fierce over civil disturbances: an unduly loud car muffler may get you a ticket; speeding even slightly over the very low speed limits certainly will do so. It is a joke, but no joke, that if you walk the residential streets at night you may be stopped for questioning, and even with a good explanation, picked up for loitering. And in an area where parking has always been at a premium, a recent regulation, petitioned by the citizens after the new Neiman-Marcus store was built on Wilshire, prohibits parking on the side streets unless you are a resident and have a verifying sticker on your windshield.

Beverly Hills has always been a place where many things are better than in Los Angeles. The school system is better; every grade at least a year ahead of the same grade in an L.A. school. The police protection is better; the city had nightly patrols long before any area in Los Angeles found it useful to hire private patrol companies, as so many do now. The library, in a magnificent rococo building, is nearly a match for the big main branch of the Los Angeles Public Library, though it is not truly "public" since it charges a yearly use fee. The streets are prettier: the exclusive residential areas north of Santa Monica Boulevard have streets wider than most boulevards, while the north side of Santa Monica itself, separating the business and residential areas, incorporates a twenty-block-long park.

Property taxes have always been lower in Beverly Hills, and for a very long time so were rentals for the apartments south of Wilshire. Even the apartments were prettier than those in Los Angeles—roomy two-story triplexes, attached only at one wall and facing broad courtyards. South-of-Wilshire, in fact, is not the place to live—the houses are small and there are all those apartments and the people who live north of Santa Monica tend to feel that that section scarcely belongs in the city. But even south-of-Wilshire has the good schools and the good city services; and it has the Beverly Hills address, which is worth a good deal in the eyes of the world.

If part of the Beverly Hills image is elite, part of it is garishly nouveau riche. In the days before Americans discovered European car chic, Cadillacs grazed at the edge of every pasture-sized lawn like herds of prize bulls. In the daytimes the streets were littered with gardeners hosing down the immense circular driveways, and with maids pushing baby carriages or walking toddlers. (Whatever happened to those children after the age of four or five? One never saw any of the other signs of childhood—bicycles abandoned at curbside, or jump ropes or balls.) The ladies who shopped at I. Magnin's or Saks or Haggarty's (now gone) or W. & J. Sloane sported Palm Springs tans and beehive hairdos and tight slacks, and they carried the requisite toy poodle. If one saw a well-dressed woman, she was usually a visitor from Los Angeles. One saw very few men on those streets because there were very few office buildings. Teenagers commuted the few blocks to Beverly Hills High School in their own expensive cars; their lunches were sandwiches ordered from Jurgensen's Fine Foods and delivered to the house each morning.

Money has always been the prime requirement for living in Beverly Hills, and from the very beginning it was new money. Originally the city was a movie star colony. It was close to the major studios, yet offered ample room for building immense mansions on fabulous estates. Its first mayor was Will Rogers. As time passed, owning property there became synonymous with "having it made." Doctors, lawyers and other professionals succumbed to the symbol as readily as film people, and each era brought its own complement of new successes—rock stars and TV directors, followed by hairdressers and real estate agents.

It is almost entirely a Caucasian community, though not so much Wasp as Jewish; Latinos, Blacks and Orientals seen in the neighborhood generally are maids, chauffeurs or gardeners. Except for the business streets, Beverly Hills has been virtually untouched by the kind of tearing down and building up that has gone on in Los Angeles. The original lifestyle is maintained with blithe unconcern for such contemporary problems as fuel, energy and water shortages: the big houses in their truly fascinating variety of styles still shine by night; the parklike lawns still drink their massive doses of water; the big cars still abound, though today they are more likely to be BMWs or Mercedes or Rolls than Cadillacs.

It was in this Beverly Hills, this gaudy city glossed with elegance, that Jackie Rubinstein grew up.

The family moved out from New York when Jackie was five, did not immediately settle in Beverly Hills, settled in fact (dear God!) in the Valley. The father, a financial manager, quickly made connections in the film industry and soon he began "hanging out with the Sinatras and so on and so forth," in Jackie's words. A Valley address was not suitable for keeping this sort of company. Her thirty-odd years of Beverly Hills life were about to begin.

Jackie Rubinstein personifies ambivalence. It has probably always been part of her nature; it certainly is part of her charm. Every positive statement is followed by its negative; sunny moments by darker moods; every smile seems framed by the possibility of tears. Thus the years at Beverly Hills High School are described as both an idyll and something of a torture. "I guess as a teenager, no matter what, you go through a lot of pain. My impression is that in those days I was an outsider trying to make my way in." Then, "I was very involved, I was in a lot of clubs and I had the lead in my senior play. I met my husband when I was fifteen and he was seventeen and a half, a senior." Somehow it does not sound so traumatic, snagging, at Lolita age, the handsome scion of one of the wealthiest families around; and yet, remembering, her face reflects a certain amount of pain and (another ambivalence) shyness mingled with toughness.

She might have become an actress. "There was a noted director, he was a client of my father's, and he wanted to put me into the movies out at Fox." She might have become a singer. "I took my little girls to a singing teacher, and this woman just became totally fascinated with me and with my voice quality, and I was told that I should be the singer." She might have become an artist. "At one point I took a little art class, from an artist who's dead now, and he ran around and told all the local artists what talent I had." She might have become a decorator or an interior designer. "A lot of people have asked me, it's all out there, I'd have instant clients . . . the editor from *Vogue* called me from New York one day, she said, 'I was told that you're the only lady with taste in that city.'" *Might have been.* She is eager to remember what might have been. But then, isn't everyone?

A sunny day. A house just at the edge of Beverly Hills, as she is now at the edge of the life that once was. The street has impressive beginnings, but dwindles off into an area of pleasant little California ranch-style houses. This one is a little larger than some: there is a semicircle of driveway at the front; the usual shiny tropical plants, palms and philodendron, edge the lawn; the usual small Mercedes sits, lonely, in the two-car garage to the side. She opens the double front doors and seems surprised to see me, though she has invited me.

She is peach colored; more exactly, peach-beige. That is the color of her velour jumpsuit, but it also is the color of her skin;

a soft, glowing peach-beige, the color you always hope you will find inside a new bottle of makeup. Her eyes are long-lashed and that clear color that is almost green. Her hair is the dark brown that looks black except in direct sunlight; it is piled high on her head, held by a barette that she readjusts constantly. Wisps of curls escape, dangle by her ears and the nape of her neck. She stands in the doorway and blinks at the sunlight; she looks like a sleepy child confused at having to face a stranger.

The house is cool inside, larger than it seemed from the front, and there is a sense of aloneness about it, as though she has been here by herself for a long while. She drifts rather aimlessly about, and the sense of drifting seems to have to do with more than her actual movements. "Would you like a drink? A glass of wine, some coffee? Would you like to sit on the couch or shall we sit at a table? Is the den all right? We could go out by the pool if you prefer." The vulnerability, the childlike quality are both intriguing and bothersome. This is not, precisely, the essence of Beverly Hills.

But then the photographs. The miles of photographs, the years of photographs; book upon book of them all right at hand, under the table next to the couch. They tell the story of her life, from sex kitten through smart divorcée, and in none of them, not one of them, does she look vulnerable. What she does look is totally different in every sequence of pictures. She is always lean and tan, and she is always flashing a thousand-watt Beverly Hills smile; her hair may be short or long, smooth or frizzed, but it always appears midnight black; yet she could pass for ten, fifteen, twenty different people.

"You look so different," I have to comment, hoping she doesn't think I am saying that she looks older now, or less attractive. But that wouldn't enter her mind. "Every picture. Every picture is different. I have to change." Perhaps this woman today, who virtually melts into the peach-beige leather couch, whose voice fades and fades so that eventually I have to move closer to catch her words, and who now seems not just vulnerable but also nervous—rubbing and scratching her long thin hands, nuzzling a large white orange-eyed Persian cat, and cooing to it as one would to a baby—perhaps this is just the latest change, the latest in a remarkable series of personas.

"I have charisma," she says suddenly, a startling remark from a nervous, hand-scratching girl-woman. "I can do anything," she says.

"Who are your friends?" I ask just as suddenly, hoping to leap to the good stuff, the big names.

"Everybody," she says. Then, "Nobody. I have no friends." She chuckles softly. There is pride in her voice.

The first book, the first picture. And one sees why the girl who can do anything, might have been anything, followed instead the path that she did. It is such a Beverly Hills picture. It is just before her Sweet Sixteen Party, such a Beverly Hills event, the nouveau-riche answer to the debutante ball. She is wearing a turquoise-colored tulle dress, off-the-shoulder style. She is sitting on something that probably could not have been found anywhere in the world in the late fifties except in Beverly Hills: a large *round* brocaded white satin love seat.

The next picture with Ronn, the husband-to-be; then lots of pictures of both families—Sweet Sixteen and that background. "I had a strict kind of father, really, I was supposed to just get married, that's all, raise a family, and that's what I did. I went from home to home." You look at the father's face, kind enough but determined looking, the overly protective Jewish father who would not let a famous director make an actress of his daughter, the father who recognized the perfect catch for her when he saw it. From mid-high school on, she was encouraged by both sets of parents to run in and out of the Rubinstein mansion as readily as she ran in and out of her own nearby house. There is no other direction her life could have taken; though her ambivalence caused her to rock the boat a bit.

She went with Ronn for six years, tried a couple of semesters at USC, a couple at UCLA ("Psychology, sociology, that sort of thing"), was even—definitely not a Beverly Hills sort of thing— a dental assistant for a brief time. "I enjoy anything while I'm learning it. But my mother couldn't stand that uniform." During all this time, Ronn begged her to marry him. One night there was a formal proposal, both sets of parents waiting for the answer. She said yes. Then she went up to her room and, "I started shaking. I wasn't ready, I wanted to try my wings. I called him at home as soon as I knew he'd be back there and told him I just couldn't do it. His mother was furious! She sent him away on a long trip to get over me. Then when he came back we got engaged." So much for rebellion.

The photographs show the dream wedding, Beverly Hills style, all the trimmings, why not? Son of one of the wealthiest manufacturers in the country, daughter of a financial wizard with film industry clients. Dream honeymoon: Caribbean cruise, of course; and two handsome rich kids looking like models for an ad on the good life—looking happy, looking in love. Lookin' good!

Then the babies come along, three little girls one after the other, lots and lots of pictures in the albums. One of Jackie in a bikini, a real cheesecake shot, another in a bubble bath, both "right after I had my second daughter." Typical proud husband shots, and she is looking very good indeed. There is a small house, Beverly Hills of course, bought by the folks of course, but suitable for a young couple just starting out. Just barely starting out on the collecting mania, too—a small pre-Columbian piece is seen in the background of one picture. It seems very unpretentious, very unspoiled—an average young family with, perhaps, more money than average.

It all happened so quickly: the bright, unspoiled beginnings; the middle part, when they started acting like rich kids, building the big house to show off the growing collections, giving the big parties for the big people; and then the dissolution, meanness and pettiness, tough lawyers, a long messy divorce. Nine years from start to finish.

Did the end begin when she began to encourage his taste for collecting? "He was always creative and I wanted to help him bring that out. So we started going to galleries and auctions— just to look, you know, but when he seemed to be interested in something, I would say, 'Well, why don't you buy it?' And so he did. This was the start of the car collection." Ronn, standing proudly beside an early thirties Bentley drop-head coupé.

"Then of course the house was created and it was a work of art in itself, it was like a sculpture." They hired a young architect with whom they had gone to school. "The house was so different that the neighborhood hated it, and the architect's work was banned from Beverly Hills. A few years later some board of architects called me and asked if a group of them could visit the house, they were studying this architect's work. Isn't that darling?" She does not mention the architect's name, and the implications are that she discovered him, that she herself was responsible for the house being like a sculpture, that she had done something so daring that it outraged an entire city; and that by the time it was accepted, she had moved on.

She finds the photographs of the house, and it is indeed a work of art: pure lines, strong verticals, powerful without being overpowering. Pool, tennis court, gardens, patios, all are design elements; yet nothing seems self-conscious; and the effect of the whole is sculptural, as she has said. It is difficult to believe that any city was so backward in the mid-sixties that it could not accept this. And yet this is Beverly Hills, where provincialism can run deep; and no one knows this city better than Jackie Rubinstein.

Did the new life, then, ruin the idyll? Did the mover and shaker shake herself out of paradise? "I had parties and *Vogue* was there and *Women's Wear* was there and the film people and the social . . . they were all there, okay? I gave a party for a very noted director and I *told* Milton how everything would be, nobody would ever come in and tell me what they were going to do, I would tell them. And it was written up and photographed and all that . . ." The voice has gone again from strong to fading, the face is wistful with memories. For the good times? Or for the fact that they led to the bad times?

But perhaps it was when she encouraged him to leave the family business that it began to go awry. "He was just sleeping at the office, he was so bored. He was interested in creative things, in music and art and film, so finally I just said to him, 'Look, why don't you quit the business and do what you want to do?' And he did."

Started writing music reviews for minor magazines.

"Did the family mind?"

"Nobody cared."

"Were there any money problems?" Small music magazines are not noted for paying their writers well. But what a dumb question.

"No problem. That never was a problem."

But that was the end of it, short and not sweet. "He was interested in films and I encouraged him. That's when he became very close with this director—they started going way out. And then he was under a bad influence from a friend he went to school with, a man who was very jealous of me. And then he was offered a chance to go to Europe to learn movie making, and he wanted me to go, but I said no. I wanted him to learn, finally, to stand on his own feet." One has to wonder why she didn't ever just keep her mouth shut. "And he got in with more bad people, with drugs and things. And then he came back and we separated.

"I always thought we'd get together again. I always thought he'd find himself. But he just kept going into these things, est and Esalen and all the self-help things, and he just kept on searching and searching. Now he lives in Europe and he married this girl he'd been living with." End of dream.

The ending was not quite that easy. "What happened was he got this lawyer who even the family now admits was a . . . pig! A sleazy, alley-fighting, crude . . . Ronn was very weak. So we went to court. I didn't want to go. I said, 'Why don't you just take this and I'll take that—or you take everything, I don't care.' And he said, 'Oh Jackie'—he was very cute and sweet but he said, 'Oh Jackie, it's all a game. Life's a game.' So we had this trial, the longest trial in I don't know how many years. It was awful."

"All the community property—I suppose that's why it went on so long?"

Laughter, not pleasant. "There was no community property. You know why? Because he never earned a dime. The money he had, he'd had before we were married. So what we were fighting over was all his. The house, built with his money. The collections, bought with his money. That's what that lawyer went for. All I know is, I married a sweet young fellow I went to school with, and I was a nice person, I was a good wife, I set him free . . . I come from a very, very lovely family, my parents now are married forty-six years, they still hold hands . . . and there we were fighting, and it was shabby, dirty, awful."

The thin hands are worrying the dark hair. "Anyhow, I finally got half the proceeds from the house and half after we sold the different collections—*after* he got his initial investments, plus interest, back! I make it all *look* fabulous, because I have a knack for that, but . . ."

"So that's it?" I ask, not without sympathy. "That's what you've been living on since the divorce?"

"Yep! That's it! Alimony and child support and that."

And that is the story of the Girl from Beverly Hills.

Or most of it. We should not leave out the Antonioni sequence. "We were invited to a special screening of *Blowup* and he was to be present. I knew how anxious Ronn was to get into films, so after the movie I went right up to Antonioni and introduced myself and invited him to the house . . . and he and thirty-five people canceled dinner at La Scala and came up. That's the kind of thing I could never do for myself, only for someone I loved." Later, after the separation, "I received a telegram saying Antonioni would be in town and he would love to have me show him the city. And he said he had admired our house and wanted to do a film there and so on. So I told him I had a wonderful story for him—about this young couple, you know, us, and what we had accomplished. And I said, 'I'll give you the story, and you can shoot it here, but you must make me a promise—at the end of the film you must blow up, I mean really blow up this house!' And do you know that his next film was *Zabriskie Point,* and it was about a young couple, and there was an explosion! And I was told that he picks your brain, you know."

We should not leave out the sequence about the European trips. She had never been anywhere alone before, but "I threw myself *right* out there, twice . . . in the same year. Was asked please to stay with so-and-so, he was the top agent for so-and-so. I don't like to stay with people, but I went to some dinner parties with them, one with James Jones, and Jimmy Jones and I rur-rur-rur [she makes gestures as though they were fighting]. I mean, he had tears in his eyes, we wound up in an intellectual thing and he started to cry . . . with *me!* at a party!"

We should not leave out this: "I was asked to star in a television series, but it was the wrong time in my life, and I didn't like the story. I was offered so many things in my life. So many things . . ." The voice fades.

And we should not leave out what has happened to Beverly Hills in these past years, the years since her heyday. Actually, only two things happened, but they were major. Some high-rise office buildings were built, giving Wilshire Boulevard a skyline and peopling the streets with more well-dressed business men and women than poodle-toting ladies. And Rodeo Drive came along and changed the tenor of the city that created Jackie Rubinstein.

The city part of the city is small. Essentially, it goes west less than a dozen blocks from Rexford Drive, and south only the three long blocks from Little Santa Monica to Wilshire on most streets. On Cañon are a few fine antique shops, most notably Peacock Alley, and Le Bistro, a restaurant much favored by film people. Beverly Drive, only two blocks west, is as tacky as they come. These business streets clearly reflect the city's dual image: fine jewelry shops flourish next to five-and-dimes; a Leed's Shoe Store (lowest price) has existed for years only a block or so from Joseph's (highest price imaginable); Elizabeth Arden and Amelia Grey and the Brown Derby pull in their customers, while just around the corner a Lerner's and a neighborhood coffee shop do the same.

Nate 'n Al's is here, the only delicatessen in southern California to come close to a New York–style deli; and Ye Little Club is here, where major musical talents have been discovered; and jt seems as though Dick Carroll's men's shop and Hunter's Bookstore and the Swiss Café, which serves cheese-and-onion pie at Friday lunch, have always been here. In between are hardware stores and pet shops and hairdressers and small boutiques that come and go; there is a supermarket and there is Jurgensen's Fine Foods, one of the most expensive places in the city; there is a department store so conservative that it features flannel nightgowns in the window, and there are men's shops so unconservative that they feature white ties with dark shirts. In its small way Beverly Hills has always been like a European city, mixing the elegant and the ostentatious and the ordinary haphazardly; catering at the same time to the wealthy, the tourist trade, and the person who lives around the corner and does his daily shopping there.

And then Rodeo Drive came along.

The street has always been there; it is only its personality that has changed. When Hermés opened its elegant shop on Rodeo some eight years ago, it was still a neighborhood street with a saddlery at one end. Then, almost overnight it seemed, it had so much international glitter that one had to wear sunglasses to walk along it. Suddenly, it became the rue du Faubourg de St.-Honoré of Los Angeles, and though few of us outside of Beverly Hills can afford its prices, we take some pride in its existence. It is a street traversed by an international set of people who have one thing in common: a very great deal of money. "Forty to forty-five percent of our customers are wealthy Japanese," says Francine Bardo, assistant manager of Hermés. "With them you don't have to make the sale, as you say, because they know the name and the quality. They buy a handbag for twelve hundred dollars and think they're getting a bargain basement price—because at Hermés in Tokyo it would cost three times as much."

The Rodeo Drive stories are entertaining. The actress who spent $2,000 on scarves in one fast whirl, then returned home to realize she had forgotten to buy the very one she wanted to wear that evening; she ordered the $86 scarf by phone, then paid $100 to a messenger service to deliver it. The insecure young Beverly Hills matron who bought a bargain-price sweater for $180 and came back the next day to ask advice on accessorizing it; $300 later she had one silk shirt, one silk scarf, and a much more secure feeling about her sweater. Or this, from Hermés. "Sometimes someone comes in, they have heard that Hermés is the best, and they say, 'I want a leather gift, I have a budget of two hundred and fifty dollars.' And extraordinary as it may seem, we have to turn them down—we have to send them to Gucci's, which we do."

"The stories are not exaggerated," says the manager of one of the great-name shops, who asked not to be identified. "People do come in and spend five or ten thousand dollars or more. But then, when you've spent half a million dollars for key money and to sign a lease and do a little remodeling, you expect to make it back." Key money! Los Angeles scarcely has heard the phrase; but Rodeo Drive knows what it means.

The advent of the new Rodeo Drive—the Rodeo of the Yves Saint Laurent Boutique and Georgio's and Ted Lapidus, of Adolfo and Zandra and Fred "le Joaillier"—caused the country's retailers to look at Beverly Hills in a new light. Fine eastern stores such as Brentano's and Bonwit Teller came to town, and in 1979 Texas's famed Neiman-Marcus joined them; among them, they changed the look and the mood of Wilshire Boulevard where it passes through this city. And it is true that the cocktails flow like wine and the wine flows like water along Rodeo; that there is valet parking at many stores for the Rolls and Ferraris. Chic has come to Beverly Hills, along with the Iranians and the Egyptians and the Saudis who have bought up many of its mansions. Nouveau riche still exists, but it is beginning to acquire a patina. The city is beginning to get used to its money.

And how does the Girl from Beverly Hills fit into this city which is moving so deliberately into internationalism, and seeking the future so eagerly? Well, she does not. She is thinking of leaving, by now may already have moved, not just out of her city, but out of the country as well. Beverly Hills has changed too much. So has she.

And so we should not leave out this footnote to her story: the solitude of the woman who once was so central to everything that happened here.

She sits in the house that is all hers, just hers. The daughters are away at school, the husband is long gone, even the housekeeper on whom she relied for so long has left. The great white Persian remains. "My angel," she says.

The house verifies the claims she has made for her taste. She bought it, she decorated it, and it is lovely—serene and uncluttered by any evidence of the collector's mania, except for some fine contemporary prints on the walls. There is an Oriental simplicity to it that seems very right for her lifestyle now. And the cleanliness! Dark wood floors gleam, floor-to-ceiling windows shine, beds are made with military precision. "I do it all myself. Just get to it, get it done. I really am a doer. People say, what do you do? At a party, you know, what do you do? And I don't know what to say. But you know, I've worked in offices, I've been around businesses and lawyers—God, I've seen enough of them!—and nobody's doing anything, everybody's faking it. I'd rather wash that window, stand back and see it shine."

Who are your friends? Everybody. Nobody. "You know, a friend once said, 'If Jackie ever leaves, she'll be *gone.*' And he was right. I'm five minutes from everything, but nobody knows where I am, they think I've left. When I bought this house I called Milton and he said, 'Where are you? What happened to you?' And I said, 'Well, I'm finally in a house again and I think I'll have a party.' I said, 'Monday night,' and he broke up; leave it to Jackie, nobody ever had done Monday night. And I set a date. And then, you know, I started to shake, just like when I said yes to getting married. And I called him back and I said, 'Milton, I can't do it. I just cannot do it.' This is my hideaway, this is mine, this is me, this is private. And do you know, I didn't have a party here until my oldest daughter turned Sweet Sixteen and my youngest daughter asked to be Bas Mitzvaed—just weeks apart. Then I did it, for that I could do it. See."

These pictures. Crowds of people, both families and yes, the ex-husband, beard and all. Sumptuous food, tables of it, trays of it: "This little place called Moveable Feast, no one had ever heard of them." The decorations done by Jackie. The invitations by Jackie. The poems written, and the poster blowups of each kid, and the T-shirts imprinted with appropriate slogans for each guest, all by Jackie. All loving hands at home, a little overdone perhaps, but rather sweet. Two parties back to back, and both done in the spirit that one would expect from Jackie Rubinstein.

But this. The last picture. Jackie and her oldest daughter in front of a microphone, in front of the crowd that includes Daddy too. "Yes, she was singing for the party. And then we sang together. I guess we kind of broke everyone up. We sang 'You and Me Against the World.' In tears. Yes."

In tears, perhaps. But she is standing there with her dark head up, flashing that Beverly Hills smile. And she's looking the world straight in the face. And even though it's all different now, even though everything has changed, the Girl from Beverly Hills still is lookin' good.

9

"I Am an American!"

October 4, 1871. The breathlessly hot days of September have passed, but the night air is balmy and there is a stirring of wind—a Santa Ana may be on the way. There is something about those winds, which occasionally rage up to nearly hurricane force, and which seem to carry some of the primitiveness of the desert with them: A restlessness precedes them. Perhaps it is a superstition, like the idea of moon-madness. Perhaps it is real.

For nearly twenty years now Los Angeles has been working hard to become both civilized and cultured. The first public school was erected in 1855. Now, there is a Library Association with a small reading room, a Masonic Lodge, a Hebrew Benevolent Society, a French Benevolent Society. There are St. Vincent's College and the Catholic Orphans' Society and the Sisters' Hospital. A newspaper, *The Star*, is printed in both English and Spanish. There is a Wells Fargo Office and a bank, and there is a railroad line all the way from San Pedro to the city. There even is a telegraph line.

There also is Nigger Alley—actually, Calle de Negros, but quickly Americanized. This is a pestilential place where shootings and stabbings occur frequently, where criminals fleeing the vigilantes of San Francisco find convenient hiding holes, where the sparse remnants of the original Yang-na Indians go every Saturday night to spend their week's wages. Every Monday they are rounded up into a corral and auctioned off to whatever employers will pay their fines for drunkenness; at the end of the week, they will be paid $1 or $2 or given a bottle of brandy and turned loose. Though Nigger Alley is the

141

worst section of town, there is much crime everywhere, and public executions vie with mob lynchings to dispose of the criminals. Despite its attempts to become civilized, Los Angeles, for nearly twenty years now, has been known as the toughest frontier town in America.

On this October night a mob of nearly five hundred has descended on Nigger Alley. They are searching for a criminal reputed to be Chinese. By the end of the evening, when the Santa Ana has begun to blow in earnest, scattering pepper tree leaves and papers through the Plaza, they have torn nearby Chinatown apart. They have looted everything they can lay their hands on. And they have lynched eighteen innocent Chinese.

The Chinese Massacre is horrible evidence that Los Angeles was far from civilized this late in the nineteenth century. It also is evidence that, despite the frontier situation of being thrown together with people from every different type of background, people still banded together against anyone who looked different from themselves.

Over a hundred years later, Mas, an American of Japanese descent, tells me, "There's just one problem. No matter how American you feel, no matter how you try to assimilate, you still look different."

The Chinese were the first Orientals to come to Los Angeles. They had worked in the gold fields up north, and on the railroads. Later, most headed for San Francisco; a few hundred drifted down here. As was consistent with their culture—and the (still persistent) Asian dream of going to a foreign country only long enough to earn the money to return home and become a landowner—they created their own section of the city, started small businesses, worked hard, and mingled mostly with one another. In many sections of the world, most especially Southeast Asia, the Chinese are disliked, and in some cases hated, because of these traits. In Los Angeles in the late 1800s, they were disliked only because they looked different.

Chinatown in Los Angeles is nothing like those of San Francisco or New York or many other major cities throughout the world. It is just a few dozen square blocks, a business center surrounded by a residential area. The business center runs from Broadway to Yale Street, with Hill Street in between, and in the two sections known as Old Chinatown, which are identified by tall gates with pagodalike tops, the streets are primarily pedestrian walkways. There is a wishing well, an exotic-looking temple, the usual restaurants and curio shops. Most of the restaurants feature Cantonese or southern-style cooking—General Lee's is one of the oldest and most attractive to tourists. There also are some fine antique shops, many of them with treasures of porcelain and fine wood pieces and jade carefully hidden away; the owners know the collectors and have no need to show their best wares to sightseers.

Outside the gates of Old Chinatown are the wonderful markets: the places where you can buy fifty-pound sacks of rice and three-tier bamboo steamers and every kind of Oriental sauce and canned goods imaginable; the usual and the unusual fresh vegetable; the ordinary and the exotic fish, seafood and meats. Large fresh shrimp, which may cost $5.75 a pound or more in other sections of town, are half that price here. A whole duck may be had for $3 or $4. Squid is positively cheap. And one could spend half a month trying all the different types of fish available, fish with strange names and shapes and unique tastes.

This business section known as New Chinatown has expanded lately. There is a large shopping mall of three levels featuring stores of all types, and the merchandise here generally is of a finer, less touristy quality. Restaurants are more venturesome too, and some northern Chinese food is available. The Hunan, for instance, features spicy dishes from that province, and a fried noodle dish available only at lunchtime is unique. Most of the shoppers and diners in this section of town are Chinese; the tourists generally don't venture beyond the exotic gates of the old sector.

It is said that of all the Orientals in Los Angeles, the Chinese care the least about assimilating. In fact, all the Orientals in the city—with the major exception of younger Japanese—tend to stick to their own communities, marry and socialize and do business within their own ethnic groups, cling tenaciously to their individual cultures. No doubt the Chinese win the prize, having been here longer and having had more opportunity than other Oriental groups to assimilate if they chose; but there is no indication that the equally tight enclaves of Koreans, Vietnamese or Thais would loosen up given an equal amount of time. Only the Japanese have fought for, and won, the title of hyphenated Americans; one almost never reads of Chinese-Americans, and never of Thai-, Korean- or Vietnamese-Americans.

Just a few blocks from Chinatown, ten or twelve at most, is Little Tokyo. Both of these Oriental sections, as well as the Mexican-American section of Olvera Street and the Plaza, are within the area known as the Civic Center, which is to say the heart of downtown Los Angeles. Unlike Chinatown, Little Tokyo does not include a large residential area; basically it is a couple of main streets and a few side streets with shops, cafés, restaurants and two large and relatively new hotels. The hotels have made tourists more aware of Little Tokyo—the New Otani, in fact, is now included on some guided tours—but no attempt has been made to Americanize the dozens of cafés that serve home-style Japanese cooking, such as soups thick with noodles and seafood or pork, and though the shops feature some tourist items, their basic appeal is to the hundreds of local Japanese who throng the streets daily. Tokyo Kaikan and Horikawa are the two restaurants that draw the largest numbers of Caucasians; the former features a sushi bar, tempura bar and cocktails; the latter is like a fine Tokyo restaurant, with a small nightclub, long sushi bar and a dining room that serves the highest level of Japanese cuisine. Angelinos were among the first Americans to learn to appreciate Japanese raw fish dishes such as sashimi and sushi, perhaps because Japanese people and their customs have been part of the community for such a long time—except, of course, during the war years.

Imagine this. You are an Angelino, born and raised. Your father and mother came from somewhere else, but in 1942 in

Los Angeles nearly everyone's parents had come from somewhere else. The only difference is that your parents came from Japan. No matter that they have lived here for thirty-some years. No matter that you are an American citizen. One morning the soldiers come.

You each are allowed to bring a few things that are important to you, but your younger brother is carrying his favorite toy, a cap pistol, and that is confiscated. It looks like a real gun, the soldiers think. There are nine in your family, and you are taken to a racetrack and put into the stalls for the horses until it is decided where to send you. You sleep on cots, on big sacks filled with straw, and the straw pokes through the sacks and prickles and makes you itch all over, and it is very dusty and everyone is sneezing. One day a truck arrives with real mattresses, and everyone is very happy; but only a few days later another truck comes and takes you away. You are put on a train—exciting! Your first train ride! You are let out in a desert, where there is nothing as far as the eye can see, except some tar-paper-covered barracks, fences, a guard tower. You are in Utah. Perhaps you are told this, or perhaps you find out later. When you are grown up and back in Los Angeles and being an American, it is a little difficult to remember the details. You were only six at the time.

Gaman. Gah-mahn. It is a very important word if your family is of Japanese origin. It means something like "keep your chin up," but it means a great deal more than that. It has something to do with saving face and with hanging on when things get tough, without letting anyone know that things are rough for you. "Things will get better sometime, so for now—*gaman.* Keep your mouth closed and your chin up."

Gaman helps when nine people live in two rooms whose combined size is, say, fifteen by fifteen, or maybe twenty by twenty, feet. There is tar paper on the outside of your barracks, but just the raw beams inside, no paneling, no insulation. So it is very cold in winter and very hot in summer. But—*gaman*—look at this! We can use the beams for shelves for our goods. And there's a potbellied stove, and nine people in two small rooms add up to a lot of body heat. You're not cold. *Gaman*!

Each block in the camp has twelve barracks. Two middle ones constitute the mess hall where you all eat, and the combination laundry rooms–latrines–showers. You go to school. There is the English school in the morning, and the Japanese school in the afternoon. But even at six, you have learned that Japanese is a bad thing to be. Along with your brothers and sisters, you learn only English and you speak only English. The only Japanese word you know is *gaman*. You cannot speak with your father at all. The communications between you are these: when he is angry, you know it; when he is not angry, you know it. It is not only the Chinese who never assimilate; your father has been in the United States since he was nineteen and he is nearing sixty now, and he has never learned one word of English. He files an alien card until he dies, at eighty. He has always worked hard and saved his money in order to return home.

You never, truly, can understand the reasoning behind all this. Because never, in your entire life, have you been able to sit down and have a conversation with your father.

The camp is not so bad. *Gaman.* It is like being in the army. There is a canteen where you can buy things, and one barracks is set up as a movie theatre, where you all sit on the floor and learn what life is really like in America. There are schools of all levels, and there is a football team, and sometimes the team from Delta is allowed to come into the camp for a game. There are sock hops and Glen Miller records are played. You're too young to participate, but you get the message, boy, do you get it. We're all Americans here. Japanese is bad, American is good. I am an American. Football and baseball and movies and Cokes and this isn't so bad. Really. *Gaman.* I am an American!

Sixty thousand American citizens of Japanese origin and thirty-eight thousand Japanese aliens were sent, from California alone, to internment camps stretching from east of the Sierra Nevada all the way to the Mississippi River. What happened to them there is important because it affected what happened to them when they returned here. And what happened to their children.

In 1976 President Gerald Ford formally rescinded the World War II order that sent something like 120,000 Japanese-Americans into "relocation camps." It was a Bicentennial gesture, and a little overdue. And yet the Nisei and Sansei community here accepted it for what it was: a formal apology for an unforgivable act of the past. Earl Warren, who was governor of California at the time, and who gave testimony to the effect that, for the safety of California, it was necessary to intern these people, also apologized in his autobiography. *Gaman.* Thank you. *Gaman.* We survived.

The Japanese arrived here much later than the Chinese. Some came around the turn of the century; but the major migrations were in the late teens and early twenties, and they frightened the land barons because so many of the immigrants were superior farmers who could get much better results from the soil than the locals. Actually, reports indicate that it was not so much their superior methods that made the landowners nervous, but the fact that the immigrants had been expected to supply cheap labor and instead they were producing cheap food. The state legislature passed laws forbidding the new immigrants to own land or to take long-term leases on the land they worked. The new immigrants had babies, American citizens, and they put the land in the names of their legitimately American children. In 1924 President Coolidge signed a bill banning further immigration of Orientals and prohibiting the men already here from sending for "mail-order brides." In 1940 this policy was amended to allow small quotas of Orientals to enter the country, but in essence it remained in effect until 1965.

One result was the invention of the Japanese gardener. It truly was an invention—a novel way for the Japanese to continue to earn a living from the land, even though they could not own it. This is not to say that Japanese truck farms did not continue to exist up to the beginning of 1942; those who arrived before the various laws and bans, and had been provident enough to buy property, continued to till the fertile soil of the southwestern sections of the city known as Strawberry Park, Moneta and Gardena—these areas were incorporated under the name of Gardena in 1930. Today, Gardena has the largest percentage of Japanese-Americans of any city in the continental United States; its mayor and one of five city councilmen are Japanese-Americans; there is a thriving Buddhist Temple (50 percent of the Japanese-Americans here are Buddhist) where Japanese language classes are taught daily. That many of the people here are pre–World War II old-timers is evinced by the fact that every night nearly 80 percent of those watching television are watching one of the two Japanese-language channels.

But the lonely, single Japanese who found themselves cut off from owning land or bringing over brides in the mid-twenties, and were restricted from going into white-collar jobs by their lack of knowledge of English, turned to gardening. At that time the area around La Brea Avenue (which seemed so far west, but today is merely part of Hollywood) was just being developed as residential. There was a building boom, new houses were being constructed constantly. And the Issei, or first generation in this country, were only a step, or rather a bicycle ride, behind the contractors, signing up the hundreds of new homeowners who needed landscaping done. It was an inexpensive profession to get into: all that was needed was a bicycle to get from downtown boardinghouses to this western area, a hose looped over the handlebars, and a few hand tools. The most important tool, the knowledge of how to carve beauty from the soil, was easily transportable. The myth of the Japanese-as-gardener came into being.

Like many stereotypes, it had its basis in truth. Just as things began to get better for these men (and most were men), just when they'd gotten to the point where they could afford trucks instead of bicycles and a few family-arranged-for brides were allowed to be brought in and a few families could be started, the war came. This did not necessarily mean a permanent loss of business; many Japanese report receiving letters in camp from their former customers begging them to come back after the war.

What it meant was that, after the war there was still so much anti-Japanese feeling that many college-educated Nisei, on returning to Los Angeles from the camps or from the service, could not get jobs in their chosen fields. And so they, too, turned to gardening. John Tokada is now fifty-four. He came out of the service expecting to continue his studies as an architect. "There simply was no opportunity at that time. All the servicemen were returning, and in spite of the fact that I'd been in the Army, people still looked at my face and saw 'Japanese.' So I joined my father in getting his gardening business back together. I've never been sorry. It's a healthy life and you're your own boss. I don't quarrel with that." Today, Japanese-American landscapers and gardeners have their own trade union, the Pacific Coast Chapter of the California Landscape Contractors' Association. Despite the amorphous name, the organization is specifically for Japanese-Americans and designed to help those with language difficulties manage. And although some of the younger Japanese-Americans look askance at the gardener image, the community as a whole has never done so. Bankers' daughters and gardeners' daughters make their debuts at the same coming-out parties. An honest profession is never looked down upon by the older members of this community.

But there has been more change among the Japanese-American community than among any of the other Oriental groups in Los Angeles, which has a larger concentration of people of Korean and Thai origin than any city outside their native countries; a larger concentration of people of Japanese origin than any foreign city outside of Hawaii; and a growing number of Vietnamese.

Mas is a handsome man, young for a Nisei, only forty-two or forty-three. He has never spoken a language other than English, and yet he speaks with a very, very slight accent—a word such as *railroad*, with that difficult combination of two *r*'s and an *l*, comes out sounding a little bit, well, Japanese. He is a noted, award-winning Los Angeles art director. He has participated in a number of panels and seminars about Orientals in this city, such as the Asian-Americans for Fair Media Association's seminars on how to eliminate stereotypes in movies, television and advertising.

"Of all the Oriental groups in this city, only the Japanese-Americans have really tried to get into the mainstream," Mas says. "Almost all of my peers have gone into professions—medicine, law, the arts. Other Orientals stick to the entrepreneurial things, the stores and restaurants—those are businesses that relate to their cultures. We have tried to move out into fields which don't relate to our culture. And, physically, the people of my age group have moved out of the established areas. I don't know anyone who lives in Gardena or San Pedro or Boyle Heights. I live in Northridge [a distant, northwestern section of the Valley] myself.

"I'll give you my Psychology I interpretation," he continues. "Right after the war there was a tendency for people of my age to reject everything Japanese. We were Americans. We had fought in the war better than a lot of other Americans. [The 442nd U.S. Army Regimental Combat Team, twenty-six hundred Japanese-Americans, was the single most decorated unit in the nation's history.] We felt that Japan had been wrong in the war, so we wanted to separate ourselves from that image as much as possible. Now, no one was frowning on the Chinese culture at that time. [During the war, some Chinese in Los Angeles actually wore buttons saying "I am Chinese."] So they didn't have to try any harder than they ever had to assimilate. They're still not trying today. We are."

Mas is in a position to know that assimilation is not easy to accomplish. He was forced to finish high school in a city near where his internment camp had been—his family did not have enough money to return to California. And yet the family was broken, as were so many others during that period of hardship. "Divorce is frowned on, absolutely, by everyone of Japanese background," he says, "yet half the people my age now have divorced parents. The minute the camp was disbanded, my mother took my youngest sister and somehow managed to get back here. She divorced, and later remarried. The kids all understood, we had no ill feeling. But her older sister never forgave her. 'I've never been happy, but I hung on,' she told her. 'Why couldn't you do the same?' Well, she was in Canada, she didn't have that daily attrition that those of us in a camp had. A lot of divorces resulted from camp life.

"I had no problem developing my profession," he continues. "I was young. By the time I got back to Los Angeles, anti-Japanese feeling had softened. Besides, I wanted to be an artist, I went to art school. Everyone accepts the Japanese as artist." He grins. "But, for example, I had a friend with an engineering degree, and he wanted to join the Department of Water and Power. He scored number one on all the tests. He was turned down. Every year he tried again, he always placed at the top, and yet for several years he was turned down. Finally, he was accepted, and worked his way up from the bottom. Now, he runs the department." *Gaman.* Maybe it really works.

"We tend to put some of the minority groups down a little," says Don, another Japanese-American. "Not the Blacks. There's no oppression to match theirs, next to the Jews. But we have little compassion for groups that do a lot of crying and do nothing to lift themselves up out of their own problems. We have a very low tolerance for that." This is another face of *gaman.* Since the first Japanese arrived in this state, they have helped one another get ahead. Ruth Watanabe, a Sansei or third-in-the-country, is an excellent example. A member of the board of directors at City View Hospital in Lincoln Heights, a prime mover in the fund-raising campaign for the Japanese Retirement Home in Boyle Heights, a former president of the Japanese-American Republicans, Japanese-American Citizens' League, Japanese Philharmonic Society Auxiliary and Japanese-American Medical Association Auxiliary, she confines all her time-consuming civic efforts to activities that benefit the community of her background. "We need to help our own," she says simply.

As recently as the fifties, the Oriental sections of the city seemed stabilized and were easy to pinpoint. The Chinese basically spread out from Chinatown all around the Civic Center, though there were pocket communities elsewhere. The areas Mas mentioned—Boyle Heights in East Los Angeles,

Gardena and San Pedro in the south—were Japanese, as were Olympic Boulevard in the midtown area and the western section of Sawtelle. No other Oriental groups were large enough to be counted as individual communities.

This delineation has changed radically. Koreans have made inroads on the Olympic Boulevard area, and while some Japanese nurseries and stores remain, a huge number of buildings feature signs with Korean lettering; restaurants advertise Korean barbeque, while markets sell giant-sized jars of the red-hot cabbage concoction called *kim chi*. In East Los Angeles the never-ending influx of Mexicans has virtually forced the Japanese out of Boyle Heights; to compensate for this, Japanese communities have spread south and west, reaching partially into areas that once were predominantly Black. Vietnamese now are found in many sections of the city, especially in south-central Hollywood; while in the eastern part of Hollywood, around Western and Vermont avenues, an immense Thai community has established itself.

This diffusion means that in many areas Oriental children are far more integrated into the school system than either Blacks or Chicanos. On the lighter side, it means that the complete spectrum of Oriental food, from the highly spiced sweetish curries of Thailand to the spinach-wrapped omelets of Vietnam, is easier to find in Los Angeles than almost anywhere outside of Southeast Asia.

Los Angeles is possibly closer to being a true melting pot than any city in the country. At some point in the early 1980s, Caucasians will no longer constitute a majority. Yet even something as innocent as the Save the Whales movement can tip the balance of harmony. Because Russia and Japan are the only two countries to refuse to set limits on whale hunting, little third- and fourth-generation Japanese-Americans have been derided in their schools. "You kill whales!" they're told.

Mas and most of his Nisei and Sansei friends call one another "Buddha Heads." "Hi, Buddha Head!" they will say when they meet. Yes, of all the Orientals in Los Angeles, the Japanese-Americans of the postwar generations have tried the hardest to assimilate. The in-joking is the single clue to how difficult this still is. Among themselves, they acknowledge that bare fact: they look different.

"Our family acts exactly like *Father Knows Best*," Mas says. "I live in the suburbs, I have a wife, a son who plays Little League baseball, a daughter who is doing very well in high school, the two-car garage, the pool. Even the dog is perfect middle-class American—a German shepherd. And yet my son is the only Oriental on that Little League team, and he knows he looks different. And my daughter is going to Granada Hills High School, and there are two Japanese-American boys there, and *she* feels she's being categorized by her friends because they picked out Gary, one of the Sansei boys, and said, 'Oh, he'd be perfect for you.' And so, what I'm finally trying to do is to let the kids know a little about what it was like. I don't want to lay anything heavy on them. But I've got a few books lying around, telling what the camps were like. And when they raise these questions, I think it's all right now for them to know what *we* went through."

He mentions that, in fact, some of the Sansei now are asking, "Why did you permit yourselves to go through that?" My own reaction is the same. "Why did you come out of the camps feeling more American than when you went in? It's difficult to understand."

"No," he says quietly, "it's not difficult. We understood that there was a misunderstanding. Also, there was *gaman*, which our children have not been brought up to really comprehend. *Gaman* allowed us to accept the fact that although we were American, more American in feeling than many Caucasians, we had to go through this trial. That was the thing which led us to be the kind of parents we are. We've given our children such a totally American lifestyle that they are now free to say 'How *could* you?' We couldn't say that to our parents. But our children have been brought up in such a way that they can say that to us."

Japanese-Americans have the highest income level of any minority group in the United States, and the largest percentage of people with higher educations.

Mas adds slowly something that still, all these years after the camp, is difficult for him to accept. "I finally have realized that there's a lot I enjoy about the Japanese culture. And that there are a lot of things I don't want to see lost. Right now, I'm very proud to say that I'm a Nisei. Because, if I'm going to get lumped with a group, that's a darned good group to get lumped with. What they went through. And what they have achieved. It's taken me all these years to say that I'm proud. I am an American. That truly is my feeling, and something which I never can refute. But today I'm proud to be a Japanese-American. I've finally recognized that. A Japanese-American is a very good thing to be."

10

Town Hall Meetings in the Big City

It is a Tuesday evening in January. There has been sunshine with a slight overhaze all day and temperatures in the sixties, but now at eight P.M. it is chilly by Los Angeles standards, perhaps fifty-four or thereabouts, and everyone is wearing turtleneck sweaters and windbreakers or blazers.

We are at the Village Coffee Shop, forty or more of us. We are huddled around the knotty pine tables and around the black potbellied stove, we take up positions at the long counter and in the high-backed booths, we go boldly behind the counter to help ourselves to the free coffee and cookies provided by the Papalexus brothers who own both the coffee shop and the Beachwood Market next door. The brothers are not present; they do not live in the neighborhood; but what affects us affects them, and they are glad to participate *in absentia*. A few of our best friends are here, but otherwise it is a crowd of familiar faces to which we can attach few names. It is the year's first meeting of the Hollywoodland Improvement Association, Inc., known to most of us as simply the Association, and we are here to elect new members to the board, to discuss local problems, to air our grievances, and to watch the Great Ballantine, a noted magician. I had never heard of town meetings featuring entertainment, but it seems to be as good a way as any of tempting people away from their television sets—the woman sitting next to me confides that she came only to see the magician. Alas, the Great Ballantine was called to Las Vegas on a paying job. The town meeting begins without him.

155

Though of course we are not a town. We are a canyon.

We are Beachwood Canyon, which climbs from Franklin Avenue on the flatlands, just a ten-minute walk from Hollywood and Vine, all the way up to Mulholland Drive, which stretches across the top of the Santa Monica Mountains from the far eastern end of Hollywood to the far western end of the Valley. We are the canyon presided over by the Hollywood sign and by the tall red-and-white television tower atop Mount Lee. We are the canyon that looks east toward the guaranteed wilderness of Griffith Park and the verdigris-covered domes of its observatory, and west toward the sunset. We are one of the oldest canyon communities in this city of canyons (the first movie ever filmed in Hollywood, though not the first in Los Angeles, was shot on Beachwood Drive in the early 1900s). We are, as are all canyon communities, a jumble of contradictions: we are intensely private, yet value the sense of community found here; we are friendly, yet it is not unusual if neighbors don't know one another's names. Neither kaffeeklatsches nor kiddies flourish here—nearly every household has a dog or a cat, but few have young children, and Halloween in the hills is as quiet as every other night, though everyone leaves the porch light on, hopefully, and the market does a good business in candy and cookies and gum.

We are an interesting combination of the elderly (some of the original homeowners of this late-twenties development called Hollywoodland still live near the market), the successful (television and movie people, noted writers and directors—Paul Newman and Joanne Woodward used to live here, as did Aldous Huxley, and Linda Ronstadt), the hopeful (young actors, musicians and artists), the transient (the lower canyon has many rental properties), the stable ("Once a highlander always a highlander," I was told when I first moved into the hills nearly twenty years ago, and certainly I cannot refute the maxim). We meet walking our dogs, hiking the hills, having breakfast in the coffee shop, riding at the stables at the end of Beachwood Drive. We meet in what we call the village, at the Oriental laundry, at the real estate office where people as often stop merely to chat as to buy or sell property, at the hairdressers or at the Château de Chanté, where Freemont clips poodles. We meet at the regular "hillside runs" (we do not jog here, we run), or at the occasional *al fresco* brunch the market sponsors in its parking lot. Mostly, we meet at the market. It is impossible to dash in there for a can or bottle or package of anything without running into friends or neighbors or familiar faces. Of course all the people who work at the market are friends also, and it serves as our bank and our grapevine. Once, stopping in after work, my husband was told by *four* different people, "Hey, Bert, you're having pancakes for breakfast tomorrow. June says to pick up some syrup."

We are of many different colors, many different ages, many different income brackets, and at least three different sexual persuasions. Politically, we range from farthest right to farthest left. But when it comes to this place, these homes, this neighborhood, we are precisely alike in one respect—we are uncompromisingly conservative.

Neighborhoods are important in Los Angeles, perhaps more so than in many other cities, for it is our neighborhoods rather than the city as a whole that determine the quality of our lives. Except in odd pockets of the city, this is not a place for street life. Most people do not walk here, do not pop into shops to browse, or drop in on museums or parks or bars. Because here nearly every such move must be a calculated one—most of us must drive to these places. There has been an admirable attempt to revive "downtown" as a central city, but despite handsome new buildings—hotels, restaurants and shops—few people have been wooed away from their suburban habits. One goes for shopping or recreation, usually by car, to the nearest suburban center: Century City, or Fashion Square in the Valley, or Beverly Hills, or Westwood, or Crenshaw Center or Pasadena. Almost from the beginning, building always was encouraged outward rather than upward; partially because of the earthquake danger (as recently as 1950 there was a thirteen-story or 150-foot-height limit on buildings, with only the City Hall and the Federal Building exempted by special ordinance); but mostly because there simply was so much space.

That has changed now, and it is amusing to people from other cities, vertical cities, to fly in over the basin and see our one little cluster of skyscrapers in the downtown area, the thin line of tall buildings that outlines Wilshire Boulevard on its east-west run, the second little cluster of skyscrapers in Century City. Try as we may—and we are not trying very hard—we cannot look like any other city in the world.

It is said that it was the incredible traffic problems in the downtown area that caused all the major department stores and many other businesses, just after the war, to start the suburban centers that now characterize this city; but, in fact, the people were already out in the suburbs and the businesses just went out to meet them. (Perhaps the Los Angeles concept of "suburbs" has been described too often in the old joke of "suburbs in search of a city"; but these suburban centers are in the *midst* of the city, as well as in farther-flung areas.) And so, we make our ways of life through the neighborhoods in which we choose to live.

It is the great advantage of Los Angeles—which, for most of us, more than offsets the fact that there is no city as such— that there are so many different ways of life to choose from.

An apartment near the Sunset Strip, or a condominium in Beverly Hills or Century City, or a house near Westwood Village, all provide some action within walking distance. The Valley offers a certain specific lifestyle—casual clothes and pools and barbecues and child-oriented families—and can be enjoyed on a three-quarter-acre lot that is zoned for horses and chickens, or in a postwar tract house or a sparkling new apartment. The beach cities, from Malibu to the north all the way down to Laguna at the south, *are* walking cities, each with its own mood and lifestyle; although the apparent general concern with health—jogging, biking, roller skating, health-food restaurants—jars with the other apparently general concern for living the swinging singles life in raucous bars, discos, jazz clubs, pickup places.

There are the old-money/big-homes neighborhoods, such as Hancock Park and Freemont Place and, far away from these midtown sections, Pasadena/San Marino to the northeast and Palos Verdes Estates to the south. There is horse country, including Hidden Hills, which is far out in the Valley, and Rolling Hills, which is far off near the ocean. There are the extremely far-flung development communities such as Valencia and Westlake, which offer, besides man-made lakes and golf courses and room for horses, at least a one-hour freeway drive to get anywhere near anyplace else. There is a running joke here that nobody lives more than one-half hour away from downtown. When I worked downtown and lived in Hollywood, which is only ten minutes away on an empty freeway, but never takes less than thirty minutes to reach during rush hour, all of my co-workers who lived far out in the Valley (including one man who lived in Saugus, which is nearly in Ventura County) insisted that they, too, could get to work in thirty minutes or less. It is this Los Angeles freeway syndrome, this psychological quirk, this insistence that no place is more than half an hour from anyplace else, that causes us to think nothing of driving fifty or sixty or seventy miles round trip to a dinner party. It also, often, makes us arrive very late.

You may live overlooking a lake here: Toluca Lake, Silver Lake and Lake Hollywood all are pretty, heart-of-the-city locations. And there are the hill and canyon areas that, like the beach cities, create their own village atmospheres, but in a country environment: raccoons and deer and skunks and coyotes roam hillside backyards, only ten minutes from Hollywood or Beverly Hills or Westwood or Brentwood or Santa Monica, depending upon which canyon you choose. A friend recently saw a confused coyote on Rodeo Drive at Santa Monica Boulevard in Beverly Hills, which gives some idea of how closely country life is linked to the city.

Other areas are identified mostly by the types of people who live there. White uniforms are a major part of the street scene around Vermont and Sunset, where so many large hospitals are located. The apartments around Vermont and Santa Monica, around Jefferson and Hoover and around Westwood Village are filled with students, because those areas are where the three major colleges and universities are located. Elderly people tend to live in apartments close to the main east-west streets, since bus stops and markets are within walking distance. Fairfax Avenue, between Santa Monica and Beverly boulevards, is a central location for elderly Jewish people because Fairfax features many kosher butchers and the east-west streets have numerous synagogues. People who work in the aircraft or aerospace industries tend to live in Hawthorne and El Segundo and Torrence and Westchester. And there are strictly ethnic areas: Watts, which is Black; East Los Angeles, which is Chicano; Little Tokyo and Chinatown, which speak for themselves; and sections around Hollywood and around Olympic Boulevard that have drawn large numbers of Thais, Koreans and Vietnamese.

We used to have so many choices. Easterners tended to head for high-rise condos with doormen and security garages; young families could buy tract houses in outlying areas for virtually nothing and trade upward as their finances grew; singles could find reasonable apartment complexes where the pools and recreation areas were huge and the apartments minimal, or they could find equally reasonable cottages in the canyons. If you were buying there was the choice—the great Los Angeles choice—of a Spanish style or Mediterranean or English or French or Moorish or town house or California ranch style or just plain modern style house. If you were renting, there were almost as many choices. And prices were so much lower here than in the East, both for renting and buying. The Angelino, even the newcomer Angelino, always thought it was a God-given right to have all of these choices.

Suddenly, inflation and the nationwide mania for investing in real estate instead of savings accounts caught up with us, and there was a building slowdown in the early seventies that *we* never caught up with. The speculators began to come in and suddenly we were stuck with the choices we had already made. Which may be why we became even more protective of our neighborhoods than we had been before.

Quite naturally, the neighborhoods that have the most distinctive characters are the most anxious to protect their individuality. And so it is in the canyons that most of the neighborhood associations are formed and the town meetings held. The canyon communities stretch from Griffith Park at the east, down the entire length of the Santa Monica Mountains to the beach, and in some instances they cut across the mountains into the Valley. There is an umbrella organization, the Federation of Hillside and Canyon Associations, which covers all these local homeowners' associations: Bel Air, Bel Air Knolls, Bel Air Skycrest, Benedict Canyon, Beverly Glen, Briarcliff, Cahuenga Pass, Canyon Drive, Casiano, Curson Canyon, Encino, Hollywood Crescent, Hollywood Dell, Hollywood Knolls, Hollywoodland, Hollywood Manor, Lake Hollywood, Laurel Canyon, Laurel Hills, Lookout Mountain, M.A.P.S., Maybrook, Mount Olympus, Mulholland, Nichols Canyon, Outpost, Roscomare Valley, Sherman Oaks, Studio City, Tarzana, Whitely Heights. (Some of these spread into flatland areas, but all are basically hillside or canyon organizations. I have not been able to discover any flatlands associations of the same type, not even in the beach cities—which is not to say that they don't exist, only that no city official could tell me they did.) All these organizations have their own officers, boards of directors and newsletters, and conduct regular meetings, usually monthly. Some of the areas covered are very small (Canyon Drive, for instance, is only about one mile long, though the streets that climb up from it into the hills on both sides might include another two miles); some associations have overlapping areas (for a while we belonged to both the Hollywoodland and Canyon Drive associations, and these two now share a patrol system); all the associations willingly join together to fight for or against new legislation that might affect any of these areas, and to oppose large development projects or changes of zoning or building codes that might change the basic characteristics of the canyons.

With the help of the Federation, our Association fought and won a case against Seven-Eleven Stores, which wanted to build on a corner site in our village. Since Beachwood Market closes at seven P.M. on weekdays and is not open on Sundays, it might have been handy to have a little place you could run into at odd hours for cigarettes or a carton of milk. But, our concern was that teenagers and riffraff (a word often used during the fight) would be hanging around the Seven-Eleven all night. We like our streets quiet at night. Also, we have a basic loyalty to Beachwood Market. There is an all-night supermarket over on Bronson, which is the flatlands end of Canyon Drive, and there is a liquor store there; we felt we didn't need anything else.

A small weekly newspaper called *The Canyon Crier* is mailed free of charge to members of all the homeowners' associations within the Federation. Its publisher is extraordinarily conservative, he is antismoking and antiabortion and anti almost everything, and I spend many late nights composing angry letters to him, which I tear up the following morning. But the newspaper itself is very useful to those of us interested in protecting our neighborhoods. It reports, in advance, hearings on issues in which we might wish to involve ourselves; and later reports the results of those hearings. It gives important information on which city or state departments to contact on specific problems. It cites which City Council people are helping us and which are hindering, and does the same for state representatives. If some major issue is up for discussion in either the state legislature or Congress, it tells us to whom we should write to express our views. It speaks for all of us in editorials advocating more fire and police protection, and it publishes the responses of public officials to the editorials. It also has a classified section, which is helpful if you need your brush cleared or your house painted and would like to hire someone local, and it has an entertainment column and a restaurant column.

But it is the monthly newsletter from each individual association that informs us of association meetings and when it is time to pay dues or pay for the patrol service, and asks us if we want to be a "tree neighbor" (that is, plant a tree and care for it), and tells us which plants repel fire and which retard dirt slippage. It is folksy and newsy and usually comes late. We

almost missed tonight's association meeting because the newsletter reminding us came only today.

At tonight's meeting of the Hollywoodland Association, the
board of directors is introduced, and then Joe Greenberg, the
president, gives a quite long pep talk. He reminds us that it was
the strength of our Association and the Federation in general
that stopped the Seven-Eleven from being built; that blocked
the building of a condominium property in Lake Hollywood that
would have brought an additional two thousand cars into the
area; that blocked the construction of a fire department heliport
on top of our very own Mount Lee and got the city to agree to
construct it on Mount Hollywood, from which we would get
the same amount of protection in the event of fires but far less
noise during cruising and training maneuvers. "It's the first
time in history that the fire department ever backed down on a
thing like that," he tells us, "and we're the ones who managed
to do it!" Applause.

He mentions that, thanks to the Hollywoodland Patrol
Service, our area now has the lowest incidence of burglary in
the city, but adds that we have only 60 percent membership in
the service (at this writing, it cost $60 for six months), and
need 85 to 90 percent to get twenty-four-hour coverage. He
announces that Federally funded low-cost flood insurance now
is available, and tells us how to get it. He exhorts: "Buy any
vacant lots next to you! Builders now have the capability for
building on strictly vertical land, so buy it before they get it!"
He informs: "If you have any problems with new homes being
built on your street, noise before or after legal hours, or trucks
blocking the road, call the chief of mechanical inspections at
the Building Department, or call Hollywoodland Realty, they're
acting as liaison on this." He gives us the telephone numbers.
He urges: "Support the zoning variance to allow additional
parking behind Beachwood Market, so we can get some of these
cars off the streets." (Obviously, canyon areas have very
narrow, winding streets; cars parked along them are not only
traffic hazards but a hindrance to fire trucks in emergencies as
well.) He politics a little: "Thanks to Councilman [Joel]

Wachs, we're getting a left-turn arrow at Beachwood and Franklin." Applause. He warns: "There are housing violations going on all over these hills. Only five people are allowed to live in an R-1 dwelling; if you see houses with more people than that, call me. And if you see traffic violations or parking problems or are bothered by barking dogs, call me. In fact, call me about any problems you have, unless I've already given you the numbers to call for specific problems. I'm posting a list of important numbers on the bulletin board." (This is the typical neighborhood bulletin board, posted on the Beachwood Drive side of the coffee shop, and offering such things as baby-sitting services and cars for sale.)

He now begins to ramble a bit, talking about keeping the balance of nature in the hills, letting the raccoons and coyotes have their share of the territory. "Call me if you see anyone poisoning or hunting wild animals. If you have problems with skunks, call Animal Regulations. They have a skunk trap that just captures them, and then they release them out in the wilds." Everyone here is very pleased to hear this. We do not want discos or condos or Seven-Elevens in our neighborhood, but we do want the wild animals; that's why we live up here. We are among the few groups of people anywhere who actually appreciate the coyote.

People begin asking questions. "What are we going to do about the defacement of the Hollywood Sign?" (It was torn down and rebuilt only two or three months ago; already it is covered by graffiti.) "The committee has money left over and they're going to build a fence around it," Greenberg answers. A very elderly lady, highly made up and oddly dressed, talks on for quite a while about dog barking and dog droppings. Greenberg finally cuts in, "Barking problems, call the number I already gave you. Droppings nobody can do anything about. Despite the new laws, nothing's happening there." Another woman mentions that there are large nests of rattlesnakes up in the area of the Hollywood Sign, and suggests that a warning notice be put up. "Doesn't work," Greenberg answers. "We all know that there are rattlesnakes, but the outsiders come up here, and they'll hike up there anyway."

Various people complain: "Trucks of dirt are driving up Beachwood and the dirt is being dumped at the top, and when it rains it will all wash down the street"; "There was a big truck with a crane, and it was filled with debris, and it had no license plate, on Hollyridge late one night"; "There's been an abandoned car near my house for days now, the windows are broken and it's just parked there on the hill"; "There's a man near me who fixes other people's cars in his driveway." And on and on. Joe has answers for most of the questions: which city department to call; which problems violate the law, which do not; and gives pats on the back to the police and fire departments and police traffic department—"They're all being very cooperative now"—and again to Joel Wachs—"The builders own the City Council, Wachs is the only one on our side, except sometimes Peggy Stevenson. We just have to fight harder. We just have to all show up, every single person in these hills, every time there's a hearing on development building." I have been to some of these hearings, and seen the small rooms crowded to overflowing with my neighbors and friends, and heard eloquent speeches given by the most eloquent among them, and seen the victory still go to the developers. But we do fight city hall. And sometimes we win.

Finally, Greenberg shuts off the questions, makes a few further announcements, and gets down to business. The first order is to elect new members to the board, and that is speedily accomplished; another hurdle is not so easily jumped. The original 1923 Hollywoodland bylaws are being updated, to which everyone agrees, except for one point: the new bylaws read that members of the Association will have only one vote per parcel of land (that is to say, a husband and wife, even if they pay for two memberships, would have only one vote); and only the legal occupant of the parcel may vote (which is to say, if you rent your property out, even if you retain your membership in the Association, your renter would have the vote). There is a great deal of argument over this, but finally persuasive Joe Greenberg gives a final speech in favor of passing the new bylaws as they stand, and the votes are taken, and the bylaws are passed, and the meeting is over.

Not really over. Some people have another cup of coffee, and some people automatically begin to help the board members who have agreed to do the clean-up chores, and little pockets of people stop to talk, both inside the coffee shop and on the street, and neighbors who don't know one another's names are introduced by mutual friends and so on and so forth. It is midnight by the time we drive back up our hill. And, as always, we feel relieved and satisfied that not only we, but so many other people, are looking out for our neighborhood interests.

There are other town meetings in this big city, and even what might be called "city hall meetings" since they are not local. But they are more personal than that; they could be called open houses.

This is a Wednesday in late January, eight A.M. About forty people are waiting in the long corridor that leads to the anterooms of Mayor Tom Bradley's office, and a few of them have been here since five or six A.M. By nine A.M., when this day officially begins, there will be at least 125 people here, and perhaps as many as 300. It is the day of Mayor Bradley's monthly open house.

It is a practice Tom Bradley established when he was a city councilman. Then it was a weekly event, but now he is so busy that he can manage it only once a month, and it never can be scheduled very far in advance—when a day frees up, that day is chosen. No press release is issued, so the open house is not announced in any newspaper. If people telephone the mayor's office to find out when it will occur, their names and telephone numbers will be taken, and when the day is scheduled, they will be informed. Occasionally a radio broadcaster will find out about it in time to announce it on the news. One man here says, "I heard about it on the five A.M. news and I came right down." Still, despite the lack of publicity, this large crowd appears.

The crowd this morning is a cross section of Los Angeles. There are very elderly people and quite young ones, there are people of all races and nationalities; many of the young ones are in Levi's, most of the older ones are spruce in dresses or in suits. Most of them seem to be alone, although a few have a friend or a child in tow. Some of them chat in the way people do when thrown together in a waiting situation. Some stand resolutely apart, willing to share their problems with no one but the mayor.

At nine A.M. the people waiting here will be admitted to the mayoral suite. Their names and a one-sentence statement of their problems will be taken, and they will be shown to a room where there are chairs and where coffee is ready for them. If it is obvious that they will have a long wait, they will be told approximately how long, so that they can leave and return later. "We're pretty well able to estimate what time they'll be seen," Bradley has told me. "The sessions usually last until about six-thirty, but at times they've gone till nine P.M. That's a long day. But we do what is needed."

Most of the people here are individuals with individual problems, not lobbyists or representatives of special-interest groups. "Oh, we get them occasionally," the mayor says. "A whole series of groups came in to discuss the library. [Whether to modernize and enlarge the beautiful, but somewhat dangerous and highly inadequate, Art Deco main branch of the public library, or to build a new main library somewhere else, has been a controversy for years.] And when a real estate ordinance was passed prohibiting the mixture of residential and commercial buildings [in the same area], many representatives of the real estate business came in to talk about it. That problem was referred to the City Council. But we generally deal with individuals, and quite a few of their problems are related to unemployment."

While names are still being taken, the first person is shown into Mayor Bradley's office, the immense room whose only indication that it is an office is its huge desk. Otherwise it looks like a homey living room, with a very long couch, several comfortable upholstered chairs, soft lighting from table lamps. The mayor always rises to greet his visitors. He is a very tall man with large hands. Luckily, years of politicking have taught him how to give a warm and generous grasp without crunching any bones. Generally, he shows his visitor to the couch, while he sits in one of the chairs, pulled companionably close. He is a man who smiles easily and laughs readily, a man who can make you feel that your reason for being in his office is just as important as anything else going on in the city. He listens carefully. He reacts.

"We try to get results," Mayor Bradley says of the open house. "If it's something I can take care of personally with a simple phone call, I'll do it immediately. If it's complicated, I'll assign members of my staff to follow through. We try to do something specific about every problem that comes through here."

An example is the young man who had been unable to find a job. He was going to have to go on welfare, which he didn't want to do. The mayor had learned that there was a meat-packing plant that had openings for salesmen, but prospects had to post a $300 bond to take the training course and have access to a van. Bradley picked up the phone instantly and spoke to the plant owner. "I told him that I was so impressed with this young man's desire to earn a living rather than go on welfare that I wondered if he would waive the three-hundred-dollar bond. He said it was something he never did, that it was an absolute rule, but since I was asking him personally, he'd do it." The next morning the young man had a job.

When this Art Deco building with the pyramid on top was erected in 1928, it was called the Lonely Tower. The City Hall still stands at the heart of the civic center and is still its core, though now it is dwarfed by glass-and-steel skyscrapers, the city and state and Federal buildings that surround it. Still, it is a handsome building in its old-fashioned way, and rather an impressive one: there is a marble-floored rotunda and marble stairways and halls, with hand-painted tiles on the walls of the main floor; there are banks of Deco elevators that run very slowly; there are long carpeted corridors that lead to mahogany-doored offices.

It is not surprising that some of the people who come here for open house come just to see what it's like inside this building, to see how City Hall functions, or merely to shake hands with the mayor. "Very often people just come to see it in action,"

Bradley says. "They tell me, 'I have no problem, but I wanted to see if it works.' Others have said, 'It's reassuring to know it's here if I ever need it.'" Does he ever get cranks or chronic complainers? "No, not really. Sometimes a person will come back two or three times with what really is an unsolvable problem, but it helps them to know that at least someone will listen. Occasionally we'll get someone with an emotional problem, but even then it's therapy for them to have someone listen.

"As far as I know, when I took office I was the only mayor in the country to do this. A number of mayors have called me to inquire how it works, and I believe some of them have adopted the idea. It's been written up in our national publication, and at conferences I've been asked about it. It's a way of opening up the lines of communication. You can't expect the people to have faith or trust in an elected official if they have no communication with him."

Mayor Bradley's official town hall meetings take place on a regularly scheduled basis, and they occur more than once a month.

Walking down Hollywood Boulevard, or up Broadway, our main downtown street, or down, say, Ventura Boulevard in the Valley, or Western Avenue, or Vermont, you might see a very tall man making his way along the street or entering some of the stores, and see people running up or edging up to shake the tall man's hand. This is the way the all-day/all-evening town hall meeting programs begin for the mayor. "I start out in the morning and I go to the stores and talk to the merchants and the customers. I always visit at least one school in the neighborhood, usually the high school. I visit other community organizations, senior citizens' clubs and the chamber of commerce. Then I just walk down the street for the rest of the day and shake hands with people and talk to them."

In the evening, if this is your neighborhood and if you are interested, you will go to the high school auditorium or some other hall or building that can accommodate a large crowd, and sit down with your neighbors, the ones you know and the ones you don't know, and listen to the mayor speak for a while, and then ask him questions and share with him your local problems.

"We've divided the city into five major areas," Bradley says, "and the areas are divided into sections, and each area has a coordinator who decides which section I should visit. The coordinator alerts the section well in advance, so we always get a good turnout for these evening meetings, which I call town hall meetings, because that's exactly the way they function. This way, an entire community can voice its desires and its own particular problems. I try to visit every section of the city this way at least once a year."

"Do people respond well?"

A huge grin is his first answer. "I get a very warm response, an immensely warm response. In a city this spread out, it's so easy for people to think that nobody cares what's happening in their community. When the people who represent them actually come out into the community, ask questions, try to answer their questions, it means a great deal to them. They feel more committed to their communities, and to doing something for the communities themselves. And they feel the isolation of the big city less."

11

In Old Pasadena

"The power still works downtown and goes home to Pasadena," the insurance executive says. He should know; his company specializes in insuring fine art for the wealthiest people in the city. He is wrong about one thing. What he is referring to as downtown is now mostly located on Wilshire Boulevard between Western Avenue and the edge of the old central city—the very land where Alyce Williamson's great-grandfather used to have his sheep ranch; the very section of the city that her father developed into the power center it is today.

But the point about Pasadena is well taken. Pasadena and the adjoining city of San Marino are where many of the third-, fourth- and fifth-generation Angelinos live, where many of their great-grandparents lived before them, and where much of the old money and much of what may be considered society has always been centered. Since Angelinos are relatively unconscious of class, we tend not to pay too much attention to the elite status of Pasadena/San Marino.

If we think about the area at all, we consider it in terms of old trees. For when the railroad barons and the land barons built their estates in this northeast section of the city a century or more ago, they planted lot after lot and street after street with nonindigenous trees, which today serve to identify that section. Life there is very private. But outsiders are aware of the trees.

Parts of Pasadena/San Marino are not as nice as they once were. Some of the big old houses have become run down, too many torn down, and some business sections have become tacky, and some edges of the two cities have been encroached upon by those little things—fast-food stands, liquor stores, gas stations, overgrown lots and neighborhoods running to seed—that imply decay. But in the heartland of the area, in that private sector where the very private people live, virtually nothing has changed since the days when Henry E. Huntington, the Southern Pacific Railroad executive who went into electric railway lines and made a second fortune connecting every section of this vast city with every other, built his incredible home and gardens just over the border of Pasadena in San Marino.

Pasadena is reached via the city's oldest freeway, the one that was built before city engineers had any idea of how to build a freeway. It is the one that curves and sidles like a snake over the old Arroyo Seco (dry wash) Road; the one that was so innocently designed that its off-ramps are fifteen-mile-per-hour hairpin turns and its on-ramps so short that most have stop signs instead of merging lanes. A pretty freeway as freeways go, it surprises the driver with views of the San Gabriel Mountains and of Heritage Square, where Victorian houses were moved and are being restored; it passes under old bridges and viaducts of decorated stone, and passes the hillside where "The City of South Pasadena" is spelled out in sculptured plants. Most freeways in Los Angeles do not end, they merge into other freeways or into major highways; it is possible to circle the city forever just by merging from one freeway to another. But the Pasadena Freeway does end, just dwindles out, stops for a traffic light and turns into Arroyo Parkway, which is simply an ordinary street.

The business and residential sections around here are innocuous; only the large complex on California Street that is the California Institute of Technology stands out. But just to its south lies one of the oldest enclaves of old money in the city.

Except for the immense and noted Huntington Library and Gardens, everything is subtle. The streets are broad, but not extravagantly so. The houses are large, but many run deep rather than wide, as do their grounds, so that from the front most do not look like mansions or estates. This is not Beverly Hills, this is not nouveau riche; no one has to prove anything to anyone else out here. The trees are older and finer and taller than anywhere else in Los Angeles, but they just grew that way. Almost as if to make up for this gaffe, the cars parked beneath their shade and along the driveways mostly are small cars that do not consume much energy, and some of them are slightly shabby. One almost never sees a Cadillac here, and only occasionally a Mercedes. Cars are not status symbols in Pasadena/San Marino. Only names are status symbols.

Names do count. You cannot belong to the prestigious Valley Hunt Club, one of the oldest (nearly one hundred years) private clubs in the city, unless you are connected to certain families. But even if you are connected, there is a waiting list for membership that often takes ten years to climb. Alyce Williamson's mother-in-law, now Lady Crocker, put her son's and daughter-in-law's names on the list seven years before they were invited to join. In the modern way, they hesitated to do so. "We have our own tennis court and pool and the children have their own friends," Alyce says, "and anyhow we're not clubby. But we finally decided we would, and now I'm so glad. It's a wonderful place to take people to lunch, and a lovely place to have parties."

When Alyce Williamson talks about taking people to lunch she almost always means people who might help on the dozen or more charities that she supports—not just with her money, but with nearly all her free time and energy. When she talks about giving parties, with the occasional exception of a family birthday or anniversary, she generally means a benefit. She does not do the things one imagines well-to-do social women doing—the day-long shopping trips on Rodeo Drive, the leisurely lunches at Le Bistro with friends. "Wouldn't that be fun!" she exclaims, laughing. "But I don't have time for things like that."

She was born Alyce de Roulet. Her father, Henry de Roulet, built what was considered one of the first skyscrapers in Los Angeles, the thirteen-story Pellissier Building (named after his grandfather who had raised sheep on the land) at Wilshire Boulevard and Western Avenue; a building that still stands as the Franklin Life Insurance Building. As early as 1923 de

Roulet had organized property owners on Wilshire to widen the
street, straighten it out, and smooth out the hills and gullies—
at their own expense. He foresaw that the power of the city
eventually would move west from downtown, and his efforts
were of major importance in that migration. In 1971 the
Wilshire Center Chamber of Commerce awarded him its first
annual Man of the Year Award.

On this French side of Alyce's family, the Pellissiers were
Catholic. There still are Pellissiers in Paris—a cousin, Hubert,
was best man at Princess Caroline's wedding; his father was
one of Onassis' lawyers. The de Roulet side was Calvinist, and
there still are relations of that name in the south of France.
Alyce herself was raised as a Catholic, and attended the Santa
Catalina School in northern California, which at the time was
associated with the Dominican Order. She still supports the
school and is on its board.

On the maternal side of her family she had a great-
grandmother "who crossed the country in a covered wagon. She
went to the Mother Lode country and discovered gold. Hard-
ships never bothered her, and she certainly profited in the long
run." This heritage, the sturdy French sheep rancher and the
covered wagon pioneer, are strongly evident in the ways in
which Alyce Williamson deals with the many facets of her
complicated life.

On her husband's side she is associated with the powerful
Chandler family, which has run *The Los Angeles Times* for so
many generations. Warren Frederick Williamson, known always as Spud ("because he looked like a potato when he was a
baby"), is a stockbroker. His great-grandfather was General
Harrison Gray Otis, credited with building the *Times* into a
nationally recognized newspaper; his grandfather was Harry
Chandler, one of the noted publishers of his time.

No one could have better connections than these in the Los
Angeles social structure. Yet no one is less pretentious than
Alyce Williamson.

She is quite tall, five feet, ten and one half inches, and
judging by the ages of her children, she is probably in her early

forties. She looks like a very tall little girl. She sometimes wears her long thick dark brown hair in a long pigtail. And she giggles. Not constantly or boringly—but when something giggle-inspiring comes along, she gives in to it wholeheartedly. She is lightly tanned, because she gets up early nearly every day to play tennis—seven A.M. is about the only hour of her meeting-filled days that is free. Between the tennis game and the first meeting at nine or nine thirty, she does things around the house—when the children were home, that was when she made their brown-bag lunches. She has one woman as full-time help, but there are many things she does herself.

She can look regal—when she piles her hair up and puts on a long slim dress for a big benefit party, she looks very regal indeed. But mostly she finds formality boring. This is not to say that she putters around in Levi's; Pasadena women do not do that, they wear skirts and blouses or casual dresses or casual suits of the Chanel type. As is evident today, an unexpectedly drizzly day in early May.

The drizzle is a shame, because today is the day of the Art Walk of the San Marino League, and by ten A.M. the women of this area are out in force. The Art Walk actually is a tour of homes in Pasadena and San Marino, and the $10 fee benefits the Art Center and the Japanese Gardens of the Huntington Gardens. This event is not open to the public, not advertised in "The Calendar" section of *The Los Angeles Times*. It is open to people who belong to certain organizations, and to their families and friends. Alyce has left a ticket for me at the door of the first house on the tour. The first house happens to be hers.

Her father is in the hospital, probably dying. (He died three weeks later.) Her six-and-one-half-foot-tall son has just had his nose broken playing basketball (the news interrupted her twentieth wedding anniversary dinner party last night); he was taken to the hospital and pronounced all right, then hemorrhaged and was returned to the hospital for surgery. Her oldest daughter has just left for Semester at Sea, a school-connected tour that will keep her away for several weeks. Her house is in the midst of being redecorated, with the help of her childhood friend Robbie Woodward, a well-known interior designer. In the midst of all this she has opened her house for the Art Walk, though she is not even a member of the San Marino League.

She has allowed the League members in to place their special flower arrangements. She has had tables set up for wine and tea and cakes to be served in the yard—the nearly one-acre yard that does not show from the street. She has told her husband, "We're having some people for tea," not mentioning that the number was close to two thousand. (Spud, however, knowing his wife, left for work early that morning.) Despite general havoc and personal strain, she appears just after ten looking as effervescent as if she were giving a private party, finds me, and gives me a welcoming hug. "Just let me find Robbie and we'll all do the walk together."

It is one of Alyce Williamson's special attributes that no matter what is happening in her private life, she accepts the fact that she also leads a public life, and does not let the first affect the second. She is very down to earth and open, and there does not seem to be a single phony nuance to her personality—nor do ideas of power or adulation seem to enter into it. She simply was raised to believe in certain things, most importantly: "If you take from a community, then you have to give something back to it. I think you should give back as much as you can, as often as you can."

What makes this altruism delightful instead of boring and Pollyanna-ish is that Alyce seems to derive so much pleasure from every single thing she does. Here are some of them:

She founded (with Mrs. George Jagels) the Pacemakers, a benefit organization to help fund the Pasadena Cardiovascular Research Foundation, which operates in conjunction with Cal Tech. The foundation itself has been in existence for twelve years or so. Alyce was motivated to start the fund-raising organization when her only brother, to whom she was very close, died of cardiovascular disease a few years ago at a much-too-young age. "At first I was devastated," she says. "It seemed like part of the world had ended. Then I realized that mourning doesn't help, you've got to do something, you've got to fight in some way. Something like sixty percent of the people in the world have or will have some sort of cardiovascular problem, and so little research has been accomplished. It seemed to me that fund raising was what was needed, and that's exactly the sort of thing I know how to do."

She belongs to two groups that raise money for the Children's Hospital. She is on the committee, and has been a member of the board, for the Las Madrinas Debutante Ball, one of the oldest, and certainly the most elite, presentation balls in the city. She also is on the committee of the Pasadena Guild for the Children's Hospital, and has organized the annual Treasures and Trivia Sale and the June Ball.

She was on the board, and now is a member of, the Costume Council of the Los Angeles County Museum. She donated her own wedding dress, the rose-point lace gown with infanta sleeves in which her grandmother was married, and which was updated and lined in satin by Cahill for her own wedding, to the museum. "They preserve the gown. We can borrow it back for family weddings any time we need it."

She belongs to the Pasadena Garden Club, and in 1979 was its program chairman, finding speakers for monthly events. "The object is to beautify the community. We planted trees on Lake Street, and built a *casita* on Arroyo. Right now we're raising money for an auditorium and pavilion at the Huntington Library, where we already funded the building of little rest areas. It's wonderful, because, you know, this really is an international organization. Wherever you travel, in the States or in Europe, you can visit homes and gardens. You learn so much about a community and its people from its gardens."

She is a sustaining member of the Junior League. "It's very good, because it gets you out into the community," Alyce says. "They train people to act as volunteers in many different organizations. You learn what the community needs, and how you can help it."

She is involved in the docent program at the Huntington Library. "You must take a course and then an examination, and you take a refresher course each year. The children's tours are especially interesting, because you help open their eyes to art."

She is an officer of the Blue Ribbon Four Hundred, the

major support group for the Los Angeles Music Center, which her inlaw, Mrs. Norman ("Buffy") Chandler, was instrumental in creating. "You donate money and time and energy. There also are a lot of programs for children revolving around the Music Center. They are bused in from outlying areas to hear special programs, and there are demonstrations of all the instruments of the orchestra, and instruments are made available for the children to try themselves." She adds, "Pasadena considers itself thoroughly part of Los Angeles. We're totally involved in what's happening in the entire city. I think I spend more time on the freeways than I do at home."

In February 1979 the new Neiman-Marcus store opened on Wilshire Boulevard in Beverly Hills. The grand opening party, attended by virtually every celebrity and socialite in the city, was a benefit for the Performing Arts of the Music Center. Alyce Williamson was one of the major organizers. Shortly before the event, for once she sounded harassed. "Will it be ready, will it possibly be ready in time?" she worried. "You mean everything for the party?" "Not the party. The store. Will the store be ready to open in time for the party!"

Most importantly—since it is one of the organizations that involves a great deal of her time—she is on the board of Girls' Club West. Here, girls from underprivileged families are taught skills and crafts, while girls from more privileged families (especially members of the Tick-Tock Club of the National Charity League) are trained to help and to teach.

Raising money for this group has been one of Alyce's most challenging projects. A couple of years ago a national foundation offered matching funds if Girls' Club West could raise a certain amount of money—the sort of thing she loves to get her teeth into. She initiated an annual Kentucky Derby Party for the first Saturday in May. The first year she arranged a spectacular at the nearby San Marino estate of her mother-in-law, which she named "Crocker Downs" for the occasion. Tents were set up throughout the immense garden, and television sets were hung in trees, so that everyone could watch the race. Official Kentucky Derby programs and official glasses were flown in from Kentucky. As usual in Pasadena/San

Marino circles, friends and family flooded in from all across the country to participate, and $75,000 was raised. "It was a wonderful party, and a nice profit but not a great one. We spent too much money on the tents and things," Alyce says. "In 1979 I decided to do the party at Hollywood Park in the Gold Cup Room. We got Cary Grant as the official celebrity, and we called the event 'Crocker Downs Goes Hollywood.' We raised a great deal more money, because we didn't have that initial outlay of expenses. Next year, I'll think of something else—I don't like to do the same thing twice.

"A few years ago," she says, "a lot of my friends were starting their own businesses, and I began to wonder if I was sort of falling behind. And then I realized that so many of these organizations couldn't exist unless we raised the money for them. Our Pasadena Guild makes over three hundred thousand dollars annually for the Children's Hospital, and we make millions annually for the Music Center. If I had a real job, I honestly wouldn't have to work as hard as I do now. But we're helping people, and I still feel that that's the most important thing you can do in your life."

Typically, she nearly always says "we." When you try to talk about Alyce Williamson, she says, "We have so many amazing women leaders. Mrs. Norman Chandler, who saved the Hollywood Bowl and created the Music Center. Mary Duque's work for the Children's Hospital has been fantastic. Marge Everette has done so much for the city. And there are so many others—"

She is about to embark on a long list when I interrupt. "But you've done a great deal yourself."

"You know how it works. You do one job and do it well, and people ask you to do other jobs, and it just spirals."

This is not false modesty. She knows that what she has done has been useful, but thinks of herself as a woman who has devoted herself primarily to her family rather than entirely to charities as some others have done. "To tell you the truth, I was very good at modern dance, and I originally thought it might be a career. But my father, with that French background, was very old-fashioned—he thought I should just get married. So I married at twenty-three and had the children, and I loved taking care of babies. Until they were old enough to be in school full time, I didn't do anything else. Even now, when they're home I try to be home also. Of course, I'm on the phone a lot, but I'm here.

"The family still is the most important thing to me. We have a big family, my mother and father [this was before Henry de Roulet died], Spud's mother, my sister-in-law and her children, our children. And we've always done wonderful things together. We used to take our children to a dude ranch in Arizona every year, and up to Big Bear for the snow. We'd spend a lot of time at the house in Santa Barbara. [Lady Crocker built two houses there, one for herself and one for all the children and their children.] And we have a lot near Del Mar at St. Malo, which is called that because it looks like Normandy. We haven't built on the lot yet, but we rent a house nearby. And you should be here for some of the family parties— the house just overflows and we all get really silly. We have the big Christmas party every year, and we did use the Valley Hunt Club for an engagement party for my niece—I had pink tablecloths and pink flowers and the place cards were done in calligraphy, and it truly was beautiful. And when my sister-in-law was out here with the Mets [Laurinda Payson de Roulet was part owner of the Mets], we did a lovely party out in the garden. Come look at the Christmas pictures!"

The baby grand piano in Alyce's living room is covered with family photographs: Alyce in her grandmother's wedding gown, pictures of all the children at various ages, photos of everyone connected with the family. But here are the two she especially wants to show me. The Christmas party with everyone, including Lady Crocker and Harry Chandler, lined up on the long stairway and looking very serious and sophisticated. The matching photograph with the same party and same lineup, but with everyone wearing fright wigs and funny hats or masks, and making faces; even Lady Crocker, even Harry Chandler.

On the day of the Art Walk, Alyce corrals her friend Robbie to show me around her own house, though there are plenty of League members there to do the job. We start in the entry, where there is a superb walnut parquet floor, "a miracle of workmanship," Robbie murmurs, just as a woman comes sprinting across it to wave him down. "Robbie, please! Talk to Malvina [her decorator, it turns out] and tell her how to get this. I must have this exact floor!" He gives me a look; this kind of floor has not been available in the United States for forty years.

The study—and in this house it is not a den—is exactly what a study should be: paneled walls, deep and high-backed chairs, a fireplace with brass fittings. There are some good art objects and paintings, and some photographs of Hunter's Moon and other winning horses in the Williamson racing stable.

"Both sides of our family have been involved with horses, always," Alyce says. There was a time, when I first knew her, when she considered this involvement frivolous, perhaps a waste of money; but now she talks readily about it. "Spud is really into breeding now, and the mares are kept near Murietta Hot Springs. We have three horses racing at the moment, and about twenty in training. Spud has a partner with some of the horses, and he's so involved himself. I don't go to every race, but if one of our horses is running, you can't keep me away. Once you're been in the winner's circle, you're addicted."

So there are racing photos. And in the living room, one room that is completed as far as redecorating is concerned, there is a racing print that Robbie had especially designed for the sofa and windows. "Ah, this is a man's room," some of the passing tour members are heard to say. And indeed, there is the flintlock rifle collection, and the Charlie Dye western paintings on the walls, both Spud's special interests. But there are also some fine old French paintings from Alyce's grandmother, and some fine pieces of antique furniture, gifts of Lady Crocker; there are Alyce's collection of frogs, and all the family photos on the piano. There are some quite mature paintings by the youngest daughter on several walls. There is the family cat curled up on the window seat in the sunniest spot, impervious to all the comings and goings and unexpected pats. It is very much a family room, spacious and comfortable, a little bit of everybody's personality included in it.

There is an immense upper hallway, extremely high-ceilinged. "Must get rid of that French blue," Robbie murmurs. The stair walls hold two handsome pieces of ancient Chinese art, and so Robbie has brought in a twelve-panel, twenty-four-foot-long Chinese Cormandel screen to bring the upper hall into balance and to tie in the themes. Spud does not care for the screen. Everyone is playing a waiting game. Will Spud get used to it? Will Alyce convince him that it is absolutely right? The tour members are making their own judgments. "Fantastic!" everyone exclaims. "Incredible!" "Robbie, you're a genius!" A pity Spud is not here to be swayed. Then again, just as well he is not here to see two thousand people sweeping through his house.

The 1930 Monterey Colonial house, its furnishings and its grounds are very much like Alyce herself: a combination of conservativeness and openness, with a lot of warmth and friendliness thrown in. There is a very long arched gallery that follows the L shape of the back of the house; sometimes Alyce puts isinglass curtains at the arches and entertains out here on winter evenings. Some very old camellias hug the arches, and there are willows and Chinese elms and birches and ferns in the lawn-covered backyard. She has held dances on the tennis court, which is far to the rear of the property, and has had parties around the brick-edged pool, which has deep green tile inside, so that the water appears green as the Nile. Everything here says "old Pasadena" in a very comfortable—and comforting—way. Throughout the day-long tour the visitors agree: "Alyce's house is the best."

The next house, around the corner and down the hill from the Williamsons', is truly wild—there is nothing subtle about it inside or out. It is an immense house on an immense piece of property and it shouts these facts the minute it comes into view. Inside, it seems as though each room were done by a different designer, each trying to express the most eclectic taste to the most extreme degree.

There is a black-and-white-tiled entryway, with black-painted arches leading to other rooms, and a black bar with glass shelves and Art Deco objects, spotlit. The dining room is red and purple, with the largest glass-topped table I've ever seen—"Five thousand dollars if it cost a penny," Robbie whispers. The room is dramatic but dark. The living room, on the other hand, is tall as a cathedral, all bleached oak floors and bleached paneled walls and bleached beams and bleached natural fabrics. Seating is on the floor, that is, in chairs without legs. There is an immense plant, seemingly part cactus and part palm, which rises in one corner almost to the height of the cathedral ceiling. It is like a church in a desert; or a desert in a church. "Can you imagine cuddling up to the fire in a room like this?" Robbie whispers.

Downstairs is a very long L-shaped gallery, the floors a wonderful old deep-green tile, the walls covered with palm-frond paper. A thatched-roof Tahitian-style bar is the focal point; or perhaps it is the tall arch turned into an aerie, with a toucan in it. One end of the L passes numerous bedrooms designed in various advanced contemporary styles; its archways are open to the long rectangular swimming pool, and ("Why, why?" Robbie moans) Mexican reed chairs hang on the walls between each arch. Upstairs are other bedrooms, some sort of semi–Art Deco, and an all-mirror black bathroom that you walk up to via one short set of stairs and down from via another. There is a tower room, with a wrought-iron-encircled outside stairway leading up to it, and other such things.

Outside is an excess of gardens and pergolas and little huts with telescopes for viewing the distant edges of Pasadena, and under the house is room-upon-room, a dark room and a Ping-Pong room and a cedar closet room with dozens of drawers and many many other rooms, all painted in lively colors, with pipes painted in contrasting lively colors so that it all looks like the Beaubourg in Paris. There also is a long string of garages where craftspeople are working today, showing their wares and methods for the tour. Some of the garages are high enough to hold fire engines, and it is difficult to imagine their original purpose. The salmon-colored stucco building, with its towers and porte-cochere and green tile roof, was designed by the same person who designed the Biltmore Hotel in Santa Barbara. And this is the way some other people live in Pasadena.

The tour members tsk-tsked their ways through this house. No one in Pasadena cares to offend. They damned carefully, simply by muttering throughout the tour, "Ah, Alyce's house! Now that's a beautiful house!"

"Let's go back to the house and get the car and go to the club for lunch," Alyce says, "and then we'll finish the tour." We walk back up the curving streets, but it is difficult to move quickly when you are in her company. Everyone milling around the usually quiet side streets on this tour day knows her, everybody has to stop her to talk about some project or some meeting or some personal subject. "This is my good friend," she says, introducing me to every person she speaks to. Pasadenans are naturally polite, but Alyce has a special kind of openness that makes her introduce me this way.

When we finally arrive back at the house, the Black man who takes care of the parquet floor has just arrived to make sure that everything is going along all right. We are introduced. "What time is the tour over?" he wants to know. "I'll come back when everyone's gone and get the scuff marks out." It will be nearly eight o'clock when everyone finally has gone, but he will return then, because people do this sort of thing for Alyce. "He cares more about that floor than I do," she says.

It takes at least another forty-five minutes to get away from the house. It is the Pasadena-San Marino tradition—all two thousand people on this tour know one another, or of one another, in some way. Alyce has opened her house for the Art Walk because "everybody helps out everybody else here. We all support each other's charities." Like Alyce, I was born and raised in Los Angeles, but I keep in occasional touch with only one girl I knew in all the long school years. "One thing I love about this area," Alyce says, "I know so many people I grew up with. Our parents all grew up together and our grandparents too. I love this sense of identity with family and friends and neighborhood."

"I'll get the Peugeot," she says when we finally escape the house, although the Peugeot is in the garage and there are about eighty people in her driveway, including the ticket takers at their card-table stands. "No," Robbie says, "we can all squeeze into the Honda, if I take the umbrellas out." The umbrellas are for some other decorating project and quickly are disposed of; the Honda is a Civic, the smallest of the line. "I live in Santa Barbara now, you know," Robbie says, "but all of my work is in Los Angeles. So I drive down nearly every day. [Santa Barbara is two hours or more north.] This is a marvelous car for it, it gets such good mileage. Sometimes, if I have a huge amount of paperwork to do and I know it's going to be a really long day, I hire an off-duty fireman or policeman to drive me. They're happy to earn the extra money, and I can sit in the back and do my paperwork."

The Valley Hunt Club is impressive, not because it is grand, but because it is charming and warm and familiar feeling. It is a large, cozy house, a real house and an old one. It has long stretches of polished wood floors, a scattering of fine old Oriental carpets, lots of comfortable print-covered couches and wing chairs, some nice old oil paints on the walls. There is a handsome staircase, and it is in the rooms above that many of Alyce's meetings are held. The dining room is immense, perhaps originally a ballroom, and there are lots of tables-for-four covered in linen and set with nice china and fresh flowers. As usual, it is difficult to get Alyce settled; too many people *have* to talk to her.

It is during lunch that she turns to Robbie with a wicked grin. "Do you think I should show June the Room?"

He grins back. "Yes, of course. You must show her the Room."

"After we finish the tour," she tells me, "I'll show you the real Alyce Williamson."

The next stop is two condominiums in the same contemporary compound, each decorated by some well-known local decorator, each innocuous. There are many polite comments to the owners, and many raised eyebrows as people leave. The best aspects of both apartments are the flower arrangements done by the members of the San Marino League, many of whom have trained ten years or more to develop their skills. They have kept the arrangements simple in these simple settings: a clutch of anemones here, a spray of wheat there. At Alyce's house, they did very dignified arrangements in the Chippendale-furnished dining room with its Meissen table service, whimsical arrangements with Italian ceramic rabbits in the garden, striking Japanese arrangements in the upper hallway, a fine balance for the Cormandel screen. It was at the eccentric house that they had their finest hour, with arrangements as striking as the house, a difficult achievement. They scooped out fresh pears to serve as holders for single flowers; set fresh pineapples, scooped out and filled with flowers, on beds of purple cabbage leaves; wrapped candles in other colorful leaves. Everywhere you looked there was a surprise, in a house already filled with surprises.

The last house on the tour is charming, and also a surprise: very small, circa 1930, in a section that scarcely could be called elite, a narrow street filled with other 1930 houses almost touching one another. But the interior has been architecturally redesigned to accommodate a fine collection of contemporary art; there are a number of delightful touches, some a result of the design elements, some a result of the art; there is a cozy book-lined study and an extremely convenient kitchen; there is a pool area with rocky ledges enclosed in a natural bower. This house is approved of by all.

Back at Alyce's there is the usual delay while she talks to guests. Then finally up the stairs, which suddenly are empty since everyone is having tea in the garden. "Quick," she says, lifting the velvet rope that has kept the master suite off limits to the tour. "We can't let anyone see us doing this." The three of us slip under. We are in an immense room, a true "master suite" with almost an entire corridor of dressing rooms and tiled bathrooms and walk-in closets attached, and a fine view across the wide lawn. It is very attractive and not very unusual. How is the real Alyce to be found here?

There is a door to the side. "The master study!" Alyce announces. She flings open the door to a large room. A room in total disarray.

There are boxes of books and boxes of photographs and boxes of all the other kinds of things, much of which can be termed junk, which people, especially people with children, tend to collect. There is a stuffed duck, lying upside down on a table. All other available surfaces are piled with old clothes.

"What do you do," she asks me, "when you know that two thousand people are going to be tramping through your house?" I would do exactly what she has done.

Earlier, Alyce has said, "I don't go in for clean closets and clean dresser drawers and writing letters. I'm involved in the details of life—I like to do everything myself and I like to do it perfectly—but the details must be for important things. You like to give of yourself and do all these details for other people. Robbie takes care of the details for my own life, he's the only one I know who can do things better for me than I can for myself."

We are standing among some of these details of her life, amid the clutter collected by a real person who lives a real life. And, indeed, it tells me something new about Alyce Williamson.

"Someday," Robbie says, looking at her in the best he can manage of a stern manner, "this will be a beautiful study."

Alyce giggles.

12

Stars and Stars Forever: Hollywood

"Hi," the man says with a nice wide grin, getting up from behind the round table to shake hands; getting, in fact, much farther *up* than one might have imagined from seeing him on television—he is quite a tall man. "I'm Dennis Weaver," he says, and Joplin, Missouri, comes through in the slight drawl, although it is tempered by twenty-five years of southern California living. "Sit down," he says. "Have an apple."

At this particular time, Dennis Weaver has long since ceased to be Chester (in which role he did not look tall—everyone looks short next to James Arness), has ceased being Gentle Ben's owner, is now McCloud. He also is president of the Screen Actors' Guild and has done numerous innovative things for, and with, that organization; he is about to preside over a Thalians' dinner honoring Debbie Reynolds ("an old friend"); he is involved in the UCLA talent award scholarships; he is on a special Bicentennial committee for the film industry; he is making appearances or taping commercials for the Crippled Children's Fund, the American Cancer Society and the Heart Fund, among other charities; and, in his spare time, he is narrating educational films on law enforcement to be shown in schools. Like so many people who commit themselves to twenty-six-hour days, he appears totally relaxed during this brief break in his office-bungalow on the Universal Studios lot, even though he is sharing the break with a stranger. "Well," he says between crunches, "tell me a little about yourself. Where're you from, to start with?"

Dennis Weaver is a man from Missouri who likes to play the guitar and to write songs (he has had several albums released), who likes to grow his own vegetables and go back-packing with his sons, who is interested in Indian weaving and basketry and all types of crafts, who believes in eating natural foods (his wife, Gerry, once owned a health-food store, and now is a consultant on the subject), who would like to "just go up to Arrowhead or Flagstaff or somewhere and hibernate for a while," but is much too busy to find even the time to daydream about that.

For a while, he did do the celebrity number, owned the big house with the immense lawns and gardens, the near-Olympic-size pool, the tennis court. "But you know," he says slowly, "that wasn't really me. You don't want a place that consumes you, I finally figured that out." He moved to a smaller place in Calabasas, far out in the Valley. "It's just like an old California town," he says. "There even are hitching posts, and they have a Pumpkin Festival once a year. A lot of craftspeople live there, and the air is fresher and you feel less hemmed in. Of course we still have a pool." He laughs. "But it's a small one."

At last, here is a celebrity who admits to liking Los Angeles. "L.A. is a city with a small-town feeling, and yet the culture is very diversified. It's more like a rainbow than a melting pot. I think more good things catch on here than just about anywhere else, the crafts, the health foods. I'd like to live here even if I weren't involved in films." He even enjoys the long drives to and from work, accomplished in a small energy-saving car. "Well, I admit it," he says, with that nice grin, "I enjoy having the people in the next car recognize me. I stare straight ahead, but out of the corner of my eye I can see them looking. I pretend to ignore them. Then, all of a sudden, I turn and I give 'em a big smile and I wave."

Dennis Weaver does not seem at all "Hollywood." And yet, of course, that is exactly what he is, as is anyone who is a success in what is known as "the business."

As virtually everyone knows by now, Hollywood-the-film-center has nothing to do with the quiet, mostly residential section of Los Angeles called Hollywood; and, with a few minor exceptions, it never did. When Hollywood was incorporated into the city of Los Angeles in 1910, it was already a well-established residential and citrus-farming community of four thousand people, with numerous churches, schools and clubs—and not one single nickleodeon, despite the instant popularity of this new fad. It had a single showplace—the mansion and incredible gardens of artist Paul de Longpré, situated almost exactly where the noted intersection of Hollywood and Vine is today. When the first eastern movie makers, Selig, the Bison Company, Griffith, came west, they settled in and around Los Angeles, but not in Hollywood. Slightly later, the Nestor Company and the Lasky Company came west, and these two fairly small groups did choose Hollywood as their headquarters—one of them taking over an old riding stable. Cecil B. De Mille was associated with Lasky—perhaps he, more than anyone, can be credited with giving this small section of town its reputation as the film capital of the world.

By the time the movies were in their heyday, only Paramount and RKO were established in Hollywood, and they were at the far eastern edge. MGM had taken immense acreage far to the southwest, in Culver City, and David O. Selznick had built his Tara-styled offices next door. Twentieth Century–Fox was almost as far southwest, right next to what is now Century City. Warner Brothers had gone over the hills to Burbank, the eastern end of the Valley. Hollywood and Vine had become famous, but for what? As long as I can remember, it has been an ordinary intersection with a drugstore (not the famous Schwab's) on one corner, the Broadway Department Store on another, an office building and a coffee shop on the other two. This famous cross-street, and all the rest of this section of the city, are major disappointments to visitors. Yet the image persists. It is rooted in myth.

Before the great equalizer, television, swept its way across the country, making the farmer in Iowa as *au courant* as the stockbroker in New York, nobody knew anything about Hollywood except what they saw in the movies or read in the movie magazines. And neither of those told the truth. So people imagined a glittering city, searchlight previews nightly, snazzy cars on every street, movie stars in every restaurant and every store.

We took a trip across the country when I was seven. We had a brand-new car, a gleaming golden-brown sedan, and the license plate frames said "Hollywood, California." Every place we stopped, every single place, people would come out to gather around our car. It did not matter that we were not celebrities. All that mattered was that we were from the golden land. We asked a motorcycle policeman in Dallas if he could tell us how to reach the section of the city where my great-uncle lived. "You really from Hollywood?" he asked. "Yes." "Okay, follow me!" And he turned on his siren and led us all the way across Dallas at a screaming seventy miles per hour, right to my uncle's door. There was magic in that name back then.

I was born in Hollywood and I grew up here and even I believed in the myth. Believed that only my family's overprotec- tiveness kept me from seeing the glitter, the stars, the snazzy cars. We shopped and went to restaurants and movies on Hollywood Boulevard, the famous street—and it was a street like any other in the late thirties and the forties. This is not to say that the great picture palaces of more glamorous times did not exist—they still do: Graumann's (now Mann's, a sacrilege) Chinese, the pagoda-shaped monster with the forecourt where generations of stars have left their footprints; the Egyptian, a wonderful monument to the Art Deco period; the Paramount, another Art Deco fantasy, now trying to earn its keep as a legitimate theatre; Warner Brothers, where the first Cinerama films were shown. Occasionally, premiers were still held at these theatres, although the majority were held at the Carthay Circle in another part of town.

But then, as now, none of these places stood out as unique or grand; the famous palaces rubbed shoulders with too many little shops and big stores and hamburger stands and banks and restaurants and smaller movie theatres to create the mood of grandeur one expected. The cars that drove this street and the people who walked it were ordinary. Then, as now, there was Hollywood the city and Hollywood the fantasy. For millions of people the fantasy was, and still is, the more real.

A childhood friend moved out of the city. A year or so later she wrote, "Oh, you're so lucky to still be living in Hollywood and seeing movie stars all the time!" I'd never seen a movie star in my life.

I wish I had known Charlie Callas then. To meet Charlie is to meet Hollywood. He greets you as Cary Grant. Not the hackneyed "Judy, Judy, Judy" number, but doing a rather elaborate conversation between debonair actor and unknown journalist. Like all great impressionists, when Callas does Grant, he *is* Grant. "Ah," he sighs, "I'm just a businessman now, my friend, you can't be interested in me. Here's the great showman of all time," and James Cagney does a quick buck-and-wing, before shaking your hand and launching into a long tough-guy routine about how he's really not a tough guy. He quickly turns into George Jessel, who gives a genuine toastmaster's speech to introduce George Sanders. "But Sanders is dead," you protest. "Never mind, my dear," says that most suave of all suave voices, "that hasn't changed my attitude about life one bit." Finally, you beg Dean Martin to let you speak to the real Charlie Callas, and Martin gives you a long, loud raspberry.

"How many times, just for the record, have you been on the Johnny Carson show?" I ask Charlie, having finally nabbed him.

"Oh, fifty, sixty times. They keep letting me try until I get it right."

Some of the stars Callas so convincingly brings to life did, in earlier days, touch down on the far western fringe of Hollywood. The Hollywood Hotel, on Hollywood Boulevard near La Brea, once had its share of celebrities; farther west, the tile-roofed bungalows of the flamboyant Garden of Allah were the scene of many a wild Hollywood party. Just across Sunset from the savings and loan building that replaced the Garden, the Chateau Marmont, an apartment-hotel where stars are reported to have lived, still exists in old Hollywood splendor. (Long after seeing movie stars ceased to matter, I once ran into Shelley Winters there.) But it was the Beverly Hills Hotel and the Bel Air Hotel, and in more recent times the Beverly Wilshire Hotel, where movie stars generally were to be found, and none of those places is in Hollywood; two of them, technically, are not even in Los Angeles.

If the Hollywood fantasy exists today, these hotels could be said to be its headquarters. Certainly they are where eastern writers come to interview celebrities and find out about the latest "big picture" deals, and discover the stories they have been looking for ready made for them.

They tell how everyone in Los Angeles lies around swimming pools all day, drinking exotic drinks and getting bronzed while they talk on the phone and make deals. Or how everyone sits in the Polo Lounge at the Beverly Hills Hotel all day, drinking and doing business as above. How love affairs are like the freeways, fast and dangerous. How people queue up in long lines to take their clothes to the "in" cleaners and get their pastramis on rye from the "in" deli. They take a few minutes away from those Beverly Hills or Bel Air enclaves to "experience the cult of the freeway" or to lunch at Le Bistro (again in Beverly Hills). And return home to write about the decadence of Los Angeles life.

It is difficult, if not impossible, for anyone who does not live here to realize how far away Hollywood is from Los Angeles. Farther away, even, than Los Angeles is from New York.

Hollywood is, of course, the motion picture industry, which has expanded and overlapped with the television industry. It is the record business and all its accoutrements. It is the public relations business and the publicity business, the business managers and the talent managers and the actors' agents. It is even the advertising business, since television commercials require actors and actresses, sound stages, cameramen, grips. It is the unions, tough as steel, that protect the talent from all the people who are trying to take advantage of it. It is the numerous agencies that have sprung up to translate the extraordinarily complicated union rules for the layman. For

instance, if an advertising agency uses SAG or AFTRA talent
to do a radio or television commercial, there is virtually no way
its personnel can figure out what must be paid in studio fees,
initial talent fees, use fees, in A markets or B markets or
whatever. There are entire companies that not only translate
all these rules and regulations, but take care of the myriad
necessary payments.

Many of the people on the business end of these businesses
actually operate out of the East; they come here only to close
the deals. When they come, they fill up these hotels, recover
from their jet lag around the pools or in the lounges, and set the
models for what are considered elsewhere as Los Angeles
stereotypes. I have been to formal dinner parties where some of
the out-of-town guests have worn loafers with no socks. "Why
are you not wearing socks?" I ask in amazement each time—
assuming that anyone so crude will not mind my own rudeness.
"Why this is the way everyone in Los Angeles dresses," I am
told, every time.

Actually, many of the people "in the business" are, like
Dennis Weaver, far more Angelino than Hollywood. Joan
Rivers is a wonderful case in point. I called her to set up an
interview. She answered the phone herself. "Oh, listen June,"
she said, as though she had known me forever, "I've got a
terrible problem right now, and I can't even explain it." She
was whispering. "Could you possibly call me Saturday morning?"

On Saturday, it turned out that the problem was a long-time
nurse who was taken seriously ill. "She's like my family," Joan
Rivers said. "I didn't want her to know we were talking about
her, I didn't want her to know how serious we thought it was."
It is an indication of how vulnerable she herself is. "I think
comedians are the most sensitive, the most vulnerable people in
the world," she tells me later. "When my mother died—and
she was the closest person to me in the whole world—when
friends came over to console me, I made jokes. When Kennedy
died, I made jokes. It's the only way I can survive these things,
to cover them up. You lose friends sometimes, but basically,
we're all manic-depressives, we can only survive trying to make

ups out of the downs. Take someone like Don Rickles. You can kill him by hitting him with a feather. One night at an opening I sat at the same table with Woody Allen and Dick Cavett. You would have thought there'd be peals of laughter coming from that table, but it was the glummest table in the room. We were discussing comedy.

"I started out as a straight actress," she says. "I went to Barnard, I appeared in things like *Othello* and *Mourning Becomes Electra*. I started to make the rounds of the New York agents, and I'd do something to make the secretaries laugh so they'd remember me. One day, an agent came out and saw me doing my number. 'You should be a comedian,' he said. So I joined Second City, with Alan Arkin and Barbara Harris. We learned, we all learned.

"All comedians are on the thin edge. Comedy is insanity pulled in. You see things upside down. That's the wonderful part, and the scary part. Listen," she asks, "have you ever watched comedians watching other comedians? They don't laugh. They sit there, and they hear a line, *the* line—because of course every comedy act is based on a one-liner—and they think, 'Why didn't I think of that line?' When you hear a great one, you kick yourself for not having thought of it.

"Come back," she says. Not wistfully, but with a certain generosity that comes through as graciousness. "Ask me anything," she says. "I'll talk for hours."

Jack Lemmon is another personality who doesn't seem to fit the Hollywood image. It is lunch break on a movie set. Lemmon does not just talk, it is as though he is in a marathon for people who can talk the longest, fastest, best. And yet it doesn't come across that he's talking for show—only that he's talking because he really likes to do it, likes to philosophize, likes to try to figure out what it is that makes certain people do certain things. Later, I report our conversation to his agent. "Not bad, for a Harvard man," he says. Lemmon never mentioned Harvard.

"Human behavior, the daily things, the things that make everyday life livable, that's the hardest stuff to do, the hardest to write and direct, the hardest to act. When I first got out of school I went to New York and I saw every single show playing on Broadway. And do you know which one had the most laughs? *Streetcar Named Desire.* Because laughter comes out of the real things in real life, the problems, the day-to-day living. You don't think of *Streetcar* as a comedy, do you? But it's funny. Funnier than all the comedies on Broadway that season.

"That's what life is all about. Not black or white, but the gray areas in between. That's what makes you able to bear life. The gray areas. And the funny things you can find to laugh at in them. Even when I do a very serious role, I try to remember that—that there is comedy in every tragedy. And, conversely, a little tragedy in every comedy. I think it's more difficult for a serious actor to do comedy than for a comedian to do tragedy. Because the comedian already has learned that there's a little sorrow behind every laugh.

"Find the character," he adds. "We're all a little bewildered today—'What are we doing here and how do we cope?' I try to find the weak spot in a character, and play on it, because I believe people will identify with that."

There are certain places in Los Angeles where you can regularly sight celebrities. There are several office buildings on Sunset Boulevard, just where it crosses the Los Angeles city line into Beverly Hills, where numerous top agents keep their odd hours and meet their famous clients; if you rode the elevators of these buildings over a period of a few days, you probably would see some of the most noted faces in filmdom. Le Bistro in Beverly Hills is a popular lunch and dinner spot with movie people, as is Ma Maison, in an unobtrusive area of Melrose Avenue just east of La Cienega. Any of the more expensive restaurants—Mr. Chow's in Beverly Hills, l'Orangerie, l'Hermitage or the Palm, all edging Hollywood— are possible spots for sightings, and I have seen Rock Hudson at the Brown Derby on Vine Street, and Zsa Zsa Gabor and Rod Taylor at Le St. Germaine on Melrose.

Special concerts at the Hollywood Bowl or the Greek Theatre may bring out the Hollywood contingent, but both of these outdoor amphitheatres are so immense that no one can stand out from the crowd. Opening nights at the Huntington Hartford or any of the theatres at the Music Center usually find famous friends of the play's stars present; on the other hand, at the opera or ballet the *Times*'s music and dance critics generally are the only stars in the audience. On the Rox, the private club above the Roxy on the Sunset Strip, is a noted hangout for hip Hollywoodians—the only problem is that you cannot get in. The more exclusive health clubs regularly draw celebrities: Jane Fonda's Workout gym in Beverly Hills is a best bet.

The Polo Lounge at the Beverly Hills Hotel remains the all-around best spot for regularly seeing stars. Incredibly crowded—you have to make reservations just to have a drink there at cocktail hour—and always more than two-thirds filled with tourists, Hollywood hangers-on and hopeful starlets, it nonetheless retains its status as a rendezvous for some of the top film people. A recent visit turned up John Huston leading an entourage through the crowds, Ginger Rogers holding court in a corner, Anthony Hopkins table hopping. And even if there are no famous faces in sight, the atmosphere of old Hollywood is unmistakable. An aging uniformed page, barely four feet tall, carries from table to table a slate with the names of people who have telephone calls waiting; when a name is identified, he hurries off for a telephone, which he plugs in next to that person's table. Many of the most important behind-the-scenes people of Hollywood eat and drink here; many of the biggest deals are consummated here. The management, the alert switchboard operators and the ubiquitous page make doing business easy.

If any place epitomizes both the fantasy and the reality of Hollywood, it is the Beverly Hills Hotel. It sprawls across some of the most beautiful and most expensive acreage in the city, fronted by Sunset Boulevard, backed by the Santa Monica Mountains. It is an immense pink-stucco-and-tile building, and the requisite giant palm trees wave their fronds high above its roof, the requisite subtropical plants bloom in its gardens, and its backdrop of sky seems always to be blue. It has established the "Hollywood scene" for many a movie over the past half-century; one of the earliest I recall was a George Burns comedy.

The years have treated both the "pink palace," as it is often called, and Burns well. Both have become legends; both manage to look and act far younger than their ages. Yet Burns often uses his age as a takeoff point for his humor. "Some of the new comedians talk very fast. I'm on the slow side with my delivery." Pause. "Outside my delivery I'm slow, too." Or, "Today comedians can say all those four-letter words you couldn't say before. I'm not against them, but I don't use them. I know what they mean." Pause. "But at my age it doesn't do any good."

The pauses, of course, are his trademark. "I time my jokes by smoking a cigar. I draw on the cigar to give the laughter time to quiet down. I don't try to get a laugh a second. Anybody who makes people laugh that hard, the audience should get paid for laughing." When he's not on the road or making a film, he's in his office every morning at ten A.M. Yet despite his schedule, he insists he parties nightly. "I'm a smash at parties. I'm always my best when I'm not getting paid. I love to go to parties because I sing. I bring my own accompanist, and if they don't have a piano, I bring that too. People love to invite me to parties."

"Of course I lie a lot," he adds. "I don't tell jokes, I do stories based on my own experience, and if you told the truth it wouldn't be funny. I went to the dentist. What's funny about that? You have to embellish it, tell the dentist's name, where he is, talk about his mother . . . you have to exaggerate to make it funny. Of course I always let the audience know I'm lying, and that always gets a laugh." Pause. "Well, not always."

"I never lie," says Milton Berle. "I'm the only actor in the world who will tell you the truth." Don't bother to ask what the truth is—the answer to that is, "Read my book, you'll find out." Like Burns, Berle has never retired or even relaxed. He spends much of his time teaching the comedic arts at seminars in universities all over the country; and he does not just preach what he practices. "Personally, I like sophisticated humor—wit, farce, satire. Mort Sahl, Nichols and May in their heyday,

I try to tune the kids into all of that. But you know, they laugh like crazy over my old routines, because they've never seen them before.

"Listen," he says confidentially, "years ago I created this character. He was brash, aggressive, insulting. He was a success. I'm not crazy about him anymore, I think he's outlived his time. But who am I to argue with success? I've been in this business over sixty years, and I guess I'll keep on doing what I do well. About forty years ago a critic said about me, 'Nobody likes Milton Berle—except the public and his mother.' Well, my mother died, but I've still got the public."

The public is called fickle, but it is loyal to the stars who seem to warrant it. And also to the idea of the glamor of Hollywood-behind-the-scenes. There probably is not an Angelino alive who hasn't received at least one letter from relative or friend saying, "Coming to California—can you get me on a movie set?" In the past, unless one was well established "in the business," the answer had to be no; movie sets were virtually impossible to penetrate. Rather belatedly, a major studio finally got the message. A few years ago Universal inaugurated its Universal City Tours, and they remain so popular that during peak tourist seasons the line of cars trying to get onto the lot is backed up for several blocks onto the Hollywood Freeway. The tours are a marvel of showmanship: cowboys fight gun duels, stuntmen fall from buildings, famous film disasters are re-created left and right of the little trams that carry the incredulous visitors through back lots and past film sets. It is glamorous and exciting and it has very little to do with what happens on an average set on an average day.

Waiting is the name of the game on any movie set. Patience is the ultimate virtue. It can take hours for the lights and scrims and reflectors and filters to be put into position. The transposition of a few props can cause aching delays. Union rules are strict; the man who is allowed to move this object specifically is prohibited from moving that one; there can be ten grips hovering, doing nothing, but if the correct grip is not present, nothing can be done. Eagle eyes check and double-check details—if today's shooting is a continuation of yesterday's scene, every hair on the actors' heads must lie in the same position as the day before, watches must show the same time, a wrinkled sleeve must keep its wrinkle intact, a belt may not be a notch looser or tighter. There are rehearsals before the camera rolls; and after it rolls a dozen or a hundred things can happen to cause the call: "Let's try it again, please." On the set of *Hotel*, Rod Taylor was doing a bathtub scene. "If you want to talk to me, honey," he called, "you'd better do it fast. I've been in this water so long I'm turning into an old man." He held up a water-wrinkled hand to prove it.

Yet the public fascination with behind-the-scenes never falters. I was on a sound stage where a scene was being set up for a commercial about a laundry product. Large cut-out letters were being lined up in front of a washing machine to spell out the commercial's message, and it was taking forever to get them straight. Somehow an elderly lady from the neighborhood had slipped in, and she was watching with fascination. "Isn't it wonderful?" she remarked, without taking her eyes from the set. "They do everything so carefully. That's what the film business is all about, you know," she said, finally turning to look at me. She was quite correct.

As has often been said, the film business is also about generosity—it is one of the thousands of stories about Hollywood that is not a myth. Actors will leap on planes by the dozens to go to a friend's opening in Las Vegas or even in New York; they will applaud the longest and the loudest if one of their number is appearing in a play—even if the play isn't very good, even if the acting is below par. They are active in their support of the various homes for aged film people. And when it comes to appearing at benefits or giving their time to supporting a charity, they are tireless.

One year, as a favor to a friend, I wrote a series of radio and television commercials for the Boy Scouts of America's annual Scout-O-Rama, inviting people to attend or to give money so that underprivileged children could join. I also was asked to recruit talent for the commercials, and it was suggested that famous names would be best. Within a couple of hours of my first tentative phone calls, my telephone was ringing off its hook. Carol Burnett would be glad to record a radio spot. Bill Cosby didn't have time to come to a studio, but if I'd send a script he'd record it and send the tape back instantly. Lloyd Nolan would love to do one of the TV commercials, if I'd pick him up and take him home; he didn't like to drive. Jack Albertson would do likewise, though he would drive himself to the Boy Scout camp nearly twenty miles outside the city limits (which is very far, indeed). The Roger Wagner Chorale would be glad to lend their trained voices to those of the real Scouts who also would sing. Naturally, this was volunteer work, no one received any pay. Agents called constantly, offering talent: "So-and-so is in Chicago, but we'll be happy to fly him back for you." "So-and-so is televising in Vegas, we'll fly out a script and shoot her there." "I get ten to twenty charity requests in any given week," Dennis Weaver says, "and I do as many as I possibly can." So do they all.

The day spent with Lloyd Nolan was an intriguing glimpse into Hollywood's past. I picked him up at the large house in west Los Angeles, with its wide green lawns and fine gardens. "We paid a fortune for this house," he confides. "Something like twenty-five thousand!" He chuckles. "Of course, we were way out in the country then. Remember the bridle path along Sunset? Well, we used to ride down that to La Cienega, then all the way down La Cienega to about where Wilshire is now. It was just a dirt riding path then." La Cienega Boulevard has been Restaurant Row for as long as I can remember—but he is speaking of the twenties. "Hollywood was something in those days. There were stars and I mean *stars.* Hollywood Boulevard on a premier night was brighter than Broadway on an opening night—lights all over and cars . . . Coop had this La-gonda . . ." He stops for a little, as though sifting through memories. "But listen, it's really better now. Television has opened up so many avenues for actors, commercials too. There are many more ways for an actor to earn a living now. Sure, some of the glamor is gone. But the living's better for all of us today."

Today, Hollywood Boulevard is the Times Square of Los Angeles. The length of the street from Vine to La Brea has a sidewalk studded with stars, and the names of Hollywood celebrities from various eras are engraved inside them. Two-thirds are recognizable only to an expert on Hollywood trivia. There is a movement afoot to change the boulevard into a pedestrian mall, to erect high-rises, to change the names of the side streets from, say, Ivar to Tara.

Meanwhile the mean street exists. There are a lot of little movie theatres beside the palaces of old, and there are discount shops and war surplus stores, record shops and shops that sell T-shirts with "Hollywood" printed on them and souvenirs in the shapes of oranges and ashtrays with palm trees. There are hamburger stands, a dozen or more; and there is Musso Frank, "established 1924," with the wood-paneled booths where movie stars used to sit, and the long counter where you can watch the chef flip the famous flannel cakes, and the long bar that used to be a hangout for the great screen writers of the thirties and forties. There is an old Victorian mansion set far back from the street, with a parking lot in front of it; no one ever parks there, because the two elderly ladies who own the house and attend the lot are never in attendance. It is a ghost mansion on a street filled with the ghosts of a wonderful myth.

Hollywood Boulevard is one of the few streets in Los Angeles that is alive by night. Old men and women, often oddly dressed, walk there. Prostitutes are out in force, recognizable by high boots and low-cut tops and short skirts and long hair. A few junkies wander about, their gazes engaging you, then drifting off to nowhere. Hari Krishnas ring their hand bells and make their pitches for peace and love. There are Blacks and Chicanos playing the pinball machines in the hamburger joints, and the street is bumper-to-bumper cars, teenagers "cruising the Boulevard" as they have done nightly for the past twenty years. Head shops and poster shops and book shops stay open late here and there is the illusion that something is happening here; although, of course, it is not. Some people are trying to transform Hollywood-the-city into something more appropriate to its international image. Even if the funds are raised, failure is inherent in the scheme. Nothing made of concrete or stone or wood can re-create the dreams or match the fantasy. "The Boulevard" is real, a living thing, colorful, tawdry, dissolute, rich—the kind of street that the other Hollywood might have tried to capture on film. Leave it. And leave Hollywood to our dreams.

13

East Los Angeles: Portraits and *Placas*

These are the Chicanos.

They are a happy people even when faced with poverty or adversity. They have brought the rhythms of Mexico to Los Angeles, the rhythms of the songs from their native states, the rhythms of the dances, the cadances of the language that can croon, that can snap. The rhythms, also, of a life devoted to the family, grandmothers and uncles and third cousins added, without question, to the core group of mother and father, teenagers and babies, babies, babies; of a life devoted to keeping alive the traditional culture, the food, the clothes, the flowers—paper or plastic or real—the colors; of a life devoted to the Church, the rosaries told, the masses sung, the saints' days and feast days and all the additional rhythms the Church imposes on each person each day, each month, each year. The rhythms, also, of the mostly rural communities from which they have come, where some worked hard and some did not and the end results mostly were the same, so that a kind of fatalism developed, and they now accept the good times as good and the bad times as bad, without much questioning or complaining. These are the people you see sitting and talking, with soft laughter, on the neat porches of the neat frame or stucco houses with the neat grassy yards that cover that section of Los Angeles known generally as East Los Angeles—though it encompasses Belvedere and Highland Park and Montebello and City Terrace and Boyle Heights and Lincoln Heights, among other sections or cities—where a huge percentage of the

Chicanos in this mother city are born and live and die. These are the people you see with the ready smiles and the *bienvenidos* attitude toward the outsiders who wander into their neighborhoods. These are the people who attend services every Sunday at the old Plaza Church or the numerous other churches, who dress their little* children in stiff, starched, ice-cream-colored clothes and take them for *menudo* or *carñitas* and *frijoles* after church, who put paper hats on their dogs and tie big red ribbons on their pet goats or hogs for the Blessing of the Animals every Easter season. These are the people who have given Los Angeles the largest urban Mexican population outside of Mexico City.

The Blessing of the Animals falls on a Saturday before Easter, not necessarily any special Saturday; it is a tradition, but not established in the Church calendar. The date is set by the Church of Our Lady of the Angels, the old Plaza Church that now stands at the edge of the center of the city and yet still seems to be at its core. You telephone and ask, "When will the Blessing be?" The answer, in lightly accented English, is traditional: "Oh, it has not been decided yet. Could you call back in a few days, or perhaps next week?" It is already mid-March.

The day, whichever day it is, will dawn bright and sunny, smog-free, warm but not hot. It is one of the few mysteries of weather in Los Angeles that Easter Sunday, though it roams all over the spring calendar, is all too often overcast or gray, while the Blessing of the Animals day is always perfect.

From a few blocks away, you can hear the music, and you will see a few people with handsomely groomed and decorated pets, but it is not until you reach the grassy slopes of the Plaza itself that the large turnout reveals itself. The line circles the Plaza, doubles up and spills over around the entrance to Olvera Street, then swings over to North Main Street and extends down that street for a block or more. The line is filled with people of every age group, from toddlers to great-grandmothers and great-grandfathers, each one cradling, clutching, leading or being led by a pet.

There is a brace of bullocks, big, sleek, gentle-eyed, their yoke covered with flowers and ribbons. There is an amazing contraption, obviously hand-made: a slatted crate on a cart, the crate studded with calla lilies and topped with pine branches and rose buds; on top of it a hand-made cage, topped with more branches and some full-blown roses and daisies; inside the crate, a young spotted hog; inside the cage, a large brown hen. There is a pair of goats on leashes, with an unfettered kid huddling near—Mama wears a fluffy pink harness with pink rosebuds, Papa is formal in black harness with white daisies. These, plus a couple of burros and one pony are the largest or most noticeable suppliants, but smaller animals are in the majority. There are dogs of all sizes and ages, from puppies with eyes barely open to white-muzzled oldsters, and a surprising (or perhaps not) number of chihuahuas. There are cats on leashes and in cages, and one large gray cat optimistically confined by nothing except the owner's arms. There are numerous rabbits and birds in cages, and quite a few small rodents, white mice and gerbils and guinea pigs, and there are glass cases with lizards and with snakes.

What is most interesting is that the cages and the animals all are decorated to the nines with fresh flowers and jaunty ribbons, and in some cases crepe-paper hats for the dogs and cats. And all the people, the babies and toddlers, the teenagers and middle-aged and old people, are dressed up. And while everyone is having a very good time, everyone also is taking this rather seriously, staying carefully in line, waiting eagerly for the moment when the priest, way over there by the bandstand, will say the few words of blessing. A favorite entry this year is the fortyish woman, plump, bleached blond, heavily made up, who carries in one arm a four- or five-month-old baby in starched white frilly dress, and in the other arm a cockapoo puppy with white feet and a white crepe-paper hat. She pets, calms and quiets each one in turn, and inches forward on swollen feet stuffed into high-heeled mules.

These are the things that Chicanos do in Los Angeles.

Or perhaps these are the Chicanos.

They are a fierce and violent people who are alienated from

the life of the rest of the city by poverty and lack of education and their own traditions of pride and machismo. They inhabit *barrios*, neighborhoods that may include only one block, and they fight, and sometimes kill, people from other *barrios* who venture into their own. The youngsters take drugs, start sniffing glue when they are kids and graduate into such things as angel dust and heroin; they drink and smoke before they are old enough to do the drugs, fight to make a reputation and have lots of babies. The youngsters have no role models because their fathers have run off and their mothers have too many other children to do anything but cook and pick up the welfare check; and often they don't even do this, they run around with younger guys, and the kids fend for themselves. The families barely subsist on the welfare, and the kids drop out of school because it is boring and because they know it won't get them anyplace anyhow, it has never gotten anyone anyplace. They are born, grow up, marry, have babies, die, within their own *barrios* (although many of them die in jail). It is not safe for Anglos to drive, let alone walk, through the streets of East Los Angeles.

"It is considered the most hazardous duty in the city," a former deputy sheriff told me. "At least one kid a week gets killed on Whittier Boulevard, and we can't do anything about it. And," he adds, "God help you if you get caught in the crossfire." These are the people who are jealous and envious, vindictive and sadistic, uneducated or just stupid, and just naturally mean. These are the people who have given Los Angeles the largest urban population of Mexicans outside of Mexico City.

Los vatos locos. The crazy guys. An estimated thirteen thousand teenage boys belong to gangs in Los Angeles County. They lead a life that could be called one of despair, except that they are so busy—stealing to buy knives and guns, stealing to buy drugs, using the latter to get up enough courage to use the former, defending their *barrios*, intruding on other *barrios* to retaliate against some real or imagined offense against their own, spraying their *placas*, their graffiti, in hopeless pursuit of an identity, beating up their girlfriends or, alternatively, loving them, telling them their dreams, begging for early marriages and lots of babies—so busy that despair seems the wrong word entirely.

They dress according to a strict code: sharply creased khakis and a Pendleton shirt worn as a jacket. It would probably unhinge them to learn that this is the favored dress of the chic Los Angeles homosexual (at least at this writing). They are *cholos*, one translation of which is "rude," and their girlfriends are *cholas*, who wear bizarre eye makeup and sometimes tattoos, and sometimes the same garb as the boys, though these styles are said to be fading. The *cholas* also fight, hair-pulling, fist-pummeling, down-on-the-ground fights, but usually not with weapons. The *cholo* role usually is a handed-down one, in the sense that the only male role model available in a particular family or a particular neighborhood—the father if he is still around, or else an uncle, an older brother, or the top guy in the neighborhood, the one to whom everybody looks up—has played this same role. Generally the people who have pulled themselves up through education or perseverance do not have *cholos* in the family. And yet there is a dichotomy here.

In its January 29, 1979, issue, *New West* magazine published an article by Tracy J. Johnston entitled "La Vida Loca," about the *cholas*, the gang girls. Sympathetically written, it made the point that they are indeed a subculture of the Chicano community, that not all Chicanas live this kind of life. The letters section of the magazine's next issue showed a frightening response, frightening because it came, not from the kids in the *barrios*, but from presumably mature, obviously educated, and in two instances professionally involved people. One, from the director of Chicano Studies at California State University, Sacramento, stated that the article "should also convince *carnales* [brothers] everywhere that we are wasting our time and energy and bullets on each other." Another, from two members of La Raza Law Students Association, Hastings College of the Law, San Francisco, stated that "equal space should and must be given to show the positive elements of the *barrios'* gang subculture, to avoid the violent rampage on your staff by the men in the *barrio*, who as Ms. Johnston affirms, make the

rules." Two specific threats and one assertation that there is
something worthwhile about the gangs. This is the way even
Chicanos who have pulled themselves out of the *barrios* feel.

Correct or incorrect—and naturally there is some truth in
both of these imperfect views—these are the images the
Chicano has in the city that his Spanish forebears founded on
September 4, 1781, under the name of El Pueblo de Nuestra
Señora La Reina de Los Angeles de Porciuncula. These are the
images that combine fact with fancy and fear to keep the
Chicano, the Mexican-American, the two-hundred-year-long
resident of Los Angeles, in a position somewhat lower than the
smallest minority group here. These are the images that have
made Angelinos dangerously short-sighted when it comes to
dealing with a phenomenon that will have a greater and greater
effect on our lives as time goes by. For the simple reason that
we don't talk about it, or deal with it, or know anything about
it.

We don't know who the Chicano is, or how he thinks, or
how he lives. I was born in Los Angeles, I have lived here all
my life, I have felt a kind of identification with the Mexican
spirit that is the founding spirit of this city. I had never been to
East Los Angeles until last year.

Part of the truth about the Chicano may be found in the
murals of East Los Angeles. There were, at last count, some
350 murals in this section of the city, which the Anglo
identifies more by the fact that five freeways cross here than by
the fact that its public buildings and private buildings and walls
show a fascinating picture of the real life and the fantasy life
and the history and the hoped-for future of the people who live
here. There are professionally executed murals done in tile or
mosaic, and there are murals done by school kids and by gang
kids. They speak equally of pride and of struggle, and they
speak also of longing and of hope.

It is a hot Sunday a few weeks before Easter, and my friend
and I are in East Los Angeles to see the murals, or rather some
of them, for it would be an exercise in futility to try to cover all
of them in a day or even a week. The Chicana deputy mayor of

Los Angeles, Grace Montañez Davis, has described some of them to me; but Joe Gonzales, who runs the Goez Gallery on East First Street, which has been involved with many of the mural projects since they began, has given me a wonderfully designed map entitled "East Los Angeles, California, United States of America [in small lettering and] Mexico Aztlan [in large lettering]." It is outlined with Aztec and Mayan symbols, and printed on it are such things as "Tierra por Libertad" (Land for Liberty) and "In Europe all roads lead to Rome, in Southern California all freeways lead to East Los Angeles." The map pinpoints 107 different mural locations. The quality of the murals is as surprising as the quantity.

East First Street is a fairly long street running from the Civic Center (where it meets West First) past El Pueblo de Los Angeles State Historic Park and across the Los Angeles River—which is optimistically outlined in blue on city maps, but which almost always is a dry wash. It continues past the Japanese Hospital and White Memorial Hospital, past three more parks and a cemetery and one police station and one sheriff's station, nearly all the way out to East Los Angeles College, where Joe Gonzales found out he was more interested in being an artist than an engineer. It is primarily a business street. Oddly, most of the signs on the street are in English rather than Spanish— "Hair Styles for Men and Women," "Weight Control and Family Planning"—and the pictures in the beauty salons are of smiling blond Anglos. Most of the shops are closed today, since it is Sunday, and most have grills guarding their doors and windows. But the First Street Store is open and doing a lively post-Mass business, as is Tom's Burgers, Pastramis and Malts, and families stroll the streets, all the children in Sunday clothes and eating ice cream. Cars packed with six or more people cruise by leisurely.

The cars. Alas, the gloriously low-slung, high-glossed, wildly decorated and startlingly individual vehicles of the noted East Los Angeles car clubs are not in evidence today, not one of them. Today all are serviceable Cameros and Mustangs and Darts, mostly a couple of years old, with the odd Mercedes or Cadillac the only diversions. On a Sunday afternoon East L.A.

looks like any other section of the city, except that there are more families doing things together, and more toddlers and babies.

The First Street Store's murals are among the most noted. They are of hand-painted tiles and they are set in arches between the flat red-tiled roof and the display windows. There are perhaps twenty of these arched panels, and they depict the history, real and fantasized, of the Mexican people from 3000 B.C. to A.D. 2000 plus. Each panel has a date span, some long (the first, which shows people working the land, is dated 3000 B.C.–A.D. 1329), some short (one, which shows a man buried among a pile of spears, is dated A.D. 1529–39). These obviously are professionally executed. The images are forceful, the historical details researched. The prevailing subject is pain.

The oppression by the Spanish invaders: skulls and spears and priests and soldiers. The Revolution: men with guns and bayonettes, women beside them, angels hovering over them. The aftermath: a Mexican standing on a piece of paper entitled "Treaty of Hidalgo" and fighting; a fat white Anglo in a top hat holding out a piece of paper that says "Law United States." In the several panels labeled 1900–74 there is a man blindfolded and in chains, while another man with grape-pruning shears attempts to cut the chains; signs that read "Don't Shoot!" and "Huelga" (strike) and "Farm Workers"; men crushed beneath a scale weighted down with money bags. Perhaps the most telling panel is this: a man sits on a book labeled "Knowledge" that has a lock on it—an angel hands him the key.

On the side of the building the future is depicted: 1974–00 shows a man caught by a huge machine and struggling to get out; 2000–00 shows men and women staring straight ahead— in their hands are swords, lances, a scythe.

"The Story of Our Struggle" says the main panel over the store's front door. It shows the Mexican national symbols, the eagle and the snake.

There is no effort here to help the Chicano reconcile the Mexican side of his heritage with the American side. Of course, these are not the communally painted murals one has heard about; this is a professional statement.

At the Little Sisters of Mercy Hospital and Old Age Home at Second and Mott streets the surrounding walls are covered with thirty-six large murals. The work here is not slick. Judy Baca, a well-known muralist, coordinated the project; one wall lists the names of every person who worked on it. Tucked in among the names such as Fernandez and Garcia and Muñoz and Sanchez and Vasquez are those of two nuns. Listed also are Tim Yamamoto and Eddie Nagasaki.

Here is a warrior with a torch in one hand and a club in another, kneeling on the Mayan calendar with the Pyramids of the Sun and the Moon rising to each side. Here are *campesinos* (farmers) raising their fists to the sky. Here are migrant workers in a field, next to a soldier who is threatening Cesar Chavez. Here are *vaqueros* (cowboys) and men in sombreros and women with long braids and a Mexican flag and Aztec and Mayan and Olmec symbols. Here are scenes of people reaching, stretching, to the heavens or to an angel for help.

Aside from the more primitive technique, there are two basic differences between these works and those at the First Street Store. One is an attempt to show some feeling of brotherhood among races: some scenes show Blacks, one shows a Japanese child, and there is a very large close-up of a man praying at a table set with food—next to it is lettered, in English, "Let us come into his Presence with thanks," and "Thank You" is written in Spanish, Hebrew, German, French, Japanese, Thai and English. The other difference is that some of these murals are covered with spray-painted graffiti.

Deputy Mayor Davis has told me, "You won't find any graffiti on the murals, even the gang kids have a sort of respect for them." More realistically, Joe Gonzales has told me, "The only ones that would be defaced are the murals that the kids do not relate to . . . or if, for instance, one gang paints a mural and another gang paints a better one, the kids from the first gang might take offense and paint their names or their *placas* on it. Then, of course, the other gang would retaliate." Perhaps that is what happened here, as some murals are defaced, some totally clean.

Some of the murals of East Los Angeles do not depict Mexican history. Some, such as the one at the Pacific Telephone Building in Highland Park, tell the story of neighborhood life. The nearby Arroyo Seco is shown here, as are local businesses such as the Sparklets Water Company, and portraits of neighborhood kids are incorporated. Others, such as the Goez-designed murals at the Benjamin Franklin Library on East First, aim for universal themes. "It's the Four Elements as Plato saw them," Gonzales says. "We wanted something the kids could learn from, yet also relate to."

But as one follows the Goez map, taking in the long side wall at the Zapateria Guadalajara and the entire façade of the Farmacia Hidalgo and the tile murals above the Doctors' Hospital and as many others of these 107 locations as time and patience allow, one sees that the murals that are purely local and those that strive for universality are the exceptions. The history of Mexico is told and retold. The struggles are lived and relived.

The Chicano virtually never intermarries with another nationality. He almost never leaves what may be called the ghetto—the *barrios* don't look like ghettos, but the ghetto spirit exists there. For the most part he doesn't mix or mingle with Anglos—there are few places, except for touristic Olvera Street, for the paths to cross. The busing program will help to change things a little; but it is hard to make friends when you cannot go over to someone's house after school; when you have to get on a bus and be driven back across town to your home. Forty-five percent of the children now in kindergarten in Los Angeles have Mexican surnames, which promises some exchange of ideas and cultures in the future. But it is estimated that 42 percent of all Chicanos in the nation drop out of school, which dilutes the promise greatly.

The Mexican has not had much luck with governments since Juarez, so the Chicano doesn't vote. Voter registration of Hispanics in California is around 50 percent, mostly the result of a huge United Farm Workers campaign in 1976. There is no indication that anywhere near that percentage actually votes.

UNO, the United Neighborhoods Organization, works through church parishes and door-to-door campaigns and is meeting with some success, but it is a slow struggle.

There was no middle class in Mexico until recent times, so the Chicano is all too familiar with the idea that some people are rich and some are poor and there is not much to be done about it. Even when this fatalism is overcome, lack of education leads to lack of opportunity. A survey conducted across the country less than three years ago showed that 23 percent of all Mexican-Americans had completed fewer than five years of school.

The Mexican has always been family-oriented—it is one of the most important aspects of the culture. So the Chicano family continues to accept, gladly, every uncle and cousin and nephew who manages to slip across the border. Paid at illegally low rates, they cannot contribute much to already strained family budgets; speaking only Spanish, they add to the uneasiness the children already feel about their "native" tongue; joining already overcrowded households, they leave no one the privacy to dream dreams or make plans. These "undocumented workers" are as welcomed by their relatives as they are by the businesses that exploit them. Yet their presence—among, certainly, numerous other causes—helps keep 19 percent of the Chicanos in California below the poverty level.

Like the murals that permeate his community, the Chicano is steeped in the traditions of Mexico, and it is a difficult task to interest him in identifying with those of the United States. Yet for the first time in recent history, there is a strong movement to put some of the power where it belongs—in the hands of 28 percent of the population of Los Angeles.

The Chicano community has not had much in the way of spokespersons in the past. There was, and is, Ed Roybal, the founder of MAPA (the Mexican-American Political Association), who was the first (and last) Hispanic on the Los Angeles City Council and now is California's first (and only) Hispanic representative in the United States Congress. There was, and is, Deputy Mayor Grace Montañez Davis, who has worked in so many different areas to help the Chicano community for so many years that it would take two pages to list her accomplishments. Dr. Julian Nava was on the school board for twelve years and is credited with having helped inaugurate bilingual education. Various organizations such as UNO, the twenty-five-year-old Community Services Organization, the GI Forum (begun after World War II) and the Mexican-American Opportunities Foundation have worked quietly and steadily over the years to help Chicanos pursue education or better jobs, and to get out the vote.

Today, new young spokespersons, many of them associated with MAPA or MALDEF (the Mexican-American Legal Defense and Education Fund), are raising their voices specifically for power. The September 11, 1978, issue of *New West,* in an article titled "Chicano Power," quotes Vilma Martinez, MALDEF's president and general counsel: "Knowledge is power. Money is power. Votes are power. And we're very slowly beginning to understand it, to articulate it, and to have access to it." MAPA's president, Eduardo Sandoval, speaks out for "full economic and political participation." Even Gloria Chavez, of the Church-oriented UNO, has said, "Powerlessness in the East Los Angeles area has been our problem. Now we have the elderly and the youth and the middle-aged becoming involved and becoming aware." Andres Torres, a college professor, has tried to get a Chicano party, La Raza Unida, on the California ballot. An attempt to make East Los Angeles a separate city was defeated by a 16 percent margin a few years ago, but only twelve thousand people went to the polls; there is a strong likelihood that that proposition will turn up again. There also is a current campaign among the new Chicano leaders to open the border, and to declare a general amnesty for all "undocumented persons" already in residence. This could assuage some financial and other difficulties for the community; whether it would lead to further Mexicanization rather than the integration of Chicanos into the mainstream of American life is another question.

Grace Montañez Davis does not think in terms of greater Mexicanization. She says, "We were called Mexicans up until the war. But afterward, after so many "Mexicans" had fought so well, and such a large number had won Congressional Medals of Honor, we fought to be called Mexican-Americans, because that's what we are. (According to Mrs. Davis, "Chicano," which also means Mexican-American, originated with the activists who began to emerge in the late sixties; "Latino" refers to people who are Spanish-speaking but come from Central or South America; "Hispanic" refers to anyone who has Spanish roots.)

She believes that the bilingual program in the public schools should either be used to phase exclusively Spanish-speaking children into English or should be a true bilingual program in which all nationalities learn both languages. "It was never meant to keep the children speaking only Spanish—that just makes them outcasts. God knows, the parents want them to learn English. But we have absolutely no control over how the system is being used, there's no overall program, it's just hit or miss, and I know that's how it's working out in some of the schools." Every one of the more than two dozen Anglo teachers I know believes that the intent of the program is to keep the children speaking only Spanish.

Joe Gonzales does not think in terms of greater Mexicanization either. In 1970 he founded the Goez Gallery in pursuit of a dream he had had for years: "We were trying to create a movement which might someday be identified as Chicano art. The Chicano artist combines the two elements—the Mexican heritage or culture, and also the American element, which we were born with here. The combination of the two, both sides brought out strongly enough, would be the Chicano art form. It hasn't developed into anything like that yet, there is nothing yet that truly can be identified as Chicano art. But I think eventually it can develop. But the thing we are striving for now is to be recognized, first, as professional artists—and then afterward by the fact that our names are Gomez or Hernandez or Gonzales. We all are Mexican-Americans here, but it is the artwork and not the fact that we are Mexican-Americans that must come first now."

The artists whom Goez represents—330 Chicanos, the largest group of its kind in the nation—have won a great deal of recognition. They were invited to paint a mural for the Smithsonian Institution in Washington, D.C., and one for the University of Southern California. They were invited by Russia to contribute works to a show for the World Congress of Peace, and two of the works they submitted were chosen for the Pushkin Museum. They have put on art shows at the Music Center in Los Angeles. Joe Gonzales himself is listed in *Who's Who in American Art.*

But most important to him and to the work he is doing here, to the effect he is trying to have on the community, is the East Los Angeles mural program that he and his brother, John, started, and which many hundreds of other artists, not all of them associated with Goez, now are involved in. "When we began, there were only two murals in the area, those at the Doctors' Hospital and at the Pan American Bank Building. Initially, it was just considered a beautification program. We called it 'The Beautification of East Los Angeles for the Fine Arts Program.' And you know, when we started it was like a Mark Twain type of thing, where you start to paint a fence, and the other kids see you and they want to help, so you give them a brush and pretty soon they're painting the fence and you step aside. And this was the way it was planned then, because we wanted to get the artists involved. And we kind of spoiled the businessman, because to prove what we could do we would tell him, 'You provide the paint and the brushes and we'll make the mural free.' And of course he was happy with that. The result of all that is that today there are nearly four hundred murals in East Los Angeles, and April 5, 1975, was declared East L.A. Mural Day as a tourist attraction, and we made sure that every artist who had contributed to five or more murals received a commendation.

"But now the important thing is that the businessman understands that it is art, that it has worked to beautify this section of the city, and now he must commission the artist. The artist must be paid just like the electrician and the plumber. That's what we're working for now, the kind of recognition which is paid for."

Joe Gonzales has gone to Mexico to study mural materials

and techniques, and it has convinced him that hand-painted ceramic tiles are the only materials to use. "Their techniques in Mexico were not much better than ours were. Even some of the Siqueiros murals were cracking. I don't want to put in all this work for something that will last ten or twenty years, I want it to last three hundred years."

He is very proud that the center, as he calls Goez, is entirely self-supporting, has never applied for grants, never used public money. "It was very important to us to show people that a group of artists can hold their own. You have to work harder, you have to struggle harder, you go hungry more. But it's a satisfying feeling when you've also accomplished more than all of those people who have received hundreds of thousands of dollars through Federal grants. We wanted to do it our way, and we did. We even supported the school, and we've made it through nine years and it's very gratifying to know that we did it on our own.

"The idea of the center has been to be a place where artists could intermingle and learn from each other, and also a place where they could help develop the talents of the youth in the area. So we have an apprenticeship school. We'd rather have them from age sixteen or seventeen up, we'd rather get the young adults who are serious about going into the art field. And we let them know exactly what is in store for them, that it's not all peaches and cream. We let them know that there's so much competition—not to discourage them, but to prepare them. We're going to start to make them pay now. Prior to this they didn't pay, but it's not good for the students and it's not good for the organization. I think the student will have more interest if he has to pay, has to give a little bit more of himself. It will be minimal, five to ten dollars for three hours, and that includes the teacher and the model.

"Yes, we've had gang members working here, we've had kids who were in jail or in juvenile hall, who were artistic and for whom we felt there was hope. Their future is our concern, you know."

The building on East First Street that houses the Goez Gallery used to be a meat-packing plant. The Gonzales brothers and their artist friends transformed a derelict plant into a handsome place with their own hands—there were no funds to hire professional labor. There is a large main gallery plus side rooms, all divided by partitions so that exhibits don't conflict with one another. The back part of the building is a studio where eight to ten people at a time design and execute murals. "It's too bad," Gonzales says. "We could have thirty or forty artists working here, so many are eager, but we just don't have the space." The gallery is in the heart of the *barrio,* close to where Joe Gonzales was born and grew up: where he was lucky enough to have teachers and employers who encouraged his interest in art; and where he worked nights and weekends all through high school so he could afford to go to the college up the street. The gallery is in a sense his real home. He comes early and works late here; his son joins him every day after school; his wife also spends much time here helping out. Like many others, like Grace Montañez Davis, for example, Joe Gonzales has stayed in his neighborhood and is raising his children here and is working hard to make it a better place.

Two East Los Angeles experiences stand out.

One is this. I had left the Goez Gallery and had decided to see something of this section of the city that I did not know. It was a Tuesday just slightly after noon, and at first I just drove through the business streets, up East First and down Brooklyn Avenue. Then I headed for the residential streets of small neat houses and small neat yards. I did, as one does under these circumstances, turn often, up one block and down another, over one and down two. At some point I noticed what seemed to be a police car behind me (later I found out that it was a sheriff's car, since part of this area is not in the city but in the county), and it stayed behind me through all the turns until I was back on a main street and ready to head home. I had done nothing incorrect, so I assumed the official car was on some business of its own—until I saw the "I mean business" lights flashing. I pulled over and the sheriff's car did the same. A man in a tan uniform got out and walked over to my car.

"What are you doing?" he said in an irritated voice, a voice that would have said "What the hell are you doing?" if law enforcement officers in this city were not required to be utterly polite. "At first I thought you were lost. What's the story?" His accent and looks indicated he was a Chicano.

"I've been sightseeing."

"Sightseeing!" Protocol abandoned, he yelled, "Don't you know this is the most dangerous section in the city? Don't you know that people get killed here every day? Don't you know that you're a moving target in that car?" I was driving my twelve-year-old Corvette.

I explained that I was writing about Los Angeles and that it seemed important to see this section of the city.

He asked to see my driver's license. "Okay," he said finally, "do whatever you want, I can't stop you. But if you take my advice, you'll go home."

He left. I lit a cigarette. Then, on this sunny Tuesday midday, I pressed the buttons to raise the electric windows, locked my doors, stepped on my accelerator and escaped East Los Angeles as fast as I could.

The other experience is this. It is the Sunday on which my friend and I have gone to see the murals of East Los Angeles. While I take pictures at the First Street Store, my friend talks to an elderly Chicano, a Sunday idler. "So you're writing a book," he says when I join them. "This mural's a good one, it shows the history of the Mexican people. Walk on down the street and you'll see some others you'll like. Good luck on the book!"

We walk along East First, taking pictures at the Pan American Bank Building and the Zapateria Guadalajara. No one pays any particular attention to us, not even the crowd of teenagers at Tom's Burgers, although a few older people smile and nod. A carful of teenage boys passes; the boys whistle at us and wave wildly until they're out of sight.

We drive to the Little Sisters of Mercy Hospital and park on a side street where people are watering lawns and weeding flower beds and talking to neighbors. While I take pictures of the murals, my friend, who loves to strike up conversations with people, goes to talk to a man and a woman parked in a car next to the walls. They are Chicano and speak, as does everyone we talk to today, in perfect and unaccented English. "We used to live here," the man says, "but you know all the old-timers have moved out now. This was a good mixed neighborhood, Mexican and Jewish and Oriental, and I guess some of the Orientals are still here, but it's not what it used to be, not as middle class now. It's gone down a little." They are here to see the murals because their daughter, who is writing a book about Mexican art, has told them that they're interesting.

We walk on down the street behind the hospital and a beautiful little girl of about seven comes running out from a back yard. "Lady, lady," she calls, "will you take my picture?" I pose her against the background of murals. Meanwhile, my friend has gone to talk to a Japanese couple who are sitting on their front porch listening to samisen music from a record player inside. She reports that they say the neighborhood still is quite nice. It looks nice, with the lawns and the flowers; a few garages have a scattering of *placas,* and the unpainted portions of the hospital's walls are covered with these, but none of the houses has been hit. As we walk back to the car, the little girl runs out again, bringing a smaller child with her. "Lady, will you take my sister's picture?" They both stand waving until we reach the corner.

Later we drive all around the residential streets of the *barrios,* enlarging on the pattern I made the day the sheriff's car followed me. The lazy Sunday mood continues, the family-day feeling, with many people sitting on porches or washing cars or watering lawns. My friend and I agree that we have no sense of this being hostile territory.

We go on over to Whittier Boulevard, where the former deputy sheriff told me a gang kid is killed weekly. Whittier is not a pretty street, it is much more bleak than, say, East First. But my friend is hungry and I am thirsty, so we find a nice-looking small restaurant and have taquitos and beer. We order in our rusty Spanish and the rather chic-looking girl who is our waitress responds politely; but later, when she asks if we want anything else, she speaks in English and we realize that, without meaning to, we have been condescending. Or perhaps not, since all the other people, the young couple with the two babies the man pets and plays with, the two older men at the counter, the little children pretending to sweep the floor, all are speaking Spanish. At any rate, the atmosphere here is a friendly one, and we forget that we are on infamous Whittier.

We left East Los Angeles near twilight, after scouting out a few more murals and browsing through a few more side streets. We had the car windows open, and the doors were not locked, and my friend did not press her foot flat on the accelerator to escape from real or imagined danger.

It would be easy to come away from these contacts with East Los Angeles repeating the stereotyped images with which one began: it is a scary place that Anglos should keep away from; it is an ordinary section of Los Angeles with some of the elements that make Mexico so charming. *Los Vatos Locos* and the Blessing of the Animals.

The murals tell a different story. If we open our eyes to them, they reveal some of the complexities of the Chicano that make the stereotypes seem as simplistic as stereotypes always are.

Fortunately, there are people like Joe Gonzales working to make the Anglo realize that there are more than two sides to the Chicano personality. Working also to help the Chicano himself understand that Mexican plus American can mesh to make a three-dimensional whole.

14

Christmas in Los Angeles: A Very Personal View

Traditionally, the Christmas season in Los Angeles begins on Thanksgiving weekend, with the Santa Claus Lane Parade down Hollywood Boulevard (movie stars! antique cars! live on TV!), and ends with the Rose Parade down Colorado Boulevard in Pasadena (movie stars! flower-covered floats! live on TV!) and the Rose Bowl Game on New Year's Day. Traditionally, vacant lots all across the city suddenly turn into Christmas tree forests just after Thanksgiving; houses of every type, from modest to mansion, begin to blossom with colored lights; every main shopping street of every section of the city is suddenly swathed with decorations; and the tall trees in the lobbies of nearly every office building are surrounded with colorfully wrapped "Toys for Tots." In short, the usual. There has never been a white Christmas in the history of Los Angeles—in fact, Christmas day reliably may be predicted to be sunny, warm and even, remarkably, clear. And yet we react to the season with as much sentimentality, as much nostalgia for childhood, as much determination to keep to our individual traditions, as anyone in any city whose Christmases are white.

My own family always celebrated Christmas to the hilt, always managed somehow, even during periods of financial difficulties, to find the largest tree, to decorate it with hundreds of saved-up-from-years-past ornaments, to surround it with at least forty or fifty beautifully wrapped presents for

223

what might have turned into a very spoiled little girl. Luckily, even as a child, I understood what counted: that someone cared enough about you to bother to collect a huge number of trifles, and wrap them and enjoy your pleasure in opening them. Luckily, as an adult, I have managed to accumulate a huge circle of friends who either had the same kind of childhood experiences, or else have joyously started their own traditions.

Christmas for us starts in mid-July (just after the last lavishly celebrated birthday) with the first flea-market gifts purchased, definitely, with Christmas in mind; moves into lots of preholiday baking and preserving and making of decorations; culminates in numerous parties, with much carol singing and a monumental exchange of gifts. Never big, expensive gifts—simply dozens and dozens of "sillies." Anyone who hasn't yet adopted some particular "silly" as a collection gets collections thrust upon him—since three of anything constitutes a collection, it is easy enough to get a slow learner started. Fortunately, even serious collectors take pleasure in "sillies."

Bobbie, for instance, besides antique dolls, cameos and fine Art Deco and Art Nouveau pieces, also collects wounded dogs! These are china or bisque or ceramic animals with paws in slings, heads bandaged due to toothaches, or noses or tails being stung by bees or flies. Jack, her husband, has museum-quality collections of pre-Columbian art and Black items; luckily, he also likes funny decanter sets. I cannot keep up with Go's beaded-bag collection, but I regularly add to her two showcases of unusual Noritake pieces. Her husband, Manny, recently discovered the joys of collecting small expensive bronzes, but fortunately magic paraphernalia also pleases him. Various teenage or grown children from the group love old embroidered items, replicas of boats, funky jewelry. Beer memorabilia and pin-up pictures thrill one friend; old celluloid bracelets another; ceramic birds a third. Anything old, cute, pretty, nostalgic, serves for most of the rest.

And so, we all are regulars at the Rose Bowl, not the New Year's football game but the flea market held on the second Sunday of every month at the same site, one of the largest in the world. We could stage wonderful reunions there every month, meeting at seven thirty A.M. and paying an exorbitant $5 to get in with the dealers, instead of waiting for the nine A.M. public opening; but we never see one another—we rush from stall to stall, eyes on the merchandise, hands clutching wallets stuffed with small bills, trying to find the particular things that will suit the particular desires of our friends before they find them for themselves.

There is also the Glendale Antique Show, the first Sunday of every month at the Glendale Civic Auditorium. This is a tonier event, with many more genuine antiques than are found at the Rose Bowl; and sometimes, especially before the holidays when the influx of extra dealers requires that the show move from the basement to the larger main floor, it is a treasure-trove. It is harder to avoid friends here, as the space is such that you physically run into people. The only solution is to be first in line for the box office (you cannot get in early by paying extra) or to come very late and hope the dealers have opened up new caches of goods. It is disconcerting to find a wonderful wounded dog a half-hour after Bobbie has made one of her fast swoops through the show. Did she somehow not see it? (Impossible, she has an eye like an eagle.) Did she see it and not like it? (Impossible, it's a delightful wounded dog.) Shall I buy it and take a chance? Luckily, my husband drifts by. "Buy it, buy it. If she's already got it, we'll start somebody else on a wounded dog collection." I hand over my $2.

The collecting of boxes is one of the most important aspects of all this.

Naturally dealers at flea markets do not provide gift packaging, so finding boxes of varied sizes is a quest that goes on all year. We save every box, no matter how prosaic—boxes that held checkbooks, or three bars of soap, or a bottle of liquor— ask for boxes for every single item purchased at a store, beg boxes back from friends after birthdays or anniversaries. "What a wonderful *box!*" is the first exclamation over any gift packed in a new, that is not-seen-before, box. Boxmania reached its peak on my birthday last year, when my stepdaughter and her mother in New York sent me a large package of gifts; at the bottom were three marvelous boxes, empty. "This is for your box collection," said the note.

Christmas in Los Angeles is many things. It is the insurance company on Wilshire Boulevard just east of Highland Avenue that imports live reindeer to its enclosed roof garden every year—we are so used to it, we don't even react. "My God!" holiday guests exclaim. "There are reindeer on that roof!" It's no surprise to *us*.

Christmas is also attending a dinner party in the hills, such long curving stretches of nearly vertical streets that even seasoned climbers avoid certain sections, and being called away from the dinner table by the sound of carolers outside. This is a group of young Chicanos on foot, complete with guitars and a trumpet. How on earth did they straggle all the way up here? "Silent Night, Holy Night," in harmony and prettily accented, drifts across the hillside. And "Adeste Fideles" and "O Little Town of Bethlehem." Standing on the front steps or leaning out the living room window, we all join in the singing. It is very moving; one does not expect carolers in Los Angeles. The men in our party run downstairs to distribute paper money of various denominations. *"Gracias! Muchisimas gracias!"* comes floating back to those of us still upstairs. As the carolers continue from house to house on foot, the old familiar songs are heard in the distance for half an hour more.

One expects a few things to be different at Christmas in Los Angeles, and a few are. The Naples Parade, for example. Naples is a sort of island community in Alamitos Bay, far south of the South Bay, south even of Long Beach. It is a community of small charming houses of infinite variety and color, most of which nearly touch shoulders on their tiny lots, but which have the unusual advantage of being separated from their opposite neighbors, not by streets, but by canals, like Venice, another beach city to the north.

Venice was ahead of its time. Its imaginative founder, Abbot Kinney, turned useless tidelands into canals connected by bridges, and tried to sell lots to the new capitalists of Los

L.A. LIVE : 227

Angeles long before the turn of the century. A few bought, but basically the venture failed (though some of the canals, now polluted, and some of the bridges, now unsafe, still exist), and Venice became one of the tawdriest beach cities, though there is currently an attempt at revival. Naples came into existence much later, and succeeded. It is such a remote area that many Angelinos don't know it exists, but those who do, try to make a point of going there at Christmas, when it truly comes into its own. Lights are strung across the canals. Every boat owner (nearly every resident) strings his craft with lights, and just after sundown the lighted boats slip through the canals, creating a lovely seasonal spectacle.

There is a similar boat parade at Newport Beach, slightly farther south. Newport people are monied people: their boats are larger, many of them yachts; their lights are even brighter, more colorful. Christmas at Newport is spectacular, but it is a little garish. The neighborhood aspect of Naples, with its tiny craft (the bridges are too low for large craft to pass beneath them), seems more in the spirit of Christmas. A California Christmas, to be sure.

Christmas in Los Angeles is also the annual series of radio commercials sponsored by Forest Lawn Memorial Park, the cemetery (now a chain of cemeteries) made famous by Evelyn Waugh in *The Loved One*. "There is a lot of drinking during the holidays, and drinking can lead to casualties. If you're driving home and feel you've had too much to drink, stop in at any Forest Lawn Mortuary. We'll be happy to give you a cup of coffee, free of charge."

It now is Tuesday, two weeks before Christmas, and time to buy the Christmas tree. It is important to do this on a Tuesday night, because first there is a flea market at the Great Western Exhibit Center, just a short distance from downtown on the Santa Ana Freeway. This place was built for stock shows, and looks it; no doubt the cows and goats and sheep that have been exhibited here were of much finer quality than most of the merchandise available on Tuesday nights. Wares are spread on the floor, or on card tables or portable stands, and during most of the year the dealers can barely fill one of the barnlike halls.

But near Christmas a second, and sometimes a third and fourth, room is opened up; the regulars exhibit new supplies of merchandise, some of them antiques; and new dealers appear, some from the East and the Midwest. There is an air of festivity, a genuine bustle of activity. As usual, our group does not wait for the six P.M. public opening; we arrive around four (yes, everyone somehow manages to sneak away from work) and pay $3 to get in to watch our favorite dealers unpack. This is close to last-chance, and so we snap up all the salt-and-peppers in the shapes of animals (50 cents to $1), the really fine old embroidered linens from the one dealer who always washes and starches and irons them before they go on sale ($1 to $5), the old-fashioned Christmas ornaments, all the other things that might possibly please someone on the list. Everything looks better tonight—perhaps one is less critical now that time is short and the list still long.

At six P.M. we meet under the clock. "The Margarita place first," we tell one another. Or, "If you're going to be late, we'll be at the carñitas place." It is our habit to go to Olvera Street, downtown at the old Plaza, after the Great Western.

Olvera Street is a short, very narrow street that holds the oldest house in Los Angeles and a couple of the oldest buildings. It also has stalls and stores full of Mexican goods of the tackiest sort: statues painted in blue and gold, three-dimensional pictures of everyone from Elvis to Jesus Christ, pictures painted on black velvet, fake animals made out of the skins of real animals, cheap sombreros, cheap leather goods. But there also are stores that carry fine Talavera de Puebla tiles, and Oaxaca pottery, and charming piñatas in every shape imaginable, and hand-blown glass and hand-dipped candles; and it cannot accurately be called a tourist trap because at almost any given time two-thirds of the people shopping and eating here are Mexican-Americans.

We do not come here to shop. We come for the tart, salt-edged double Margaritas at the place at one end of the street, where one can sit outdoors and watch and hear the passing mariachis; and for hand-made tortillas and carñitas (roast pork, chopped) and refried beans at the cafeteria-style place with the lovely tile decorations at the other end, the Plaza end, of the street. The drinks are superb, the food is wonderful—our idea of soul food.

And then it is time to buy the Christmas tree. It is a short enough walk down Alameda Street along the railroad tracks; but this is a rather eerie section of town after dark, and besides, the trees we buy will be huge ones, and we will need someone to help us tie them on top of our cars. So it is better to drive to this special place for buying trees—not one of the tree-filled vacant lots that cover the city, not one of the supermarkets, but a place down by the railroad yards, where the freight cars bring in the fresh trees daily.

It is very dark and very strange. Old factories and derelict buildings line the street. There is little traffic. Have we missed the way? No. Suddenly there is a blaze of lights ahead and what amounts to a small traffic jam. And then yard after yard of Christmas trees, block after block. "Get your trees here!" men shout from the standing freight cars. "Freshest trees, lowest prices!" The smell of pine and fir fills the sharp air. There are no trees painted in strange shades of pink and blue here, or trees flocked to look as if they had snow on them. What you will find are exactly what the barker is yelling—the greenest and freshest trees at the lowest prices in town.

You spot the exact tree you want instantly. It is the tallest and fluffiest and most perfectly symmetrical; its branches are the fullest, and its needles the greenest and sappiest. Naturally you don't buy it. First you must look at every other tree on every other lot; then stand around the freight cars, listening to the spiels. You see other friends; admire or question their choices, discuss the possibility of having two small trees instead of one huge one. Suddenly nervous, you rush back to the first lot—your tree is still there. The salesman hoists it to the top of the car and ties it down. "Have a *very* merry Christmas!" he says, seeming to actually mean it.

The tree is so wide it can barely be squeezed through the double French patio doors. It is so tall it just misses the beams of the twenty-five-foot ceiling. It takes hours and hours of several evenings to decorate; and when the decorating is finished and the ladder put away, the floor is covered with silvery icicles and broken pieces of the ornaments that have slipped out of your hands or off their devilish little hooks. A mess. But the tree is gorgeous, and when the tiny lights are turned on, the kind that flicker on and off at random, it is as though childhood Christmases, with all their extravagant beauty, somehow are re-created. Extra branches cover the mantle and every available shelf and table, with red and gold and blue and silver and green ornaments tucked into them. A battery-operated Santa Claus toy rings his tiny bell; another climbs up a chimney, while "Silent Night" plays on his music box. Long-playing tapes play every carol ever recorded. Christmas starts early and ends late in Los Angeles.

As Christmas nears, other rituals come into effect. My friend Go and her Los Angeles Culturally Curious Club make a traditional visit to a place called Stat's in Pasadena, where every imaginable type of ornament and decoration is displayed, and where all the ribbons and papers and flowers and birds are available for people who like to make their own decorations. They spend the morning there, have lunch at Emily's, a charming Pasadena restaurant in an old house filled with antiques, then go to Descanso Gardens in La Cañada, which has an incredible selection of unusual ornaments and crafts every holiday season.

Mosketel's, in the old wholesale section of downtown Los Angeles, still sells real ribbon and a variety of papers (two-sided foil florists' papers make lovely varicolored wrappings) and the bells and bows and birds that make decorating presents so much fun. The object, of course, is to have gift wrappings that look unique. My friend Bobbie gets to Mosketel's in October, and skims the cream. Going later, I have to rummage for pretty materials, but my gifts *will* look totally different.

Around this time we get sneaky about finding the important last-minute gifts. There is a thrice-yearly flea market in Ventura, seventy or so miles up the coast, which no one knows about but us. We get up at dawn on the requisite Sunday and drag ourselves up there to find the goods and the goodies that no one else will think of looking for. Hello, here's Go, with two of her daughters. They've already been here for an hour.

However, I have one source for gifts that, thus far, is secret: Riverside and Redlands, two towns at least an hour and a half south of Los Angeles on the San Bernardino Freeway. Redlands is a small, perfect southern California town, the kind of place that is still surrounded by orange and lemon groves and still has a wonderful section of early thirties buildings. But I go there for the covered antique marts—there are four of them, thirty or forty shops each, and one never fails to find a carload of "sillies" with special appeal for special friends. Nearby Riverside also has a covered antique mart, and quite a few antique shops; but the Mission Inn is the place to head first, because unique shops surround it.

The Mission Inn is the place remembered from childhood as a castle. Indeed, it is: an immense complex that is California Mission style around the outside, and wanders off into exotic architectural wonders, bell towers and Gaudí-like extravagances, on the sides facing the many courtyards. It is a wonderful place to spend the weekend. There is the Presidential Bar, where Richard and Pat Nixon were married; there is the immense chair built for corpulent President William Howard Taft when he visited; there are long lobbies filled with Mission furniture; there is a cabaret theatre and a lovely restaurant with an interior entirely of hand-painted tile. The Mission Inn nearly failed, but was revived when a foundation was established to help it recover. Now there are a number of apartments (and a waiting list) for rent by the month; and twenty to thirty rooms, with no television or room service, but all charming and truly Old Los Angeles, available by the night. It is a lovable place, typical of what used to be here before the freeways bypassed the tiny towns, and the citrus groves were turned into tracts, bedroom communities for Los Angeles.

The galleria around the Mission Inn has the nicest concentration of unique shops anywhere in the city (though this distant area can scarcely be considered "in the city"). There is the Snow Goose, which has fine crystal, fine imported wooden items, lovely gift paper and cards, Scandinavian furniture, and many small gifty things. The Freckled Frog is a very special place, with a fountain splashing and a live bird singing; it offers unusual basketry, including mainland Chinese animal baskets, all sorts of small goodies, real ribbon to buy by the yard and an upstairs section with clothes. Tiggy Winkles is a charming source of miniatures and all types of small toys. Second Nature specializes in shells and rock crystals and nature books, the finest of everything of this sort. There is a shop of heavenly scents, which specializes in unique teas and spices, and china; there is a lingerie shop with a store of things so silky and lacy that they look as though they descended from the Jean Harlow era; there is an art gallery; there is a dress shop. If you cannot find unique gifts for every friend here, you cannot find them anyplace.

We do not just wrap presents and address them; we write clues to what is in each package. The clues must be riddles, and sometimes they are in verse form. I don't know exactly where we got the idea—it is a tradition in Holland, I recently learned—but we often spend more time deciphering clues than opening presents.

We used to begin Christmas Eve at a normal dinner hour, say eight P.M., and were still unwrapping at four or five A.M. This presented difficulties, since everyone had something of importance to do the next morning. Now we begin Christmas Eve at five P.M., and end at a reasonable hour: two or three A.M.

Christmas Eve is reserved for our "family," which is to say our best friends, Bobbie and Jack and their grown children plus any house guests any of us happen to have. The tree is surrounded by at least sixty or seventy gifts; our friends arrive with at least equal amounts. Gift opening begins. Clues are read. Rippers and tearers are applauded; careful unwrappers are hissed and booed. I am against being neat on a night like this, so everything is left lying around on the floor. Extra time is taken up, because each donee has to kiss each donor after every gift. The chef—my husband, Bert—announces dinner. We are barely a third of the way through the presents.

It is traditional that Bert, noted for his Chinese cuisine, cooks on Christmas Eve—yet on this night his wonderful food is slightly ignored. We gobble the hot-sour soup and the *jao-tze* (meat-stuffed fried dumplings); we chatter our way through the *kung-pao* shrimp, the green beans with beef, the *cha-sew* (a baked pork dish in a savory sauce). Around the fourth course, everyone starts grumbling slightly: "Can't we open more presents now? Can't we have dessert later?"

The following morning is a disaster because CBS always arrives at nine. My husband collects, literally, by the thousands, Japanese battery-operated toys. Every Christmas CBS decides it would be delightful to have a Christmas night program showing him and some of his toys; Christmas morning is always the time they come to shoot. He gets up to welcome the crew; I sneak into the den (his toy room is directly over the bedroom) to sleep as late as the day's demands allow.

We are having more "family" for dinner on Christmas night, and this is the only night of the year when I cook. And it must be the dinner I consider traditional: the roast turkey with extra amounts of stuffing, mashed potatoes with gravy, sometimes sweet potatoes too, cranberry sauce, Waldorf salad, peas or green beans, mince pie and plum pudding with whipped cream.

By three o'clock the large dining room table is extended to its nth degree and reset, a card table is set up in the room for "the kids," order has been restored, and it looks as though all will be ready on time. Naturally, that never happens—every Christmas night guest knows he or she will receive a phone call about six forty-five saying, "Don't come at seven-thirty, come at eight," and everyone kindly gives me the benefit of the doubt by coming at eight-thirty.

On Christmas afternoon we open family gifts and the ones from "outside"—friends at the office or in the East or in Europe. If Bert's daughter and her mother are with us, the tree area will be as full of unopened presents as on the previous night, and we will have hot mulled wine or something similarly festive. If we are alone, we settle for a glass of white wine and carols on the FM station that plays them all through the day.

And then it is time for phone calls to distant friends, and for other friends to drop by for a glass of wine or champagne, and to exchange even more presents. At this time of day, it is *de rigueur* for everyone to sport every wearable present, so I may be wearing a sweater and a hat with my traditional red velvet long dress, and Bobbie's gift of a plastic doggie pin next to my husband's gift of a coral rose. If Christmas dinner is late, it is because so many unexpected people drop by, or call up; a messenger arrives with flowers; someone's son charges up on a motorcycle to drop off gifts; there is an endless coming and going.

And finally, Christmas night. Our natural family, Bert's sister and husband, their two sons, and any live-in girlfriends arrive. We accept live-ins in this instance, but do not have room for too many other extras. Then Manny and Go and her three gorgeous daughters. Their boyfriends, live-in or not, are invited for drinks and presents, but not for dinner; the most the old table now will hold is ten, the card table, four. Finally, Mike and Lorain, dear old friends, arrive. Again the tree is swamped with presents. Go, purely for self-protection, has brought two extra hors d'oeuvres—she knows I will serve some, but she also knows I will not serve dinner until midnight. There are too many clues to read, too many presents to open, too many kisses to be exchanged. The phone has been busy for days: "Exactly who will be there Christmas night?" Everybody brings two or three presents for everybody else, even if they are people they don't know. They will be things such as jalapeño jelly, or cranberry nut bread or decorative candles or boxes of candy, but nobody, not even someone's visiting house guest from the East, will feel left out.

And so Christmas Day straggles to its three or four A.M. conclusion, with lots of singing at the end. As everyone is walking out the door, a few of us put our arms around each other's shoulders and do one final chorus of "Silent Night."

Midweek, there are more parties, some by day and some by night. But one evening is reserved for a very special outing, typically Los Angeles, yet something many people don't know about.

It occurs on the borderline of Pasadena and Arcadia, covers numerous blocks, and is so brilliant that it can be seen all the way from the freeway. It is a veritable fantasyland of Christmas decorations—kitsch or splendor, take your choice. In this section of the city a Christmas theme is selected every year; and each block of houses chooses how it will express the theme. If the theme is, for example, "Santa Claus Is Coming to Town," one block may be entirely decorated with Santas, another with elves making toys, yet another with reindeer—depicted by papier-mâché figures on lawns, by lights in the shapes of figures, by designs of crepe paper or flowers, by all sorts of ingenious touches. Everyone competes so that the decorations and lighting and groups of figures are bigger and brighter and better at each house along the way. Even families who do not believe in Christmas as a religious holiday join in—several houses include Stars of David among their decorations. And if one can recapture the child's-eye view, remember what it was like when colored lights and ornaments and pretend-angels had the true quality of a fairy tale, there is enchantment here.

As a child, every Christmas season I was taken to the top of Mulholland Drive, the long east-west road that crosses the Santa Monica Mountains. We would park in one of the little carved-out "view areas" and get out of the car and look at the city down below. It was not as much of a city then as it is now; there were no skyscrapers. But it stretched from the mountains to the ocean, and at Christmastime the sparkling lights of every color made even the flat stretches interesting, made the entire city look like something that did not even exist then—Disneyland. It is worthwhile to make this trip to the mountaintop to see Los Angeles in a different aspect. It still is not a tall city, and maybe it is not a city at all in the usual sense. But from this height, and with those lights gleaming—gleaming even from Catalina, twenty-six miles offshore—you catch the fantasy of it, and also some sense of its vibrancy and its power. Millions of lights celebrating Christmas. Millions of lights connecting old areas and new, rich areas and poor, connecting Anglos and Blacks and Chicanos and Orientals. Christmas lights cover the city. Millions of Christmas lights connect us all.